Transformative Ecological Economics

When we look at the state of the world today, what is most evident is the fact that the major problems of our time – energy, environment, economy, climate change and social justice – cannot be understood in isolation. They are interconnected problems, which means that they require corresponding systemic solutions. Today's global economy has brought about critical distress for ecosystems and societies and we have to go to the very root of the problems to find a way out.

This volume develops a synthesized interpretation of ecological economics integrating different levels: (economic) system, (business) practice and the (economic) actor. It discusses how changes on a systems level are connected to changes in practice and development of individual consciousness. *Transformative Ecological Economics* delves into the insight and knowledge from different sources of inspiration (thermodynamics, Darwinism, anthroposophy and Buddhism) as well as into an integrated story describing and illustrating the core ideas, principles and values that characterize a utopian society anchored in ecological economics. Implementation of the deep changes demanded depends on our ability to write a new story, a utopian one for sure, but one which is in accordance with and based on the reality in which we live.

This book will be of interest to those who study ecological economics, political economy and environmental economics.

Ove Jakobsen is Professor in Ecological Economics at Bodø Graduate School of Business, Nord University, Norway. He is co-founder and leader of the Centre for Ecological Economics and Ethics.

Routledge Studies in Ecological Economics

For a full list of titles in this series, please visit www.routledge.com/series/RSEE.

Transformative Ecological Economics

Process Philosophy, Ideology
and Utopia

Ove Jakobsen

Routledge
Taylor & Francis Group

LONDON AND NEW YORK

First edition published 2017 by Routledge

2 Park Square, Milton Park, Abingdon, Oxfordshire OX14 4RN
52 Vanderbilt Avenue, New York, NY 10017

Routledge is an imprint of the Taylor & Francis Group, an informa business

First issued in paperback 2018

British Library Cataloguing in Publication Data
A catalogue record for this book is available from the British Library

Library of Congress Cataloguing in Publication Data
A catalogue record for this book has been requested

ISBN: 978-1-138-63776-4 (hbk)
ISBN: 978-0-367-19417-8 (pbk)

Typeset in Times New Roman
by Out of House Publishing

For Julie and Rasmus

Contents

Figures

Boxes

Foreword

by Fritjof Capra

When we look at the state of the world today, what is most evident is the fact that the major problems of our time – energy, environment, economy, climate change, social justice – cannot be understood in isolation. They are systemic problems, which means that they are all interconnected and interdependent, and they require corresponding systemic solutions. As Pope Francis puts it in his remarkable encyclical *Laudato si'*:

> Our common home is falling into serious disrepair [...]. [This is] evident in large-scale natural disasters as well as social and even financial crises, for the world's problems cannot be analyzed or explained in isolation [...]. It cannot be emphasized enough how everything is interconnected.
>
> (Francis 2015, Paragraphs 61, 138)

The global economy, in particular, is an integral part and, in fact, the main engine of our multifaceted global crisis. In recent years this fact has been widely recognized, and many eloquent critiques of our current system of global capitalism have been published. However, there have been very few, if any, comprehensive narratives of an alternative economic system. In my view, this is the main achievement of the present book.

The author, Professor Ove Jakobsen, has been researching and teaching what he calls "ecological economics" for more than twenty years, and in this book he distils the insights he gained during those years into a coherent narrative, establishing ecological economics as a transdisciplinary field that integrates economy, nature and society. In doing so, Jakobsen uses two meanings of the term "ecological." In the strict scientific sense, ecology is the science of relationships between the members of an ecological community and their environment. In this sense, ecological economics refers to an economic system that is consistent with and honors the basic principles of ecology. In a broader sense, ecology refers to a pattern of relationships that define the context for a certain phenomenon. In this broad sense, ecological economics refers to economic theory and practice that see the economy as operating within, rather than dominating, the spheres of nature, society and culture.

To convey the radical nature of ecological economics, Jakobsen introduces the contrast between ideology (a set of values and ideas that define the dominant paradigm, or status quo) and utopia (a set of values and ideas that transcend the existing order). Accordingly, he distinguishes between green economy and ecological economics. While the former attempts to reduce negative impacts within the current ideology of neo-liberalism, the latter involves fundamental changes of the dominant conceptual framework.

These fundamental changes can be seen as part of a broader change of paradigms from a mechanistic to a systemic conception of life, which has gradually been emerging over the last few decades. At the forefront of contemporary science, the universe is no longer seen as a machine composed of elementary building blocks. We have discovered that the material world, ultimately, is a network of inseparable patterns of relationships; that the planet as a whole is a living, self-regulating system. The view of the human body as a machine and of the mind as a separate entity is being replaced by one that sees not only the brain, but also the immune system, the bodily tissues and even each cell as a living, cognitive system. Evolution is no longer seen as a competitive struggle for existence, but rather as a cooperative dance in which creativity and the constant emergence of novelty are the driving forces. And with the new emphasis on complexity, networks and patterns of organization, a new science of qualities is slowly emerging.

The new conception of life has important applications in almost every field of study and every human endeavor, because most phenomena we deal with in our professional and personal lives have to do with living systems. Indeed, the fundamental shift of perception from the mechanistic to the systemic view of life is especially relevant to economics. In Jakobsen's words, "The only valid purpose of the economy is to serve the life processes in all kinds of social and ecological systems."

I would like to highlight this fundamental connection between economics and life with a few examples, which are discussed extensively in this book. Throughout the living world, we find multi-leveled structures of systems nested within systems. Each individual system is an integrated whole and, at the same time, part of larger systems. For example, the human organism contains organs made of tissues which, in turn, are made of cells. On the other hand, the organism as a whole is embedded in larger social systems which, in turn, are embedded in ecosystems.

For economics, this implies that nature is superior to the economy rather than the other way around. The economy is a living system nested in other living systems – society, culture, politics, nature and ultimately Gaia, the living Earth. Thus, in ecological economics, the economy becomes the servant rather than the master of nature. The economic system is integrated into the organic network of reality, the web of life. Every economic activity is designed to contribute to the development of viable societies within resilient ecosystems.

The basic pattern of organization of a living system is the network. Ecosystems are understood in terms of food webs, that is, networks of organisms; organisms are networks of cells, and cells are networks of molecules. More precisely, a living system is a self-generating network. Each component of the network helps to transform and replace other components, and thus the entire network continually creates, or recreates, itself.

According to this systemic conception of life, neither the economy nor society can be understood as collections of objects, but only in terms of relationships between subjects. They cannot survive in an atomized state any more than an organism can survive in fragments. Moreover, the fact that the basic pattern of organization of all living systems is the network implies that an economy will be truly alive – flexible and capable of creative adaptations to changing circumstances – only if it is organized as a network, composed of smaller living networks and integrated into larger social and ecological networks. Indeed, Jakobsen argues that a new ecological economy might be best developed from a network of decentralized and globally interconnected eco-villages.

A living system is materially and energetically open and always operates far from equilibrium. There is a continual flow of energy and matter through the system. All living systems need energy and food to sustain themselves, and all living systems produce waste. But in nature, organisms form communities, the ecosystems, in which the waste of one species is food for the next, so that matter cycles continually through the ecosystem.

For a living economy this means that all economic processes need to be circular. Circular value chains make it possible to reduce both the consumption of virgin natural resources and the amount of waste that goes back to nature. To establish efficient material cycles in practice, as Jakobsen emphasizes, collaboration between governments, manufacturers, distributors and consumers is essential. To build such a circular economy, our technologies and industrial systems need to be fundamentally redesigned, mimicking the natural ecological cycles.

In living systems, the metabolic flows of energy and matter are necessary for the continual regeneration and recycling of organic components, as well as for growth and development. However, there is a significant difference between the concepts of growth from a mechanistic and from a systemic perspective. Growth in nature is not linear, nor unlimited. While certain parts of organisms, or ecosystems, grow, others decline, releasing and recycling their components which become resources for new growth. This kind of balanced, multifaceted growth is well known to biologists and ecologists, and it is in stark contrast to the concept of unlimited quantitative growth used by virtually all of today's economists.

Unlimited economic growth on a finite planet is, of course, logically impossible. The objective of boundless quantitative growth is thus a dangerous misconception, which can be seen as the ultimate dilemma underlying most of our global problems. In his vision of ecological economics, Jakobsen advocates a fundamental shift from quantitative growth to qualitative development. Such qualitative development involves growth that enhances the quality of life through generation and regeneration. In living organisms, ecosystems and societies, qualitative development includes an increase of complexity, sophistication and maturity.

The aim is to change the economy in a direction where it is possible to create a high quality of life without material growth. Ecological economics, the author explains, is intrinsically dynamic and assumes continuous development without increased consumption of natural resources. Instead of using one-dimensional instrumental thinking aimed at increased growth and profits, our energy and efforts should aim at greater complexity, beauty and harmony. This fundamental change of perspective is perhaps the most radical, but also the most urgently needed proposition of this inspiring book.

Preface

When we get our story wrong, we get our future wrong.

David Korten

This book is based on my reflections after working for more than twenty years researching and teaching ecological economics. My intention is to develop a synthesized interpretation of ecological economics integrating all the different levels: (economic) system, (business) practice and the (economic) actor. The concept "ecological economics" is established as a term for a transdisciplinary field of (social) science that integrates economics, nature and society. When I use the concept "ecological" it means that the economy is learning from nature and not dominating her. In the following chapters "economics" is used as a broad concept and covers both science and real-world activities. In the same line of interpretation, I will use the concept "economy" as a term to cover both economic practice and the theory behind it. My intention is not to delve deep into the theories of classical and neo-classical economics, and for that reason "mainstream economics" is used as a term describing the contemporary economy. The term "mainstream economics" came into common use in the late twentieth century to describe the combination of a neo-classical approach to microeconomics and a Keynesian approach to macroeconomics.

To draw a real, clean and proper distinction between green economy, as part of the dominating system, and ecological economics, as a description of an alternative system, I refer to Karl Mannheim's analysis of the tension between ideology and utopia as an important driver of development. In theory it is easy to draw a clear, distinct and unquestionable demarcation line between green economy and ecological economics. Green economy can be described as an initiative to reduce the negative impacts within the existing neo-liberalistic economic ideology. Ecological economics contends that the problems we face are largely due to systemic failures and demands a fundamental utopian change in the system itself. In practice it is problematic to differ between green and ecological measures. It is often difficult to decide if a concrete activity is implemented to reduce negative symptoms in order to save the system or as a tool to change the system.

Colored by Schopenhauer's and Nietzsche's philosophies, my interpretation of ecological economics is deeply rooted in commitment to life. In other words, life itself – not growth or profits – is the fundamental value yardstick of ecological economics. Based on this fundamental assessment my interpretation of ecological economics has developed within an ongoing reflection inspired by several disciplines: economics, business administration, marketing, natural science, social sciences and philosophy. In addition, cooperation with artists in literature, music and drama has been essential for my holistic understanding of ecological economics. Extensive contact with the practical world of companies, authorities and NGOs – through dialogue, speeches and lectures in symposiums, seminars, workshops and conferences – has added fact and value to my interpretation of ecological economics. The outcome is what Anthony Giddens called "a realistic Utopia."

The philosophical basis for my interpretation of ecological economics is inspired by Alfred North Whitehead's philosophy of organism. Because Whitehead integrates the rationalistic and the empirical positions in philosophy of science, philosophy of organism represents a dynamic and integrated context for a theoretical, practical and relevant understanding of ecological economics.

This book was triggered, if you like, during the process of writing a large number of articles and giving brief presentations on the ideas of approximately thirty pioneering contributors to ecological economics. To ensure diversity as well as depth I have chosen contributors who represent a wide range, both in space and time, and stem from all parts of the world and span a time period of more than a century.

In the final chapter I synthesize the combined insight and knowledge into an integrated story describing and illustrating the core ideas, principles and values which characterize a utopian society anchored in ecological economics. According to Albritton, "utopias may free the mind from the despair of remaining entrapped by seemingly unalterable reified structures of thought and practice" (Albritton 2012, p. 141). Implementation of the deep changes demanded depends on our ability to write a new story, a utopian one for sure, but one which is in accordance with and based on the reality in which we live.

It is of great importance to stress that utopian stories are nothing more than beacon lights which help our understanding of the challenges we face and to find practical solutions which will lead us in the direction of an ecological economics which is in harmony with nature and society. Today it is more essential than ever before to find solutions based on creative thinking that is not only removed from but stands far outside the ideology (paradigm) that caused the problems.

Acknowledgments

I wish to express thanks to my friends and colleagues who have been a great source of inspiration over the years. My interest in alternative economic thinking began to gain momentum in 1987 when I wrote the book *Miljø, myter og markedsføring* (Environment, myths and marketing) together with Jan Mehlum, who was an engaging motivator. During work on my Dr. Oecon. thesis at the Norwegian School of Economics in the late 1980s, Leif Holbæk-Hansen inspired me to delve deeper into anthroposophy and phenomenological philosophy to develop a philosophical basis and foundation for my work with ecological economics. Gunnar Skirbekk (University of Bergen) convinced me that a wider perspective on philosophy was crucial to advance ecological economics into a transdisciplinary context. Philosophical reflections have been an important part of my work ever since.

As guest researcher at Aarhus Business School in the early 1990s Erik Kloppenborg Madsen introduced me to continental perspectives on environmental management. Some years later as a guest researcher at Stockholm University, Søren Bergstrøm invited me to take part in an interdisciplinary research group which included researchers representing different perspectives on environmentally responsible business administration and leadership. As guest researcher at the Business Ethics Center, Corvinus University Budapest, Laszlo Zsolnai motivated me to delve deeper into Buddhist-inspired economic thinking and practice. Participating in his numerous projects has been a stimulating source of inspiration over many years.

The most important parts of my research have been developed in cooperation with Stig Ingebrigtsen (Bodø Graduate School of Business) and Knut J. Ims (the Norwegian School of Economics). Others who have encouraged and inspired me in my research and teaching are Øystein Dahle, John Skår, Christian Egge, Sveinar Kildal, Emil Mohr, Jostein Hertwig, Jakob Bomann Larsen, Anders Lindseth, Viggo Rossvær, Pierre Guillet de Monthoux and Stephan Harding.

Over the last few years inspiring conversations with Johan Galtung, David Beake and, of the greatest importance, Fritjof Capra have given new momentum to my work.

But the most important sources of inspiration have been and still are my colleagues at the Centre for Ecological Economics at the University of Nordland: Stig Ingebrigtsen, Øystein Nystad, Are S. Ingulfsvann, Vivi M. L. Storsletten, Jean Jaminon and Nils Gilje,

I owe special thanks to Laszlo Zsolnai and David Beake, who took time to read the manuscript and provided indispensable advice on how to improve both language and content. Advisor Hege Vatne Arntsen at Nord University has provided very helpful support during the preparation of the manuscript of the book. I am grateful to Retura Iris A/S for financial support.

Introduction

Be realistic, demand the impossible!

Che Guevara

We are living in complex and turbulent times,

> with amazing scientific discoveries, technological inventions, industrial and commercial expansion, population increase, social transformations, new systems of transportation and communication, vast educational and research establishments, ventures into space.
>
> (Berry 2007, p. 57)

No matter how you may wish to describe it, there is no denying we live in brilliant times. Nor can we deny that while the increase in physical power from rapid techno-scientific advance has handed civilization great opportunities for much social betterment, "it has also brought us perilously close to destroying ourselves" (Segall 2013, p. 30).

In the year 2000 the United Nations set eight millennium goals to solve some of the most serious problems of our time and set a 2015 deadline to meet them. They included the eradication of extreme poverty and hunger and ensuring environmental sustainability. But as Levitas tells us: "These aims will not be met in the foreseeable future and can only be met with a qualitative change in global social and economic organization" (Levitas 2013, p. xii).

As Korten points out "when we get our story wrong, we get our future wrong" (Korten 2015, p. 1). As long as the stories told by most politicians and economists are based on a worldview which is in fundamental conflict with reality, it is impossible to make the qualitative changes needed. "New problems arise which cannot be solved by the old methods" (Johnson 1962, p. 3).

According to the World Economic Forum, "the difference between rich and poor is becoming more extreme, and as income inequality widens the wealth gap in major nations, education, health and social mobility are all threatened" (www.weforum.org). These major problems are systemic, inter-connected and interdependent.

> Since modern economic life followed an inexorable momentum of its own without anyone being in charge of it, it reduced human beings to helpless and passive spectators and represented a new form of slavery, more comfortable and invidious and hence more dangerous than the earlier ones.
>
> (Parekh 2001, p. 80)

Gandhi argued that an entire civilization which had been inspired and energized by a mistaken concept of reality would end up corrupted by it and facing disastrous consequences from it. "In his view that was the case with modern civilization" (Parekh 2001, p. 78). On the more destructive side of modern society,

> mountains are ripped apart for the underlying coal and ore deposits; rivers are polluted with human and industrial waste, the air is saturated with toxic substances, the rain is turned to acid, the soil is sterile with chemicals, the higher forms of life are endangered, the great mammals have been killed off almost to the point of extinction, the tropical forests are being ruined, and many coral reefs are endangered beyond repair.
>
> (Berry 2007, p. 57)

Pressure from continuing ecological losses may soon begin to stress both our economic and social systems. Greater degradation of the ecosystems brings about the greater risk that these systems will be pushed over the edge. From this analysis, which picks out the contradictions, we can surely agree that world history cannot by any means be described as a triumphant march of reason; instead we may and should, along with Nietzsche, ask if the one-dimensional focus on rationality leads us off in the direction of disaster. Tanner refers to Nietzsche's underlying view as follows:

> [I]f we don't make a drastically new start we are doomed, since we are living in the wreckage of two thousand and more years of fundamentally mistaken ideas about almost everything that matters.
>
> (Tanner 2000, p. 4)

In this very challenging state of affairs the clear and avowed intention of national, European and international bodies so far has been to try to restore economic growth and put up the "business as usual" signs which are as comforting as they are deceiving. Eisenstein dismisses this approach because it is difficult to solve the problems within the existing system as solutions are unavailable "through the types of efforts that have brought us to where we are today" (Eisenstein 2007, p. 394).

Fundamental change seems to be blocked by the failed existing systems themselves, which are, rather like viruses, determined to achieve their own survival. And so much so that Bruno Latour, the French philosopher and sociologist, was led, with great insight, to say: "Nowadays it seems easier to imagine the end of the world than to imagine the end of capitalism" (Latour 2014, p. 1).

Today's global economy has put ecosystems and societies into critical distress and we have to go to the very root of the problems to find a way out. First of all, it is obvious that modern civilization involves an outstandingly awful amount of violence against nature. Natural resources are ruthlessly exploited and nature's rhythms and balances are being dramatically disturbed. Second, the economy itself is in a bad state, so much so that "the economic shockwaves of 2008 and the ensuing global recessions laid bare the instability of global capitalism and its inability to provide sustainable livelihoods for the world's population" (Levitas 2013, p. xi).

Fortunately, the first elements of a new system are emerging. According to Lindner "we […] live in historically unprecedented times of risk, but also in historically unprecedented times of opportunity" (Lindner 2011, p. xxv). We have the opportunity to create a future consistent with "our true nature and possibility as living beings born of a Living Earth born of a Living Universe" (Korten 2015, p. 1). "Scarcity can be overcome, conflict can be eliminated, and moral dilemmas and psychological frustrations can be resolved" (Davis 2012, p. 129).

What we need is a ground-up reconstruction of both economy and society based on a combination of imagination and a far deeper understanding of reality. According to Capra and Luisi, the problems require systemic solutions "and since the only viable solutions are those that are ecologically sustainable, they must incorporate the basic principles of ecology, or principles of sustainability" (Capra and Luisi 2014, p. 363).

Utopian thinking offers an interesting resource which is able to serve the need to consider new alternatives when existing systems begin to break down. Utopia can have a constitutive role in helping us to rethink the nature of our social and economic life. "Utopia" as a word was first coined by Thomas More for his book *Utopia,* published in 1516. Quite simply, More coupled the Greek words for "no" and "place" to invent a name that has since passed into wide currency and exactly 500 years later it is still with us today.

Today utopia is often thought of as "the good place." The distinction between hope and desire reflects the location of utopia. Various visions of utopia have recurred throughout the modern age and are more than mere propaganda – so much so that they indicate a possible world which is "far more beautiful than what we have wrought today" (Eisenstein 2007, p. 394); in addition, it indicates some of the tension in the concept.

Utopia will not be achieved by better science, or by more precise technology, or even by finer control of our inner and outer reality. It will not happen by trying harder to be good, and not even by better control of the ecosystems or human nature. In accordance with Nietzsche's philosophy, the problems we have created are caused by the program of objectifying and controlling nature. So the solution is, in fact, quite the opposite. Only by "transcending that program and its accompanying conception of the self can we expect to create anything other than a further intensification of what we have today" (Eisenstein 2007).

Anthony Giddens, the eminent sociologist, was working along these lines when he pointed out that we had to look for an alternative to the existing worldview, which is determined to pursue nothing more or less than a sure course of self-destruction. As an example he claims that "the pursuit of capitalist accumulation could not be carried out indefinitely since it is not self-sustaining in terms of resources" (Giddens 1990, p. 165). David Korten goes a major and distinct step further and claims that "we have created a global suicide economy designed to make money with no concern for the consequences for life" (Korten 2015, p. 29).

Ruth Levitas' slogan (inspired by Che Guevara) illustrates the need for a change on a deeper level: "Be realistic: Demand the impossible" (Levitas 2013, p. 129). What Levitas really means is that utopia is not about the impossible. What is really impossible is to carry on as we are with our old and tired social and economic systems that enrich a few but destroy the environment and impoverish most of the world's population. "Our very survival depends on finding another way of living" (Levitas 2013, p. xi).

Since different societies have different histories and traditions, the search for a single model is rendered both illogical and dangerous. However, we must note that if we imagine worlds too perfect for the fallible creatures that we are then we may discourage ourselves from even making the effort to attain them. Instead, maybe it's better to look for practical and relevant visions of an alternative society, economy and culture that preserve enough of the familiar and the habitual to see ourselves living in them comfortably. Anthony Giddens (1990) called this position, "utopian realism."

In the following chapters I point out and argue that it is not enough simply to find and identify effective tools to reduce the negative symptoms of the modern society. It is necessary to make changes on a far deeper level. To elaborate on these topics I have divided the book into three parts. Part I, "Context of interpretation," gives a frame of reference for interpreting the content of Parts II and III. Part II, "Perspectives on ecological economics," gives an overview of some of the main ideas presented by innovative economists who have shifted their thinking outside the traditional economic concepts, theories and models to find new and exciting challenges which are relevant to a changing and, sadly, deteriorating world. In Part III, "Ecological economics: a utopian narrative," I draw a creative picture of a utopian economy which is based on inspiration from the context of interpretation (Part I) and the contributions to ecological economics (Part II). My aim is to present an inclusive sketch describing some main characteristics of ecological economics in harmony with nature, society and human beings.

The first part is divided in three chapters. In the first chapter, I establish an organic context for interpreting the world we are living in based on a description of Alfred North Whitehead's "philosophy of organism." According to

Whitehead everything consists of combinations of actual entities. Nature is a theatre for the interrelations of activities. "All things change, the activities and their interrelations" (Whitehead 1977, p. 15). Whitehead seeks to replace the traditional scientific concept of the universe as a mechanism with a novel conception of the universe as a living, self-organizing organism. From Whitehead's perspective, a successful worldview (categorial scheme) should aim to exhibit itself as adequate for the interpretation of the complex texture of both nature and society. In addition, the humanizing of technology is likely to involve introducing moral issues more and more into the now largely "instrumental" relationship between human beings and the created environment.

In the second chapter, I present and evaluate the relevance of the concept of utopia as a frame of reference for understanding the existing worldview and as a context for developing models for an alternative future society. André Gorz, the Austrian philosopher, argued that it is the function of utopias "to provide us with the distance from the existing state of affairs which allows us to judge what we are doing in the light of what we could or should do" (Levitas 2013, p. xvii). Utopia is the expression of the desire for both a better way of living and a better way of being, and, seen like this, is woven through human culture. Utopian thinking "requires us to think afresh about preconditions we have long taken for granted, and therein lies its greatest contribution to true originality" (Parekh 2001, p. 115). "The informed imaginings of alternative futurists have generally demonstrated a capacity to think large but not small, globally but not locally" (Sommer 1985, p. 129).

Hungarian sociologist Karl Mannheim argued that a state of mind is utopian when it is incongruous with the state within which it occurs. "The incongruence is always evident in the fact that such a state of mind in experience, in thought, and in practice, is oriented towards objects which do not exist in the actual situation" (Mannheim 1936, p. 192). Ruth Levitas, a current researcher on the concept of utopia, claims that the utopias existing in a society tell us much about the experiences of living in it, because they tell us in a way that we cannot "directly ascertain where the felt absences are in people's lives – the spaces, that is, that utopia offers to fill, whether in fantasy or reality" (Levitas 2011, p. 219).

To illustrate the difference between mere change within the existing system and the more fundamental changes actually required I present the concepts of ideology and utopia based on contributions from Karl Mannheim and Paul Ricoeur. Both argue, along with Whitehead, that societal development depends on creativity, or the existence of utopia. Fifty years after Karl Mannheim, Paul Ricoeur considered the similarities and differences between utopia and ideology. At the core of utopia is the desire for being otherwise, individually and collectively, subjectively and objectively. Ideology has a conserving effect on the established system. Ricoeur claimed that the capacity of utopia to break through "the thickness of reality is what interested me" (Ricoeur 1986, p. 309). Any critique of the present ideology must be combined with an exploration of the institutionally specific alternatives that are desirable, viable and achievable. One general conclusion about utopia is that all utopias have the ambiguity of claiming to be "realizable but at the same time of being works of fancy, the impossible" (Ricoeur 1986, p. 301).

Utopia is the driving force in the change processes in human societies. The first step is to recognize that "the differential feature of ideology and Utopia is that Utopia is situationally transcendent while ideology is not" (Ricoeur 1986, p. 272), and the second step is to accept that "Utopia is fundamentally realizable" (Ricoeur 1986, p. 272). In ahistorical perspective, utopian descriptions identify the main problems in society and function as a searchlight to help the change processes. Based on these perspectives I clarify the many and clear differences between green economy and ecological economics.

In the third chapter I draw a distinct demarcation line between green economy and ecological economics and point out that green economy stands and operates within the established neo-liberal ideology while ecological economics represents utopia. To illustrate and throw light on the contrasting perspectives I refer to Robert Merton's definition of unintended consequences, Abraham Maslow's distinction between low- and high-synergy societies and Johan Galtung's analysis of negative and positive peace. Merton states that human action quite often has consequences that are unintentional. On an aggregated level he points out that the effects can be very serious in both negative and positive ways. Maslow argued that human behavior depends on cultural characteristics concerning both individual values and social institutions. Along the same lines Galtung explained war and peace by pointing to different individual and structural characteristics in a culture. He used the term "negative peace" to describe and define peace by its negation. Hence, we can see negative peace as the absence of war, conflict or other forms of large-scale human violence. Galtung used "positive peace" to describe and define what it actually is – the presence of harmony, well-being and social systems that serve and create values such as equity and fairness.

Negative and positive peace are conceived as two entirely independent concepts, where the one is possible without the other. Green economy, in harmony with these examples, focuses on reducing the negative symptoms of mainstream economy such as "rationalism, secularization, industrialization, the scientific culture, individualism, [and] technological mastery of nature" (Parekh 2001, p. 78). But, on the other hand, and in stark contrast, ecological economics presupposes fundamental changes at both the systems level and the individual level such as holism, process, networks and living in harmony with nature.

Part II consists of a presentation of a number of contributions relevant to understanding the development of ecological economics. My aim is to describe and explain, and, over a range of nine chapters, I describe the ideas of thirty contributors. To choose between a vast variety of possible candidates I have used several criteria: time, geography, culture, sex, topics focused on and occupation (academics and practitioners). I structure the presentation in the following way. Chapter 4 lays out the four paths which lead to ecological economics. These paths are illuminated by a connection between scientific and philosophical contributions and the references economists make to the various positions:

- thermodynamics: Rudolf Clausius ► Nicholas Georgescu-Roegen (bio-economics) ► Herman Daly (ecological economics);
- evolutionary theory: Charles Darwin ► Kenneth Boulding (evolutionary economics) ► Peter Söderbaum (ecological economics);
- Buddhism: Mahatma Gandhi ► E. F. Schumacher (Buddhist economics) ► P. A. Payutto (Buddhist economics);
- anthroposophy: Rudolf Steiner ► Leif Holbæk-Hanssen (collaborative economics) ► Otto Scharmer (Theory U).

Chapter 5 focuses on the question of transdisciplinarity in terms of the contributions of Herman Daly, Johan Galtung and Peter Söderbaum. Chapter 6 itself with economics as a moral science as seen in contributions from Amitai Etzioni, Amartya Sen and Laszlo Zsolnai. In Chapter 7, the Eastern perspective is represented by P. A. Payutto, Vandana Shiva and Peter Pruzan. In Chapter 8, to illuminate the management perspective, I have chosen the work of Archie Carroll, Waldemar Hopfenbeck and Richard Welford. The practical perspective is dealt with by contributions from John Elkington, Tim Jackson, Manfred Max-Neef and Willian Rees in Chapter 9. In Chapter 10 the focus is on institutions. Law and money are discussed through the work of Ross Jackson, Polly Higgins, Margrit Kennedy, Bernard Lietaer and Malcolm Torry. The last chapter in Part II focuses on the future perspective and to represent the future I have chosen Evelin Lindner, Charles Eisenstein and Otto Scharmer.

In Part III, "Ecological economics: a utopian narrative," I provide a comprehensive and integrated presentation of ecological economics inspired by the contributions in Part II and interpreted in the frame of reference presented and discussed in Part I. To come up with a utopian description (story) of ecological economics I am inspired by narrative research methods and I create a narrative sketch of some central dimensions in ecological economics. As an amplifier in these processes art is essential. "Art cannot change the world, but it can contribute to changing the consciousness and drives of the men and women who could change the world" (Levitas 2013, p. 16).

Chapter 13 looks at utopian narratives of ecological economics in terms of worldview, economic system, business practice and personal development. My intention is to create an example of a utopian narrative of ecological economics in harmony with nature, society and human beings. I describe a realistic utopia that differs from the existing society without being in conflict with the fundamental knowledge represented by the organic worldview. My intention is to generate an example of a utopian narrative, functioning as a beacon to inspire others to create even more utopias leading to the further development and enhancement of ecological economics.

Part I

Context of interpretation

Part I gives a frame of reference for interpreting Parts II and III. Whitehead's philosophy of organism represents a holistic description of how everything in nature (and society) is constituted and how we can acquire knowledge of the nature of reality. Since the nature of reality is described as process, and everything is changing all the time, it is impossible to explain everything once and for all. Becoming is more real than being. According to Whitehead, philosophy starts with wonder and the task is to develop a consistent context of interpretation relevant for understanding the world we are living in.

Whitehead states that as the context of interpretation is not static we have to reflect on how to develop the best possible interpretive framework, or, in his language, "categorial scheme," to describe and understand reality. All change depends on creativity, "the universal of universals," the process of becoming develops in the field of tension between actuality and potentiality. If we can see the universals as no longer abstract and eternal they could be applicable to interpret reality.

I describe and discuss social change, in the spirit of Mannheim (1936) and Ricoeur (1986), as it results from the tension between ideology (referring to actuality) and utopia (referring to potentiality). Ideology always sustains the existing system while utopia aims to transform the status quo. Utopia attacks the orthodoxy of the dominant paradigm and provokes its agents. Utopia generates disturbance and alteration and is a necessity for a living society. A society without utopia would be dead.

Transferring this reasoning to economy I find a corresponding tension between green economy, rooted in the established neo-liberal economic ideology, and ecological economics as a utopian description of a potentially developing economy. Ecological economics represents a paradigm shift, suggesting solutions to many of the negative unintended consequences of the current economic system. Instead of reducing the symptoms ecological economics suggest changes on an ontological level often inspired by Whitehead's philosophy of organism.

1   Philosophy of organism

ALFRED NORTH WHITEHEAD

> No period of history has ever been great or ever can be, that does not act on some sort of high, idealistic motives, and idealism in our time has been shoved aside, and we are paying the penalty for it.
>
> Alfred North Whitehead

Introduction

Modern society is characterized by increasing production and consumption, resulting in a higher standard of living for some people and a lower quality of the environmental life conditions for all of us. To solve the most pressing problems we need a change which moves away from the existing mechanical worldview toward an organic understanding of the world.

> We all live in the midst of an ecological crisis. It is well known that human beings have been destroying nature and the environment with science and technology. Without overcoming the ecological crisis we cannot exist any longer. The ecological crisis is fundamental and complicated in its character and scope.
>
> (Lee 2006, p. 128)

Ormerod pointed out that mainstream economics offers a misleading view of how the world operates and that the ontological presuppositions in economics need to be critically reconsidered and discussed (Ormerod 1994). Boulding's view is that "economics has rested too long in an essentially Newtonian paradigm of mechanical equilibrium and mechanical dynamics" (Boulding 1981, p. 17). What we need is a critical understanding of the relationship between ontology on one hand and economics on the other. The problematic assumptions about human nature and the relationship between human beings and the natural world are directly tied to the ontological presuppositions in the current economic system. If we are to change direction, we have to rethink the underlying worldview of modern economics.

In order to describe a worldview showing the fundamental interplay between human activity and environmental conditions, I find it relevant and promising to discuss Whitehead's "philosophy of organism." Whitehead's work in cosmology and philosophy is a major contribution to the ongoing development of the transdisciplinary field of ecological economics as an alternative to neo-classical economics. Whitehead's way of putting things in perspective is both pertinent and illuminating. I do not think Whitehead's philosophical position is the only view which can give a deeper understanding of holistic ontology and cosmology, but it certainly does represent a perspective that could be understood within both the Western philosophical tradition and the Eastern spiritual philosophies. Whitehead was convinced that "what is called modern science had reached a turning point, which demanded a new philosophical thought" (Stenger 2011, p. 11). Science is threatened today by the way the state and (military) industry have undertaken to enslave it "through what is called the economy of knowledge [...] which blindly serves those who actualize that power to transform the world" (Stenger 2011, p. 11).

Abstractions

Ricoeur reflects on the following question: "what is reality and for whom?" Reality, ineluctably, includes all sorts of appreciations and judgments and values. Reality is not only objects but involves human beings and their thoughts and "no one knows reality outside the multiplicity of ways it is conceptualized, since reality is always caught in a framework of thought" (Ricoeur 1986, p. 171). A science that seeks to explain the concrete by way of the abstract all too easily falls prey to a form of knowledge production whose adequacy is judged instrumentally, that is, in terms of its capacity to transform and control nature, rather than ecologically, that is, in terms of its capacity to understand and relate to nature. Gandhi focused another great weakness of modern civilization when he pointed to "its failure to understand the nature and limits of reason" (Parekh 2001, p. 83). "Modern science has sacrificed intuitive understanding of the concrete passage and organic unity of the actual universe for the abstract knowledge of its mathematical formulae and mechanical models" (Segall 2013, p. 9).

Our use of abstractions is dangerous, as we tend to forget that they are indeed no more than abstractions. Even worse we also tend to mistake abstractions for concrete reality. Many of our abstractions lay claim to a completeness that they do not actually possess. Whitehead refers to this error as the fallacy of misplaced concreteness. But we have to be aware when we discuss this topic that "no man and no epoch can think of everything at once" (Whitehead 1967a, p. 51). Boulding points out that abstractions are essential, but, along with Whitehead, he warns against mistaking abstraction for reality. "We would be foolish to try to go for a walk across a map, but a map may be very helpful if we are going for a real walk" (Boulding 1970, p. 75).

Fallacies of misplaced concreteness flourish because the disciplinary organization of knowledge requires a high level of abstraction. The more successfully a discipline meets the criteria established for it, the higher is the level of abstraction involved as they are directly proportional and the problems connected to the fallacy of misplaced concreteness are rapidly evolving in our specialized societies. This is the reason why many practitioners of successful disciplines, socialized to accept the established paradigm, apply their conclusions to the real world without recognizing the degree of abstraction involved. To see (abstract) information as a literal product, or to make concrete things out of (abstract) cognitive and communicative matters, is to commit the fallacy of misplaced concreteness.

According to Daly and Cobb Jr. no field of study outside the physical sciences has more fully achieved the ideal form of academic discipline than economics. The success of economics as a science has involved a high level of abstraction. "Precisely because of its success, it has been particularly liable to commission of the fallacy of misplaced concreteness" (Daly and Cobb Jr. 1994, p. 25). They argue that the organization of economic knowledge in a productive perspective has been successful but it has many built-in limitations and dangers too. The result is that there is an overwhelming danger of "misplaced concreteness" involved in the conclusions drawn about the actual world. "More generally it is the fallacy involved whenever thinkers forget the degree of abstraction involved in thought and draw unwarranted conclusions about concrete actuality" (Daly and Cobb Jr. 1994, p. 36).

The consequence of abstracting economics out of nature and society is "lifeless" concepts, theories and models. Economics deprived of emotion and value is reduced to no more than a mishmash of numbers and statistics. Some of the conclusions drawn about the real world by deduction from conceptual and theoretical abstractions indicate little awareness of the dangers outlined above.

This means that economics scholars are insufficiently aware of the fact that the economic laws are dependent on the historical characteristics of the society. This leads economists "to apply them beyond their limited sphere of relevance" (Daly and Cobb Jr. 1994, p. 29). One consequence is that the laws governing an actual economic system will change if the system changes. Often when economists find "laws" that are valid in the existing system they perceive all such "laws" to be universal. Today we can observe many examples where liberal economic theories, established and validated centuries ago in Europe's Age of Enlightenment, are implemented all over the modern world.

Economists have lost touch with, and maybe even lost the concept of, the living society because of a one-sided focus on the scientific rather than the historical study of the economy. The temporal dimension is overshadowed by the spatial. One of the main statements in "philosophy of organism" is that time and space are inseparable. Whitehead asserts that "it is not necessary for the intellect to fall into the trap, though [...] there has been a very general tendency to do so" (Whitehead 1967a, p. 51). An awareness of metaphysical assumptions can help us to see the limitations of some of the scientific truth of today.

Organic ontology

Whitehead's motivation to develop the philosophy of organism was to frame a system of general ideas in terms of which every element of our experience can be interpreted. "Here 'interpretation' means that each element shall have the character of a particular instance of the general scheme" (Whitehead 1967b, p. 222). The philosophy of organism is often difficult to grasp, and many interpreters report problems in understanding Whitehead's texts. Latour illustrates these problems in the following way:

> I have always felt that Whitehead-watching had a lot to do with whale-watching as it is practiced, for instance, on the coast of San Diego in the winter. You stay on the boat for hours, see nothing, and suddenly, "There she blows, she blows!", and swiftly the whale disappears again.
>
> (Latour 2011, p. xv)

Whitehead wanted his theories to perform a social function and to make human life richer and more meaningful by helping us to understand our experiences in a more dynamic way. Instead of construing the task of science to be that of overcoming subjective illusion in order to reach objective reality, as many modern thinkers have done, Whitehead takes the speculative risk of defining nature "quite simply [as] what we are aware of in perception" (Segall 2013, p. 20). Whitehead's scientific method can be compared with Goethe's gentle empiricism which rejected simple mechanical explanations and pursued instead nature's reasons by learning to participate more fully in the archetypal patterns interwoven with experience itself. One of the main differences between mechanistic and organic models is that "a machine can be controlled, a living system can only be disturbed" (Capra and Luisi 2014, p. 318).

I have chosen Whitehead's philosophy of organism as an ontological frame of reference for interpreting ecological economics because it opens up a deeper understanding of economy as integrated in social and natural systems. Another reason for choosing Whitehead's ontology is that it is often referred to as a source of inspiration in academic texts in ecological economics. Among others, distinguished scholars such as Georgescu-Roegen (1971) and Daly and Cobb Jr. (1994) refer to Whitehead's philosophy in their analysis and descriptions of the principles of ecological economics. They argue that many of the environmental and social problems connected to mainstream economics are due to the underlying mechanistic ontology of economics. Accepting an organic ontology has important implications for both economic theory and practice. For example, it leads to an acceptance of the actors' "co-responsibility" for the whole lifecycle of the product they use or produce.

My interpretation of "philosophy of organism" is mostly based on Whitehead's trilogy of books, *Science and the Modern World* (first edition 1925), *Process and Reality* (based on his Gifford Lectures at the University of Edinburgh, 1927/1928, first published 1929), and *Adventures of Ideas* (first edition 1933). These books supplement each other, and according to Whitehead represent "an endeavour to express a way of understanding the nature of things, and to point out how that way of understanding is illustrated by a survey of the mutations of human experience" (Whitehead 1967b, p. vii).

In *Science and the Modern World* Whitehead introduced the main themes in the philosophy of organism and traces the tremendous impact scientific ideas have on all phases of life. Most important is the differentiation between the "mechanistic" and the "organic" worldviews. To characterize Whitehead's philosophical position it is illuminating to point out that his explanation of the philosophy of organism is an inversion of Kant's transcendental philosophy.

Kant describes the process by which subjective data pass into the appearance of an objective world, while Whitehead seeks to describe how objective data pass into subjective existence. "For Kant the world emerges from the subject; for the philosophy of organism, the subject emerges from the world" (Irvine 2003). This utterance indicates that all entities, including human beings, are integral parts of the whole and cannot be understood as separate atoms in a mechanistic perspective.

In *Process and Reality* Whitehead argued that the world is organic, and that nature is a structure of evolving processes. Whitehead's conviction that Newton's laws are misplaced is an explanatory factor of great importance to understand his commitment to metaphysical philosophy. To explain the reality as a process Whitehead claimed:

> A new metaphysically primitive notion which he calls an actual occasion. On Whitehead's view an actual occasion is not an enduring substance, but a process of becoming [...]. It is customary to compare an actual occasion with a Leibnizian monad, with the caveat that whereas a monad is windowless, an actual occasion is "all window."
>
> (Irvine 2003)

Whitehead's *Adventures of Ideas* provides an impressive indication of effects connected to the intellectual and moral grandeur of the human soul (or mind). He argued that as we think so we act. "In other words, civilization is impossible unless the ideals of civilization are clearly before us" (Lowe, Hartshorne and Johnson 1950, p. 46). Whitehead made himself clear in pointing out that ideals work slowly and that they must be understood before they could be applied by human beings.

Bifurcation

One feature of Western thought that occupied Whitehead for most of his career was "the bifurcation of nature." Bifurcation is what happens whenever we think the world is divided into two sets of things: for example, one which is composed of the fundamental constituents of the universe, invisible to the eyes but known to science through advanced instruments, and the other which is constituted of what the mind has to add to the basic building blocks of the world in order to make sense of them. Latour supports Whitehead's argument, as he states that if nature really is bifurcated no living organism would be possible since being an organism means being the sort of thing whose primary and secondary qualities are endlessly blurred. "Since we are organisms surrounded by many other organisms, nature is not bifurcated" (Latour 2011, p. xii). According to Segall, "our scientific way of knowing – constructed on the metaphysical assumption of the bifurcation of subject and object, fact and value, meaning and matter" (Segall 2013, p. 19), threatens the continued existence of the community of life on Earth.

We can conclude that scientific materialism leaves us in the impossible position of having to deny in theory what we are unable to deny in practice. This means that we use a map based on mechanism even if we experience reality as living. Whitehead claimed that the only way to avoid bifurcation is to develop and elaborate a new theory of the fundamental concepts of science. To solve the problem of bifurcation it was necessary to construe our knowledge of nature as being an individual experience, being more than personal. This means that we must reject the distinction between nature as it really is and how we experience it. Whitehead's theory of prehensions embodies a protest against the "bifurcation" of nature. "It embodies even more than that; its protest is against the bifurcation of actualities" (Whitehead 1985, p. 289).

Griffin (1985) provides the basis of a solution to the problem of the interaction of mind and matter by arguing that we do not have to conceive of mind as having a direct influence on matter, or vice versa, but we can see that the correlations are due to resonances in the implicit order. This indicates that mind or consciousness is an example of the explicit order as matter.

How to bridge the gap between how we experience the world and how we think and speak of it is the essential problem. Whitehead states that we are concerned with nature and that nature is what is given to us in sense-experience. The Earth and the material universe of human experience are the manifestations of the mind. There is essential reference to three simultaneous events when sensing, for example, the color green:

> [T]he event which is the bodily life of the observer, called the percipient event, and the event which is the so-called situation of the green at the time of the observation, and to the time of observation which is nothing else than the whole of nature at that time.
>
> (Anshen 1961, p. 58)

In other words, nature is what we observe in perception through the senses, and what we experience of these sensations depends upon our categorial schemes.

- natural science is the science of nature;
- nature is what we observe in perception through the senses.

So, in essence, we are integral parts of nature and our experience of nature "is" nature, so bifurcation has paradoxical implications. It tells us that, for example, colors, sounds and scents are, in fact, mind-dependent elements, despite the fact that common sense and common belief take them to be the most obvious and characteristic features of nature. Capra and Luisi conclude that "the sharp Cartesian division between mind and matter, between observer and the observed, can no longer be maintained" (Capra and Luisi 2014, p. 74).

The philosophy of organism says that everything is integrated; this indicates that sense awareness of a local event may give knowledge of all other events in nature. The extension of all intuitively given nature in the process of passing is the initial fact disclosed in sense awareness. Passage and duration are immediately perceived as constituting its very nature.

We do not immediately sense nature in an instant, nor do we immediately sense geometrical points with a minimum of extension. Instead, we immediately intuit an extended manifold which is enduring through time and passing. Thus sense awareness supports the primacy of passage (Northrop 1991, p. 195).

Categorial scheme

Whitehead was fully aware that there is no such thing as theory-neutral observations. Our observations are always guided by an interpretative framework and this is not *a priori* in any sense. Contrary to Kant, there is no gap between things experienced and things in themselves. According to Whitehead, particular experience is an "abstraction" from experience taken as a whole. Particular background assumptions that guide our finite observations are largely inherited from our theoretical, linguistic, social or biological environment.

> Interpretative schemes are contingently evolved constructions that function to highlight or bring into focus certain features of experience, moving them from the background to the foreground of experiential awareness.
>
> (Rose 2002, p. 11)

To solve these problems Whitehead sought to reconstruct science itself on an organic basis. It is essential to capture the environmental, social and ethical dimensions of economy, to broaden the time horizon both in the past and in the future, and to expand the spatial focus from local to global. In addition, he questions the anthropocentrism that dominates as a key assumption of Western rationality. Whitehead's questioning and line of argument is urgently needed at a time when we face the prospect of ecological catastrophe and when we are forced to recognize that the fate of humanity is deeply intertwined with the fates of all sorts of other living (and non-living) entities. He articulates an ontology that elucidates the common-sense values of civilized life, such as moral responsibility, beauty and truth with a conception of organic process as starting point. Rooted in creative processes, rather than static substance, Whitehead constructs an interpretative scheme that is based on fundamental categories such as actual entities, eternal objects and "creativity." Actual entities are small momentary drops of experience or feelings. Actual entities are contrasted with eternal objects, which are pure potentials for actualization. Creative processes express themselves through combinations of actual entities and eternal objects.

Actual entities and eternal objects

In Latin, an entity is an equivalent for the concept "thing." Actual entities refer to all the things there are. An actual entity may be loosely defined as any event that functions as a self-conjoined actuality containing the conditions of its unity entirely within and for itself. Therefore it is not possible to go behind actual entities to find anything more real. The final facts are, all alike, actual entities, and these entities are drops of experience, complex and interdependent. Hence, it is easiest to think of an actual entity as a "moment of experience."

This idea is close to the teachings of the Gnostics, who held that consciousness, not matter, is the fundamental essence of reality. "Without the conscious experience of living, we would be unaware of existence; nothing would exist for us, and we would not exist for ourselves [...] I, the subject, am only conscious when there is something, an object, of which I am aware" (Korten 2015, p. 63).

However, actual entities are not static beings but dynamic and interactive beings in the process of becoming. The constitution of an actual entity is a process of becoming. In other words, in the philosophy of organism, all actual entities, from unperceivable atoms and electrons to the macro cosmos, are perceived realities that are related to each other. Since the existence of an actual entity is a function of the existence of others it follows that nothing exists in itself. This leads to the holistic principle, saying that there is no separated and isolated substance and there is no self-contained and self-closed substance. Every living entity, no matter how small and seemingly unimportant, is contributing to the creative potential of the whole. It follows then that an event represents the interpretation of all the various aspects at some particular standpoint. This does not mean that the actual world is a construct, but that the actual world could be observed from different angles in time and

space. Even if the basic structure is fundamentally the same, some actual entities are much more complex than others. The actual entities differ from each
other in their realization of potentialities.

The actual entities are the becoming realities which are open and accept
other realities through process. In other words, actual entities are dynamic
and interactive things in the process of becoming. Whitehead is convinced
that the actual world is ultimately composed of processes of "becoming," not
"being" (i.e. it is not only our knowledge of nature that is in a state of becoming). Since the constitution of an actual entity is the result of the process
of becoming, we can word this relation in an apt and concise way by saying
that an actual entity's being is the result of its process of becoming. Because
an entity's being is constituted by its becoming, becoming is a more basic
category than being. From the statement that events involve the notions of
beginning, ongoing and consummation, Whitehead concluded that an actual
entity was "alive" or "living." When "becoming" ends up in "being" the actual
entity is "dead," in the sense that it is no longer becoming.

Since the actual world is distinct from the potential world, we must
account for the capacity of thought to go behind the sphere of actual entities.
The sphere of potential realities consists, according to Whitehead, of eternal
objects. An eternal object does not need a reference to any definite actual
entity. Since they are merely possible forms of definiteness they are in fundamental contrast with actual entities. "They are pure potentials for the specific
determination of facts" (Whitehead 1985, p. 32).

Eternal objects are forms of definiteness capable of specifying the character of actual entities. The eternal objects are subjective in the sense that
they are elements in the definiteness of the subjective forms. Eternal objects
are defined as the particular ways in which actual entities form their energy
or "emotion" and present themselves to the world. The eternal objects are
always a potentiality for actual entities. In themselves, as conceptually felt,
they are neutral as to the fact of their physical ingression in any particular
actual entity of the temporal world.

This implies that considered in reference to the existence of things, eternal
objects are universals. In their own nature, eternal objects refer to the general
public facts of the world without any disclosure of the empirical details of
their own implication in them. By saying that eternal objects transcend their
relationship to any actual occasion Whitehead is arguing that they transcend
their relationship to any determinable finite set of relationships. Actual entities do not, in themselves, tell what is possible, they only represent concrete
facts. The process, the becoming involved in the decision of an actual entity is
dependent on the eternal objects involved. Eternal objects are involved in the
process of change in the sense that they define the very process and give the
actual entity its specific character. Despite that, eternal objects in themselves
are neutral and they represent potentiality for actual entities. Each eternal
entity adds its own unique contribution to each actual occasion. This contribution is identical in each case. From this we conclude by saying that "the

realm of eternal objects is the realm of possibility" and that "the realm of events is the realm of actuality" (Jones 1975, p. 82).

Eternal objects could be understood as universals because they are given as pure potentials. An eternal entity functions as a determinant which determines the realization of actual entities by having ingression into actual entities. It is important to be aware that eternal entities could not be separated from actual entities because they are potentialities which are realized in actual entities.

Prehensions

Whitehead named the process of connecting actual entities and eternal objects "prehensions." Prehensions, or relations, describe how complex organisms come into being as a combination of past experiences (actual entities) and potentials (eternal objects). According to Emmet, prehensions are "a general word for the grasping, or taking hold of one thing by another, and so connoting an active coming together" (Emmet 2012, p. 41). A prehension is realized through the gathering of things into a unity. This unity of a prehension exists here and now, "and the things so gathered into the grasped unity have essential reference to other places and other times" (Whitehead 1967a, p. 69). So space and time are simply abstractions from the totality of prehensive unifications as mutually patterned in each other. Nature is a structure of evolving processes. The development in nature can therefore be described as a process from prehension to prehension.

Prehensions can be either positive or negative. Positive prehensions concern the process of integration: the actual entities connect into complex and interdependent nexus or societies. Negative prehensions mean blocking out those elements of the past and possibilities of the future that will not be incorporated into the present. In Whitehead's theory of prehensions, "the notion of 'negative prehensions' constitutes how the extensive continuum is 'divided' and 'decided' by the organism" (Scarfe 2002, p. 116).

> A nexus enjoys "social order" when (i) there is a common element of form illustrated in the definiteness of each of its included actual entities, and (ii) this common element of form arises in each member of the nexus by reason of the conditions imposed upon it by its prehensions of some other members of the nexus, and (iii) these prehensions impose that condition of reproduction by reason of their inclusion of positive feelings involving that common form.
>
> (Whitehead 1967a, p. 203)

New aggregated entities confront the whole past actual world, and bring the world into new entities. Because of this interconnectedness in time (and space) everything that has happened in the past has some impact on the present. What happens in the present has impact on the events of the future. This is the principle of relativity: "everything is related to everything else." The final real things are individual living organisms, each dependent on their relationships to others for their continued existence as themselves.

In short, the basic functions of negative prehensions are the elimination of irrelevant data from experience. Negative prehensions, working in concert with positive prehensions, are "the primary vehicles of organic selectivity, enabling [...] 'self-realization'" (Scarfe 2002, p. 116). Self-realization implies a prehensive process where objective data are fused into one datum, and, in addition, subject and object grow together and are unified.

According to Whitehead, creativity comes into existence through the interplay between the actual entities and the eternal objects. "Reality is constituted by entities which are brief pulses of creative activity [...] constantly developing in reaction to what has been and to what might be" (Hosinski 1993, p. 23). Whitehead thus affirms both the deep interrelatedness of all things and the ways that their interactions and variations continually lead to consequences that are new and unforeseen. Nature is a theatre for the interrelations of activities. "All things change, the activities and their interrelations" (Whitehead 1977, p. 15).

Networks

In this perspective, everything is integrated as part of a dynamic network. Nothing can exist as an isolated atom. An important feature of the philosophy of organism is that everything is interdependent both temporally and spatially. This interconnectedness between organisms and their natural and social environment has several consequences. First, relations become more important than objects. This means that every organism is constituted by its connections to other organisms. From this ontological position it is reasonable to claim that all entities derive their character from the social and ecological networks of which they are integrated parts. Second, every organism develops as integrated parts of numerous different processes which are interwoven with one another. This process can be understood from both an individual and a systemic perspective. We can consider the formation of the system from the characterization of the individuals, "or we can characterize the individuals and conceive them as formative of the relevant process" (Whitehead 1966, p. 98). According to Latour, the guiding principle is that "an actor is defined by its alliances; if alliances shift, then by definition the actor has changed" (Harman 2009, p. 105).

When things are understood solely in terms of their relations an entity is nothing more than its perception of other entities. "These entities, in turn, are made up of other perceptions" (Shaviro 2014, p. 31). Third, all organisms have inherent value as parts of social and ecological networks. Organisms cannot be characterized merely by mass, extension and velocity, "they are creatures enjoying the value of their own experience, which itself is intuitively inherited from the feelings of others" (Segall 2013, p. 26). Capra and Luisi argue that "living systems relates to its environment structurally – that is, through recurrent interactions, each of which triggers structural changes in the system" (Capra and Luisi 2014, p. 135).

In other words, organisms are co-creators of their own environments and they are bound together as co-creators. Cooperative interaction becomes the essential factor for long-term survival. Wherever resilient ecosystems are found, whether at the atomic, biotic, or anthropic level, it is evident that their success is a result of an association of organisms providing for each other a favorable environment" (Segall 2013, p. 52). According to Capra, twentieth-century science has shown repeatedly that all natural phenomena are ultimately interconnected and that "their essential properties, in fact, derive from their relationships to other things" (Capra 2007, p. 159), completely in harmony with the philosophy of organism. A system's resilience will increase as the pattern of interconnections becomes more complex.

Whitehead's philosophy of organism is deeply relevant to our contemporary concerns because he thinks about how novelty can emerge from selective repetition and how all entities in the world are deeply interrelated and mutually dependent even in their separation from one another, and how nonhuman agents, no less than human ones, "perform actions and express needs and values" (Shaviro 2014, p. 5). Things both differentiate themselves absolutely from one another and refer themselves incessantly to one another. Value and sense are intrinsic to all entities and thereby immanent to the world as it actually exists. "The attempt to speak of a thing apart from its relations gives us only what Whitehead calls 'vacuous actuality'" (Harman 2009, p. 101). All kinds of life are arranged in networks: "Whenever we look at life, we look at networks" (Capra and Luisi 2014, p. 95).

Concern

Even if the distinction between self-enjoyment and concern is fundamental, Whitehead refuses to choose between them because every actual choice or decision involves both. They are closely bound together. "You cannot have the one without the other" (Shaviro 2014, p. 15). Concern is relational, rather than absolute, and allo-affective, rather than auto-affective. Enjoyment (of life) belongs to the process and is not a characteristic of any static result. Concern or other-directedness is therefore a necessary precondition for even the most intransitive self-enjoyment. Concern opens the self to the outside; it is an involuntary experience of being affected by others. "When something concerns me, I cannot ignore it or walk away from it. It presses on my being and compels me to respond" (Shaviro 2014, p. 14).

Concern and self-enjoyment exceed the tendency, found in philosophical rationalism, to homogenize individuals and suppress their diversity. Rationalism marginalizes, ignores or even suppresses many valuable human faculties and forms of knowledge and has "a deep anti-pluralist bias and a strong streak of intolerance" (Parekh 2001, p. 84). Kant's categorical imperative is an illustrative example of identical ideals for all human beings. The consequence is that only one kind of life is accepted as the highest or truly human and everyone is expected to conform to it.

Consciousness

Philosophy of organism describes consciousness as consisting of three interdependent elements that could not be torn apart: instinct, intelligence and wisdom. They integrate, react and merge into hybrid factors. The primary element, which is presupposed in consciousness, is termed "instinct." Instinct is the mode of experience directly arising out of the urge of inheritance, individual and environmental. Instincts are the most primary elements which are presupposed in consciousness. With reference to the discussion of the interconnectedness of nexus and societies, it is reasonable to suggest that the thought of the behavior of an organization or a nation has many similarities with the way individuals behave. The instincts of organizations and nations are traced out by the established routines. Beyond the routines there lies spontaneity of thought, which is subject to control and efficiency. On the one hand, the claim for freedom of thought is without meaning without the spontaneity, and on the other hand, the control is "the judgement of the whole, attenuating or strengthening the partial flashes of self-determination" (Whitehead 1967b, p. 47).

Routine is essential for every society. "It is the seventh heaven of all business, the essential component in the success of every factory, the ideal of every statesman" (Whitehead 1967b, 90). When a well-functioning routine is established the system is maintained by a coordination of conditioned reflexes. A perfect running routine reduces the demand for intellectual understanding. Society requires stability based on routines. But, since the routines counteract the possibilities of a progressive society, complete routines can never be realized in a civilized society and the need for understanding (intelligence) is increasing. Progressiveness has become even more important in modern times, but to decide whether the change goes from worse to better or from better to worse presupposes values (wisdom). Today, the local, national and global society is changing so fast that the mere compulsion of tradition and routines has lost its position as the fundamental force.

Intelligence is the mode of rationality. An essential part of the intellectual operations consists of coordination of notions derived from the primary facts of experience into a logically coherent system. One of the most serious problems connected to intellectual understanding is the necessity of excluding some of the background variables. When the primary facts are selected so as to resolve the complicated aspects of things into intellectual subordination, intellectual coordination is more readily achieved.

Science's main task, in order to illuminate the actual future possibilities of development, is to expand the understanding of the constitution of society.

> Such a complete understanding is a cooperative enterprise; and a busi-
> ness community maintains its success for long periods so far as its average
> foresight is dominated by some approach to such general understanding.
> (Whitehead 1967b, p. 89)

In Whitehead's view intelligence separated from emotions and values can be a problem. "The folly of intelligent people, clear-headed and narrow-visioned, has precipitated many catastrophes" (Whitehead 1967b, p. 48). In addition to the entire internal functioning of society, the interplay between economics, society and nature represents the general topic to be understood. With reference to the different perspectives on the laws of nature, society can be understood as an integrated, dynamic organism, constituted by immanent relations, or as an atomistic, static mechanism, constituted by external laws. Depending on the choice of perspective, science can focus either on intellectual understanding of the immanent constitution of society or on a description of the different parts of the social machinery. Both are possible and relevant depending on the topics to be studied. We have to be aware of the fallacy of misplaced concreteness when studying part of the constitution of society.

Wisdom is in constant pursuit of deeper understanding, always confronting the intellect with the importance of its omissions. It is the function of wisdom "to act as a modifying agency on the intellectual ferment so as to produce a self-determined issue from the given conditions" (Whitehead 1967b, p. 46). Wisdom is the final determination, or the subjective aim, with its limits set by the inherited factors. According to the holism in Whitehead's philosophy, the whole is emerging from its parts, and the parts are emerging within the whole. This leads to the following conclusion:

> In judging social institutions, their rise, their culmination, and their decay,
> we have to estimate the types of instinct, of intelligence, and of wisdom
> which have cooperated with natural forces to develop the story.
> (Whitehead 1967b, p. 48)

Since the individual is a complex entity whose physical form of existence and mental life are both functioning under definite patterns, there is no such a thing as an act of free choice. In addition, the individual as a subject is embedded in a social pattern. In congruence with Aristotelian philosophy, goodness and morality do not come from outside the person but from the potentials of the human being himself or herself. To realize this potential, society is very important. In other words, human strengths and virtues must be cultivated in a cultural context. A good life is not a permanent state but is in continuous development and growth in concert with the surroundings. The individual, immersed in society, is subject to the directive character of the "values" prevalent in the group. Values cannot be limited to the individual being; it must always be a matter of value for others. "Morality controls the 'ends' which find their realization in the life of the individual as 'satisfactions'" (Goheen

1991, p. 454). Therefore, the likes and dislikes, adversions and aversions of the individual to some extent are controlled by the act of "valuation."

To understand the relation of our personal experience to the activities in nature we have "to examine the dependence of our personal experiences upon our personal body" (Whitehead 1977, p. 35). Body and soul are inescapable elements in our being and each has the full reality of our immediate self. In a wider perspective, this means that our knowledge is an integrated part of the larger field of nature. All sense-perception is merely one outcome of the dependence of our experience upon the bodily functioning character of group "values."

Perception

There are two sources of information about the external world. They are closely connected and at the same time distinct from each other. The first perspective is called the mode of "causal efficacy" and the other mode is "presentational immediacy" (sense-perception). On the one hand, Whitehead argues that to associate conscious sense-perception (presentational immediacy) with experience has fatal consequences for philosophical and scientific views of the natural world. He states that perception in the mode of presentational immediacy involves a high degree of abstraction from the most basic experience of the world since actual entities are separated in time and space. This kind of "objectification implies the process by which an actual entity is atomized out from the backdrop of the extensive continuum" (Scarfe 2002, p. 115). Sensory objects are immediately present to our conscious awareness.

On the other hand, he proposes "causal efficacy" as the primary mode of perception. Perception in the mode of "causal efficacy," there is no perception of separation of actual entities. In this mode of perception we directly perceive the interconnectedness of other actualities. All actual entities are functionally interrelated and no entity can be conceived as separated from the system as a whole. According to Whitehead, our basic experience (conscious or unconscious) of the world is based upon perception in the mode of "causal efficacy." Causal efficacy is the mode of perceiving things as given conditions or determinants to which our immediate experience must conform. We experience the push from the past and the influence on the future, in other words the world as temporally extended. On the other hand, presentational immediacy is the mode of perceiving things from a specific point of view in space.

> The weakness of the epistemology of the eighteenth and nineteenth centuries was that it based itself purely upon a narrow formulation of sense-perception. Also, among the various modes of sensation, visual experience was picked out as the typical example. The result was to exclude all the really fundamental factors constituting our experience.
>
> (Whitehead 1977, p. 39)

It is only in the mode of causal efficacy that we are faced with the stubborn fact of the givenness of the real world. Presentational immediacy provides us with a world that reflects the interests and purposes of particular organisms. "The primary function of Presentational Immediacy is to lay clear those elements of the world disclosed through Causal Efficacy that are of particular importance to living beings such as us" (Rose 2002, p. 72).

Creativity

Whitehead's highest value is creativity, which he calls the "universal of universals." Creativity is the actualization of potentiality and the process of actualization is an occasion of experiencing. Actuality and potentiality are organically integrated so as to allow for a genuinely creative cosmos where, though the past is settled, the future remains wildly open. New forms of fact are always emerging, though none ever exists in isolation from its environment. Life constantly reaches out into novelty. The initial situation with its creativity can be termed the initial phase of the new occasion. In Capra and Luisi's words, "Creativity – the generation of new forms – is a key property of all living systems" (Capra and Luisi 2014, p. 161).

Creativity is Whitehead's term for the inherent tension between actuality and potentiality, in the actual world and every actual entity in it. This in-determination, rendered determinate in the real concrescence, is the meaning of "potentiality." It is a conditioned in-determination, and is therefore called a "real potentiality."

> The mutual independence of contemporary occasions lies strictly within the sphere of their teleological self-creation. The occasions originate from a common past and their objective immortality operates within a common future. Thus, indirectly, via the immanence of the past and the immanence of the future, the occasions are connected. But the immediate activity of self-creation is separate and private, so far as contemporaries are concerned.
> (Whitehead 1967b, p. 195)

Hence, the process of becoming in the present is a reaction to what is inherited from the past and is caused or "created" by the creativity of the present actual entities themselves. The occasion, empowered by creativity, brings itself into being by unifying its past actualities. "The creative agency is that which achieves the final unity, which is the occasion itself. In this sense the occasion is creator or more precisely, its self-creator" (Ford 2002, p. 391). Whitehead points out that nature does provide a field for independent activities and our claim for freedom is rooted in our relationship to our contemporary environment.

Whitehead states that organisms create their own environment. According to Capra and Luisi, there is no environment in some independent and abstract sense. "Just as there is no organism without an environment, there is no environment without an organism" (Capra and Luisi 2014, p. 141). For this purpose, societies of cooperating organisms are needed as the single organism is almost helpless. "But with such cooperation and in proportion to the effort put forward, the environment has a plasticity which alters the whole ethical aspect of evolution" (Whitehead 1967a, p. 112). By defining a general principle of creative self-production, Whitehead tries to account for the objective character of the subjective experience. The process of self-creation is the transformation of the potential into the actual.

It is interesting to notice that Ricoeur connects actualization of potentials to the concept "utopia." He ascertains that "at the social level the role of potentiality is assumed by utopia" (Ricoeur 1986, p. xxxii). If utopia opens the possible, it does so on the basis of a metaphoric transformation of the existing. This line of reasoning is in accordance with Whitehead who points out that "the past has an objective existence in the present which lies in the future beyond itself" (Whitehead 1967b, p. 191). Each moment of experience confesses itself to be a transition between the two worlds of the immediate past and the immediate future. The future belongs to the essence of present fact and has no actuality. "The future is prepared in the present, but at the same time there will be more in the future than in the present" (Ricoeur 1986, p. 280). Whitehead elaborates this argument by pointing out that "the world dreams of things to come, and then in due season arouses itself to their realization" (Whitehead 1967b, p. 279).

Civilization develops only where considerable numbers of people work together for common ends. Such unity is brought about not so much by a community of bare ideas as by a community of the feelings by which ideas are "emotionalized" and become beliefs and motives. Whitehead called this utopian process an "adventure of ideas" and he claimed that a society without adventure is in full decay. The philosophy of organism has an irreducibly aesthetic dimension which requires new and bold inventions rather than pacifying resolutions.

Whitehead points out that life is enjoyment of emotion, derived from the past and aimed at the future. A model that sets adventure or utopia in opposition to reality is inadequate because reality is not given but a process. "Reality is always caught in the flux of time, in the process of change that utopia attempts to bring about" (Ricoeur 1986, p. xxxi). Utopias appear during a time of restoration, and this perhaps makes sense for our time, too. Any account of the "adventure of ideas" is concerned with ideas threading their way among "the alternatives presented by these various phrases" (Whitehead 1967b, p. 199).

To get an overview that permits a holistic approach to the problems we are facing today we must fly high. Subjectivity must be defined in terms of present immediacy, derivation from the past and signification for the future in terms of unity or individuality.

In order to establish and discuss a scheme of interpretation, applicable and adequate for ecological economics, I will apply the method "descriptive generalization" to get a deeper understanding of the paradigmatic fundament in Part II of this inquiry. This means that ideas taken from the thirty alternative economists contribute to the understanding of both the basic elements and their interrelatedness. One of the most important assumptions is that there are no self-evident axioms to start from. An integrated theory of ecological economics must start, therefore, with a set of concepts that seem to form a satisfactory scheme of interpretation from some other region of experience. While neo-classical economics refers to a mechanistic paradigm, the understanding of ecological economics presupposes an organic categorial scheme. But even though ecological economics must shape its approaches and research questions based upon human life situations and the conditions of today, it is necessary in the analysis to inquire into the historical roots.

Civilization

Whitehead claims that even if the notion of civilization is very confusing, we all know what it means. "It suggests a certain ideal for life on earth, and this ideal concerns both the individual human being and also societies of men" (Whitehead 1967b, p. 273). Whitehead puts forward a general definition of a civilized society as exhibiting the five qualities of "truth, beauty, adventure, art, peace" (Whitehead 1967b, p. 274). Johnson adds that "all five qualities should be exhibited in all phases of experience" (Johnson 1962, p. 1).

Adventure and art, including spontaneity and freshness, are the most important ingredients in civilization. Art involves freshness and spontaneity and the contrast of what is (actuality) and what might be (potentiality). A work of art is an impressive demonstration of creative powers. "It not only expresses, but also arouses, new ideas and 'freshness' of emotion" (Johnson 1962, p. 8). Johnson points to a very important aspect in philosophy of organism when he states that "if something new and better is to be enjoyed, something old and less valuable must be discarded" (Johnson 1962, p. 3). Whitehead expresses the hope that "our present epoch is to be viewed as a period of change to a new direction of civilization, involving in its dislocations a minimum of human misery" (Whitehead 1967b, p. 278). To succeed in this change process, he argues that thought has to run ahead of realization. "The vigour of the race has then pushed forward into the adventure of imagination, so as to anticipate the physical adventures of exploration" (Whitehead 1967b, p. 279).

Civilization also includes peace, not peace as absence of war, but peace as a notion of harmony which binds the other four qualities together. It is a positive feeling which is hard to define and even difficult to speak about, but it is "a broadening of feeling due to the emergence of some deep metaphysical insight, unverbalized and yet momentous in its coordination of values"

(Whitehead 1967b, p. 285). The first effect of peace, according to Whitehead, is a surpassing of personality and the removal of the stress of acquisitive feelings arising from the soul's preoccupation with itself. Peace is thus self-control at its most extensive: "at the width where the 'self' has been lost, and interest has been transferred to coordinations wider than personality" (Whitehead 1967b, p. 285). A very important function of art is "to constitute civilization by stressing the principle of the harmony of individuals" (Johnson 1962, p. 9).

In a civilized society, based on organic interdependence, economics is characterized by cooperation instead of ruthless competition. In addition, "the new economic system must take into consideration the basic rights of men to develop their potentialities of value experience" (Johnson 1962, p. 92). As far as work is concerned, according to Whitehead, it should challenge the intellect and have moral and aesthetic worth and produce useful consequences which further the welfare of society.

Concluding remarks

Philosophy of organism is relevant as a frame of reference to understand many of the challenges in the present. Economic organization creates some of the greatest problems in human relationships. The idea that all entities are connected in cooperative networks is in opposition to neo-liberal economics, which postulates atomistic competitive markets consisting of autonomous actors. According to Whitehead, we are now passing into a phase of change where mankind is shifting its outlook. New directions of thought arise from flashes of intuition which bring new material within the scope of scholarly learning. The mere compulsion of tradition has lost its force.

It is the business of philosophers, students and practical people to recreate and re-enact a vision of the world which includes those elements of reverence and order without which society lapses into riot and a society penetrated throughout by an unflinching rationality. Evidently something new is developing. Nineteenth-century individualistic liberalism has, quite unexpectedly, collapsed. "As long as the trading middle classes were dominant as the sole group whose satisfaction mattered its doctrines were self-evident" (Whitehead 1967b, p. 62). Today, the whole concept of "absolute individuals with absolute rights, and with a contractual power of forming fully defined external relations, has broken down" (Whitehead 1967b, p. 63). According to the philosophy of organism, human beings are inseparable from their environment. Even stronger, the environment is immanent in them, and conversely they are immanent in the environment which they help to transmit.

Any statement of a philosophical argument is "always an oversimplification not just of the world as a whole, but even of what the statement itself discusses" (Harman 2009, p. 169). While Whitehead's ontological principle states that everything that happens is a consequence of the reality of specific entities, Latour's conversed theorem is equally fruitful: all entities have consequences.

In the next chapter I will delve into the concept of utopia to find out how it is possible to change to a new direction of civilization. According to Whitehead "these quick transitions to new types of civilization are only possible when thought has run ahead of realization" (Whitehead 1967b, p. 278). Thus in a live civilization there is always an element of unrest. Sensitivity to new ideas means curiosity, adventure and change.

2 Ideology and utopia

KARL MANNHEIM AND PAUL RICOEUR

> The intention of a utopia is to change – to shatter – the present order.
>
> Paul Ricoeur

Introduction

In the preceding chapter I elaborated on Whitehead's philosophy of organism. Creativity was characterized as "the universal of universals." Whitehead noted that creativity is only possible on the basis of, and in response to, stubborn facts which cannot be evaded. Creativity represents the connection between actuality and potentiality. So "newness always depends on something prior" (Shaviro 2014, p. 101). All creativity involves "an adventure of thought regarding things as yet unrealized" (Whitehead 1967b, p. 279). Following Whitehead's line of argument it is possible to connect his understanding of creativity and adventure with the concept "utopia." Utopia was introduced as an expression transcending (potentiality) the description of reality (actuality). Mannheim stressed that utopia "breaks the bonds of the existing order" (Mannheim 1936, p. 192).

Utopias are usually constructed against a background of severe problems or crises in the current society. They are meant to address the major challenges and can therefore be seen as mirrors for inherent problems in the established ideology. Utopias provide "a fictional reference to which ideology can be compared and by which it can be criticized" (Steeves 2000, p. 2.). When we study a phenomenon from a new perspective we discover things that we don't see when we are in the midst of the situation. (As an example, Lovelock discovered Gaia – the living Earth – when he first saw a picture of the Earth taken from space.)

In other words, utopia starts as utopia when it distances itself from the established ideology. Utopia can be characterized as a description of something that does not exist, as an exercise in imagination unrelated to the present reality. Utopias are connected to reality as a projection of what could be possible. The tension between what is and what could be is of vital significance for change processes. Ricoeur has formulated the process of change even more strongly. "The intention of a utopia is to change – to shatter – the present order" (Ricoeur 1986, p. xxi).

The utopian impulse orients itself toward possibilities that are not constrained by what is. "The field of the possible is [now] often beyond that of the actual; it is a field [...] for alternative ways of living" (Ricoeur 1986, p. 16). Utopia is an expression of a desire for a better way of living in a better society. To be applicable for forming a better society the utopia must be formulated as concrete as possible and at the same time refer to eternal ideals.

Utopia as a driving force

Since we normally grasp the world in terms of pre-imposed concepts, utopia helps us to locate new opportunities in the future society. Utopianism is defined as a conception of social renewal either by ideas or ideals themselves or embodied in definite agencies of social change. Utopia refers to radical engagements which seek to further the possibilities of a fulfilling and satisfying life for all members of the society. It is recognized that "our wishes and thoughts, our dreams and our reasoning, our fears and our knowledge, our interests and our energies" (Popper 2002, p. 44) are all forces in the development of society.

Utopia is a kind of rebirth of fantasy essential for the development and survival of our civilization and acknowledges that every period in history has contained ideas transcending the existing order. Utopia, inspired by the Aristotelian idea of the good life in the good society, strives to contradict the negative in society and, more generally, the negative in human existence. Therefore it is a relevant requirement for calling something a "utopia" that it should offer new kinds of benefit to both individuals and society.

Ecological economics represents a utopian description of alternative development based on critical reflections on contemporary society and economy. Most of the contributions in ecological economics refer to negative consequences or symptoms of modern society that they try to overcome in the descriptions of an alternative future. The changes, individually and collectively, are both a prerequisite for utopia and a justification for why utopias are necessary. In the next chapter I will discuss to what extent ecological economics satisfies these requirements.

According to Levitas a key question is connected to the practical implementation of the measures required to fulfill utopian ideas in practice. "If the function of utopia is to bring about change, then the question of practical possibility and the problem of transition are real ones" (Levitas 2011, p. 204). She claims that the possibilities to succeed in moving from utopias to practice lie in utopia itself more than in external factors. From this line of argument it is realistic to conclude that the process of being realized depends on the quality of the utopia.

Box 2.1 Different meanings of utopia

- In the classic sense, a non-existent (good) place.
- Description of imaginary societies held to be perfect or much closer to perfection than any society in the real world.
- Philosophies of history which culminate in a vision of achieved perfection.
- Perceived as desirable, as a world not so much bound to come as one which should come.
- Critical of existing society, in fact a system of ideas remains utopian and thus able to boost human activity only in so far as it is perceived as representing a system essentially different from, if not antithetical to, the existing one.
- A utopia tends to shatter, either partially or wholly, the order of things prevailing at the time.
- It may appear to those bent on reforming society that overstatement is necessary for some degree of success.
- Definition of what is peculiar to man, of what is genuinely human rather than merely conventional, or of man's potentialities.
- Involving a measure of hazard, for an image of the future opposes the qualities of utopia, it must be ascertained that it will not come to pass unless fostered by deliberate collective action.

Levitas claims that the more concrete a utopia is, the stronger is its transformative power. However, it is important to be aware that the introduction of utopian ideas is often met with massive resistance from those who benefit from the existing system. New ideas are always a danger to the existing order. To prohibit change, representatives of the given order have a tendency to label all utopian conceptions as unrealistic and claim that they never could be realized.

On the one hand, all creative ideas which do not fit into the current order are "situationally transcendent" or described as unreal by the establishment. "According to this usage, the contemporary connotation of the term 'utopian' is predominantly that of an idea which is in principle unrealizable" (Mannheim 1936, p. 196). On the other hand, ideas which correspond to the existing social order are designated as adequate and situationally congruous.

Utopian realism

Utopias developed in a society have significance for understanding the main challenges in that specific historical epoch. Ricoeur emphasizes "the connections which exist between a concrete utopia and the corresponding historical time-perspective" (Ricoeur 1986, p. 275). Mannheim pointed out that the utopia of the ascendant bourgeoisie was the idea of "freedom." "It contained elements oriented toward the realization of a new social order which were instrumental in disintegrating the previously existing order and which, after their realization, did in part become translated into reality" (Mannheim 1936, p. 203). Today many utopias are focused on how to build a society where problems connected to climate change and CO_2 emissions are eliminated. As we will see in Part II of the book, present-day utopias also provide an explicit impression of a global society characterized by injustice, violence and massive environmental destruction.

Even if knowledge about a specific society does not affect development directly, the circularity of social knowledge has an indirect influence on the change processes. "New knowledge (concepts, theories, findings) does not simply render the social world more transparent, but also alters its nature, spinning it off in novel directions" (Giddens 1990, p. 153). From a utopian perspective, that is, modern society seen from outside, it is possible to uncover hidden assumptions, contradictions and limitations in the existing system. According to Ricoeur, "utopia is the view from 'nowhere' – the literal meaning of the word – that ensures that we no longer take for granted our present reality" (Ricoeur 1986, p. xxix). In the introduction to *One-Dimensional Man* Marcuse developed a critical philosophical perspective (a utopia) from which he could "criticize existing forms of thought, behaviour, and social organization" (Marcuse 2002, p. xiii).

Social change depends on our ability to envisage alternative futures. To be realized the utopian models must be realistic, that is, they must not violate what we know of nature and society, including knowledge of human nature. "A realistic utopia is one that 'could and may exist'; it is achievable and consistent with what we know of the laws of nature, including human nature" (Levitas 2013, p. 131). In accordance with philosophy of organism, utopias connected to immanent trends of development are more realistic than utopias imposed from outside. Utopian realism combines the description of an alternative future with analysis of ongoing institutional trends whereby political futures are immanent in the present. Giddens points out that it is necessary to "balance utopian ideals with realism" (Giddens 1990, p. 155).

Utopian dreams are unrealistic if they don't take into account knowledge of historical development. Such a methodology would lead to the study of general laws of social life with the aim of finding all those facts "which would be indispensable as a basis for the work of everyone seeking to reform social institutions" (Popper 2002, p. 41). According to Popper there is no doubt that such facts exist, and he argues that many utopian systems are impracticable "because they do not consider such facts sufficiently" (Popper 2002, p. 41). Whitehead claimed that in all change there must be something unchanging in the same way that improvisation requires knowledge about fixed patterns and systems.

Utopian realism as an idea is not without its problems, because it sets limits on its legitimacy which potentially confine it to a conservative reading of the present and binding imagination too closely to "what can be imagined as possible rather than what can possible be imagined" (Levitas 2013, p. 129).

The relation between realism and utopia may therefore be considered a tension of a contradiction, because the idea of a realistic utopia troubles both concepts, surfaces the politics of perceived possibility and interrogates the relationship between present and future.

Davis suggests a clear analytical distinction between transcendent and grounded utopias (Davis 2012, p. 136):

- Transcendent utopias are constructs of the perfectionist imagination that abstract from existing reality.
- Transcendent utopias confront realism as irreconcilable opposites.
- Grounded utopias both emerge organically out of, and contribute to, further development of historical movements for grassroots social change.
- Grounded utopias are not restricted to written texts; they find expression in an almost endless variety of cultural practices, from eco-villages to small scale transition processes.
- Grounded utopianism, focused on concrete social action intended to develop and implement practical solutions that restore ecological and social balance, documents that another world is possible.
- Grounded utopianism has greater explanatory power with respect to social change processes.

Based on the preceding paragraphs we can summarize that utopian descriptions on the one hand open new perspectives that offer a vantage point from which to perceive the given, the already constituted. On the other hand, utopia offers new possibilities above and beyond the given. Utopia is then not just a dream to be enjoyed, but a vision to be pursued. Utopia does not express desire, but enables people to work toward an understanding of what is necessary for "human fulfilment, a broadening, deepening and raising of aspirations in terms quite different from those of their everyday life" (Levitas 2011, p. 141).

Utopia entails not just the fictional depiction of a better society, but the assertion of a radically different set of values. These values are communicated indirectly through their implications for the whole way of life in order for utopia "to operate at the level of experience, not merely cognition, encouraging the sense that it does not have to be like this, it could be otherwise" (Levitas 2011, p. 143).

It is not necessary for utopia to pass into action; even if utopia is desired and fought for, it does not have to be won. "Utopias are seen as unattainable goals which, despite 'constantly receding', nevertheless lead us onward and upward" (Levitas 2011, p. 21).

Utopia is like the rainbow, even if the rainbow could lead us in the right direction we can never reach the exact point where the pot of gold is. To be utopian it is not enough to represent a quality of otherness. There must also be an element of transformation. Utopia may indeed have a transformative and emancipatory function; its defining characteristic is the capacity to

---

Box 2.2 Utopia has several functions

- Its cognitive function as a mode of operation of constructive reason.
- Its educative function as a mythography which instructs men to will and desire more and better.
- Its anticipatory function as a futurology of possibilities which latter become actual.
- Its causal function as an agent for historical change.

(Levitas 2011, p. 117)

---

transform the situation and realize itself. The transformation process connects the present with the future.

Mannheim was worried about a possible disappearance of utopia as it represented the power or will to change the world. Utopia is required to make humanity able to imagine, will and affect the future. We should regard as utopian all situationally transcendent ideas which in any way have a transforming effect upon the existing historical-social order. "The unfinished nature of reality locates concrete utopia as a possible future within the real" (Levitas 2011, p. 104). The world is essentially unfinished; the future is brought into being by human agency; our participation in this process is inescapable (Levitas 2012, p. 98). Since the function of expressing, anticipating and affecting the future can be identified in a vast range of cultural forms, the subject matter of utopia is identified in terms of the shared characteristic of the intention toward a better life. Levitas states, in accordance with Whitehead, that the world is a "process of becoming" (Levitas 2012, p. 98).

Utopia and art

To open up prospects which would have been lost without utopian anticipation it is of great importance to accept different forms of utopias. To initiate actualization of utopia the understanding of the power of transformation in utopia is important. Ricoeur pointed out that "utopia attempts to confront the problem of power itself" (Ricoeur 1986, p. xxi). Since utopia as composed by scientists and industrialists lacks passion, many contributors in utopian method argue that art has an important utopian function. According to Ricoeur, "the artists will open the way and develop 'the poetic part of the new system'" (Ricoeur 1986, p. 294). Artistic expressions play on many strings to build powerful harmonies, for example, intuitive perceptions, feelings, experience and imagination. Artists play an important role in building utopia because they bring with them the power of imagination. In his book *The Science of Leonardo* Capra argues that Leonardo's paintings were both art and science. He expressed a scientific knowledge which was quite different from the abstract and lifeless mechanistic science that emerged 200 years later.

"Leonardo's forms are living forms, continually shaped and transformed by underlying processes" (Capra 2007, p. 3).

Artistic work often expresses people's longing for beauty and the true pleasure of life and this is also the essence of utopian thinking. The utopian function of art is even more active as it encourages the sense that something is missing, and it is an indispensable inspiration to social transformation. The utopian mentality is anti-violent; the effort is to convince others to make the break with the past. In his book *The Power of Art. Hundertwasser: The Painter-King with the Five Skins*, Restany points out that "visionary utopias have the appearance of a truth progressively revealed by the inexorable logic of an exemplary humanist fate" (Restany 2011, p. 7). Utopia based on free intuitive thinking attacks the conformity pursued by the representatives of the dominant ideology and utopian messages are looked upon as provocative and subversive. By establishing strong network-based relationships anchored in egalitarian dialogic cooperation it is possible to empower the influence from art. "Without art to embody the dream of a matter, we will not be able to possess it in reality" (Levitas 2011, p. 129).

Ideology and utopia

Mannheim contrasted ideology and utopia on the basis of their social function. On the one hand, he argues that ideology preserves the status quo. Ideologies are explanations or interpretations of the social reality "concerned with the characteristics and composition of the total structure of the mind" (Mannheim 1936, p. 56) in a certain epoch. On the other hand, he provided powerful arguments that utopia transforms the status quo by indicating that "a state of mind is utopian when it is incongruous with the state of reality within which it occurs" (Mannheim 1936, p. 192).

Ricoeur nuanced the differences between the two concepts by arguing that "both ideologies and utopias deal with power; ideology is always an attempt to legitimate power, while utopia is always an attempt to replace power by something else" (Ricoeur 1986, p. 288). Steeves states that imagination takes the form of a dialectic process with two poles, "one being ideology which establishes the images and goals of a given society, and the other being utopia which exposes society to an open horizon of new images and ideal" (Steeves 2000, p. 225). Ideology and utopia combined constitute social imagination. In other words, ideology and utopia are distinguished in terms of their function in relation to social change; ideology operates to sustain the status quo, utopia aims to transform it.

Ideologies are directed toward the past, whereas utopias have a future-oriented element. "In reality, utopian and ideological elements are often intertwined" (Levitas 2013, p. 94). Ricoeur points out that both ideology and utopia presuppose processes of imagination. Ideology is important to create and preserve the self-image in a society, while utopia provides alternatives to the status quo. To illustrate the distinction between ideology and utopia we can say the ideology is imagination as a picture which describes what exists, while utopia is imagination as a fiction, re-describing what exists. The correlation between ideology and utopia typifies what Ricoeur calls social and cultural imagination.

Utopia is a way to escape from the circularity in which ideologies engulf us. To understand the time we are living in we must step outside the established ideologies and develop a utopian position from where we can observe it. Ideology is always judged from utopia. The distinction between ideology and utopia gives meaning in order to indicate a path for social change processes. Without utopia, ideology becomes static, and without ideology utopia becomes an illusion. Utopia provides a critique of the current ideology by providing alternative values and norms. Steeves states that "the goal is not to replace ideology with a new self-understanding, but to expand ideology into a broader and more open conception of society" (Steeves 2000, p. 226).

Ideologies relate mainly to dominant groups and serve to comfort the collective ego of these dominant groups. Ideologies reflect the general way in which groups determine what differentiates them from other groups and establishes an identity that satisfies the interests of the entire group. "Ideology can take the form of a common set of values and norms, basic principles that are treated as fundamental and mutual goals for the future" (Steeves 2000, p. 222). In addition, ideology legitimizes authority and allows the authorities to convince the public that its regulations are necessary.

Utopias, on the other hand, are more naturally supported by ascending groups and therefore more commonly by the lower strata of society. If at the first level the correlation is between ideology as stability and utopia as change toward the (im-)possible, at a second level "ideology is the legitimization of present authority while utopia is the challenge to this authority" (Ricoeur 1986, p. xxi). From Ricoeur's (1986) perspective, there are two explanations of why the ideological mentality assumes the impossibility of change. First, an ideology accepts the system of justification, explaining the non-congruence. Second, the non-congruence has been concealed by factors ranging from unconscious deception to conscious lie.

Ricoeur concludes by observing that the correlation between ideology and utopia forms a circle, a practical circle: "the two terms are themselves practical and not theoretical concepts" (Ricoeur 1986, p. xxii). This means that utopia in one period of time could be the ideology in a later period of time. In order to make the circle a spiral it is of the greatest importance to imagine new utopias as ongoing processes. A spiral in the dialectic of ideology and utopia would occur if "the utopia of a given society challenged current ideologies at least to the point where they could be reflected on and compared to alternatives" (Steeves 2000, p. 226). "The death of utopia would be the death of society. A society without utopia would be dead, because it would no longer have any project, any prospective goals" (Ricoeur 1986, p. xxi). This is in harmony with Whitehead's assertion that a society without adventure is in full decay and the conjunction of ideology and utopia typifies the social imagination. Imagination is constitutive of social reality itself.

Concluding remarks

Because some utopias are constructs of the perfect society that abstract from existing reality in a transcendent fashion, critics argue that utopia is "hopelessly impractical, or dangerously idealistic, or both" (Davis, 2012, p. 128). In a historical perspective utopian movements have substituted fanaticism for open democratic dialogue. If utopia is equated with impossible perfection it could lead to totalitarian outcomes. There are numerous examples of utopias based on wishful thinking that failed to acknowledge the constraints of reality. In addition, perfect solutions are impossible in human affairs, therefore any attempt to implement them in practice will be unsuccessful.

Popper argues that utopian systems do not consider the general laws of social life. The course of historical development is never shaped by theoretical constructions, however excellent they may be. The idea of a philosopher-king who put into practice some thought-out plans is nothing but a fairy-tale. "Social revolutions are not brought about by rational plans, but by social forces, for instance, by conflicts of interests" (Popper 2002, p. 42). Such schemes, or blueprints for a new order, are doomed to fail because all utopias are illusionary dreams. Admittedly, according to Popper, utopias have some influence "along with many other less rational (or even quite irrational) factors" (Popper 2002, p. 42).

Plato, the pessimist, believed that all change is decay, therefore his utopian blueprint, "aims at arresting all change, it is what would nowadays be called static" (Popper 2002, p. 7). The utopian blueprint of Marx, the optimist, was one of a developing and dynamic society.

From this critique we can draw the conclusion that utopias contain both errors and the potential for manipulation and domination but also contain a residue or surplus that can be used for "social critique and to advance progressive politics" (Kellner 2012, p. 85). Grounded utopias focus on the possibilities for better societies latent in the present and help to initiate change processes converting the potentials in the actual situation. The problem is that utopian thinking is often blocked by enormous economic, political and ideological structures which wish to preserve the system. "They have a vested interest in maintaining the system within which they are powerful; and they have the capacity to reproduce and enlarge themselves while they maintain or expand the system" (Albritton 2012, p. 142).

Utopian society's meaning lies not in its future actualization as an ideology but as a reflective horizon that may guide society and criticize current ideologies. The present moment is constituted by the unrealized potentialities latent in the present. Just as the future of an individual provides an horizon for the present, so utopia provides a future horizon for the social imagination. Steeves point out that "utopia must be understood as unrealizable to the extent that it is not a future ideology waiting to happen, but a dimension of possibility that holds the social imagination in question" (Steeves 2000, p. 228).

In the next chapter I dig deeper into the differences between green and ecological economics, arguing that ideology is represented by complexes of ideas which direct activity toward the conservation of the existing order, while utopias are complexes of ideas which tend to generate changes in the prevailing order. In this perspective green economy seems to preserve the established system while ecological economics contributes to system change through the development of utopian ideals. The challenge of ecological economics is "simultaneously critiquing the present, exploring alternatives, imagining ourselves otherwise and experimenting with pre-figurative practices" (Levitas 2013, p. 219). Of great importance and in accordance with the philosophy of organism, utopia must be continually reinvented. In this interpretation utopia critiquing is never static but is, rather, an enduring process.

3 Green economy and ecological economics

ROBERT MERTON AND THOMAS KUHN

> Crisis alone is not enough. There must also be a basis, though it need be
> neither rational nor ultimately correct, for faith in the particular candidate chosen.
>
> Thomas Kuhn

Introduction

Eisenstein argues that it is impossible to solve today's major challenges of "money, energy, education, health, water, soil, climate, politics, the environment, and more" (Eisenstein 2011, p. xx) within the current economic system, which is strongly anchored in a mechanistic paradigm. The ongoing crisis indicates, and could be explained as, a collapse of the traditional economic and financial institutions. If this is true then the problem shakes the neo-classical economic system to its core. At one level the problem is related to a dualistic economic system where the financial economy is floating without contact with the real world. According to Daly, "it's an economy built on the abstractions of numbers on paper – air money" (Stuckey 2009). Air money floats like a balloon out of reach of the ground. The only economic step that will make the economy sustainable is to stop multiplying numbers on paper and connect economy more firmly to the real world, which means, ultimately, to the world of ecosystems and social systems. In line with Whitehead's argument, in order to avoid bifurcation we have to develop a new kind of economy. On a deeper level the problems are interlinked with the ontological presuppositions in the dominating Western worldview. Rees expresses clearly that "modern economic society operates from an outdated mechanistic perception of the natural dynamics of the Earth" (Fabel and St. John 2007, p. 104).

In this chapter I elaborate on economic change that provides meaningful and life-enhancing development. When we look upon the future through the lens of neo-classical economic theory, with its focus on short-term profit and utility maximization, the time horizon is too short and the perspective is too narrow to contain complex phenomena including the relationships between ecological sustainability, social welfare and quality of life. In the first chapter I delved into Whitehead's ontology and concluded that creativity and adventure are main characteristics of philosophy of organism. In the second chapter utopia was contrasted with ideology and I concluded that utopia is an agent for change and ideology is to maintain stability. Adventure and utopias are of great importance to initiate change on the individual, organizational and social level.

My aim in this third chapter is to describe criteria that make it possible to draw a demarcation line between green economics (as ideology) and ecological economics (as utopia). To do this I will discuss different theoretical positions that are relevant to identify the difference between the two versions of environmentally oriented economics. As a starting point I give a brief presentation of paradigms and paradigm shifts. Next I analyze the change on three levels: symptoms, pathology and etiology. After that I argue that many of the problems we are facing are aggregated unintended consequences of a system which is in conflict with reality. Then I point out that it is not enough to reduce the symptoms but rather we have to invent and develop new structures that lead to a viable economy. To exemplify these changes I refer to the differences between low- and high-synergy societies. I lay out clearly some of the main differences between green economy and ecological economics.

Paradigms

The tremendous instrumental success of the mechanical worldview has led many economists to fall into the fallacy of overgeneralizing its simplified abstractions.

> Since the world is not mechanistic, as supposed by neo-classical economists, but organic, as understood in ecological economics, it is no surprise that [...] mainstream economics create economists who don't understand the real world.
>
> (Max-Neef 2014, p. 152)

Max-Neef follows up this argument by claiming "it is no longer acceptable that Universities still teach economic theories of the nineteenth century in order to tackle twenty-first-century problems" (Max-Neef 2010, p. 200).

From this thinking it is reasonable to ask if our current environmental and social problems are due to distorted ontological assumptions about reality. Economists are educated to believe that the mechanical worldview can explain the complexity of nature, society and economy. Metaphysical questions are entirely absent at business schools, and universities have "dodged fundamental conflicts among economy, nature, and culture" (Ims and Jakobsen 2010, p. 17).

This conflict can be illustrated by referring to research which points out that most alternative measures of human well-being (alternative to the conventional measure of money flows as reflected in GDP) show that "quality of life in the industrialized world peaked in the mid-1970s and has been going downhill ever since" (Dawson 2006, p. 12). In the same period GDP as currently measured has continued to climb. According to Daly in addition to a loss of well-being we also face a "possible ecological catastrophe" (Daly 2007, p. 14).

An UNCTAD report entitled *Wake Up Before It Is Too Late* points in the same direction. "The world needs a paradigm shift in agricultural development: from a 'green revolution' to an 'ecological intensification' approach" and "the required transformation is much more profound than simply tweaking the existing industrial agricultural system" (UNCTAD 2013, p. i). A shift to an organic paradigm would have several consequences: local and ecologically produced food for local markets based on diversity of decentralized farms, and the elimination of fertilizers and pesticides.

In order to work toward these ends the UNCTAD report prescribes a fundamental systemic change. This paradigmatic shift in agriculture gives a realistic idea of the massive and fundamental changes required in economics as a whole. This paradigmatic shift means that we have to change from green neo-classical economy (ideology) toward ecological economics (utopia).

Evolution, both biological and cultural, is characterized by slow development over long periods of time, followed by sudden revolutionary leaps of profound change. In much the same manner long periods of what we might call normal science are suddenly jolted by scientific revolutions. Kuhn (1962) argues that fundamental changes occur when the established explanations no longer solve the most serious problems. Problems that could not be solved within the established paradigm were simply dismissed as anomalies. If the anomalies increase in number and severity then science goes into a crisis which ushers in a paradigm shift. The scientific revolutions were the availability of an alternative paradigm, ready to step in and deal with the anomalies.

Today actual anomalies connected to, for example, finance, economy, food and nutrition security, the gap between rich and poor, and energy, remind us of the gravity of the problems. The fact is that these crises are converging to reach their maximum level of tension simultaneously in present-day society. Max-Neef sees this as "a crisis for humanity" (Max-Neef 2010, p. 200). These multifaceted and integrated challenges have prompted organizations and governments to take a critical look at systemic and structural issues affecting national and global economies. To solve the most urgent problems an increasing number of scholars accept that economic paradigm has to go through radical changes.

Three levels of change: symptoms, pathology and etiology

The ecological, social and economic crises that we face at the beginning of the twenty-first century provide exciting opportunities for change. The moment for change depends on our ability to see the weakness of the existing system. In order to delve deeper into the underlying explanations I wish to draw distinctions between the symptom level, the pathology level and the etiological level.

At the symptoms level we find, among other anomalies, pollution of the air, water and soil, hunger and violence: the challenge is to find the most efficient measures to reduce these worst negative symptoms. Simple "end-of-pipe" solutions could be introduced to reduce symptoms without disturbing the existing system. As the problems are defined as one-off occurrences, companies will often hire external consultants to solve the problems. In agreement with the dominating economic system "the environmental efforts are usually linked to individual efforts" (Ingebrigtsen and Jakobsen 2007, p. 45) complying with the legal requirements. All solutions take place within the framework of the established business ideology.

On a pathological level we come up with solutions which focus on the causes behind the symptoms. We use the neo-classical economic tool box of price mechanisms, market forces and laws and regulations to repair the damage in the system. To prevent negative symptoms getting too bad an increasing amount of resources is expended on developing new technological and organizational solutions. Basically the idea is that social and environmental responsibility will "improve their product provision and consequently improve their competitive standing" (Ingebrigtsen and Jakobsen 2007, p. 47). Psychological research shows how actors can be nudged to make the "right" decisions (Thaler and Sunstein 2008). Again, the strategy behind these solutions is to prevent negative symptoms from growing with the underlying condition so that the existing system remains undisturbed, much less challenged.

On the etiological level we consider the metaphysical assumptions to understand the world we live in. We accept that the existing system is the problem and has to be changed. Instead of preventing negative symptoms we introduce changes on systems level to promote positive social, economic and

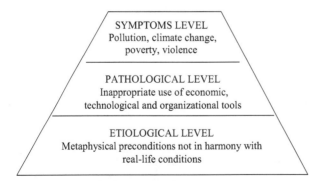

Figure 3.1 Symptoms, pathology and etiology
Source: Jakobsen 2013

ecological development. "Economics must be based on a holistic and eco-centric foundation that is able to register and respond to the complex interactions existing between the economic sector and the ecosystems" (Ingebrigtsen and Jakobsen 2007, p. 40).

Etiology refers to the actual causes of disease; pathology describes the mechanisms of disease. A systems change at the etiological level necessarily requires a paradigm shift because it cannot be implemented within the existing neo-classical ideology. To succeed in this change process, Capra and Luisi argue that a radical shift in "our perceptions, our thinking, our values" (Capra and Luisi 2014, p. iii) is required.

Accepting that the anomalies (negative symptoms) cannot be handled in a proper way within the existing economic paradigm we need a paradigm shift that offers the economy harmonious interaction with ecosystems and social systems. It is not enough to moderate our irresponsible behavior to limit the burden we impose on the living Earth, "we must learn to work with all the members of Earth's community of life to restore her to full health" (Korten 2015, p. 78).

We seem to be approaching an ecological turning point in human history that will "impact upon life on earth much more radically than any previous turning point" (Albritton 2012, p. 142). "An overall system of planetary care might be created, which would have at its aim the preservation of the ecological wellbeing of the world as a whole" (Giddens 1990, p. 170).

Unintended consequences

In 1936 Robert Merton warned against "unanticipated consequences of purposive social action" of modern society (Merton 1936, p. 894). Unintended consequences are unforeseen effects that occur due to the implementation of technology or strategies. A great number of the negative symptoms we face today are unintended consequences caused by intentional human actions.

There are numerous factors that lead to unintended consequences, including ignorance, short-sightedness and limited cognitive processes. Another possible explanation for unintended consequences is a failure to account for the world's inherent complexity. This is not surprising, and Whitehead and others have pointed out that the mechanical models do not reflect the interrelatedness and dynamic processes in the living world.

Merton differentiated between the unintended consequences in the following categories: (1) consequences to the actor, (2) consequences to other persons mediated through (a) social structure, (b) culture and (c) civilization (Merton 1936, p. 895). According to Merton, we can, to a large extent, interpret the destructive aspects of modernity as unintended consequences of a structure, culture and society in conflict with the real world conditions.

To exemplify these explanations Cobb Jr. states that we, in a historical perspective, have had a tendency to describe aggression as behavior done by cruel people, but today we also explain violence as an unintended consequence of the behavior of righteous people living in a harsh culture. "This is especially

---

Box 3.1 Classification of unintended consequences

- A positive, unexpected benefit (e.g. aspirin is a pain reliever but also acts as an anticoagulant, which can help prevent heart attacks and reduce damage caused by thrombotic strokes).
- A negative, unexpected detriment occurring in addition to the desired effect of the policy (e.g. environmental damage as a result of economic growth).
- A perverse effect contrary to what was originally intended (e.g. Peltzman Effect – the tendency of individuals to respond to safety regulations by engaging in more dangerous behavior).

---

true of economic violence" (Cobb Jr. 2000, p. 3). Stern regards climate change as "caused by market failure" (Levitas 2013, p. 171), not by evil individuals.

Spash states that interconnectedness in nature is atomized as an unforeseen consequence of the introduction of ecosystems services valuation that "give[s] new life to the use of monetary valuation" (Spash 2013, p. 16). Those making use of monetary values to represent environmental values appear to be motivated by contemporary economic theory. This results in support of the neo-liberal ideology which is anchored in the logic of price and market mechanisms.

According to Barash and Webel it is not always easy to discover and be aware of unintended consequences caused by structural violence: hunger, for example, political repression and psychological alienation, because they "work slowly to erode humanistic values and impoverish human lives" (Barash and Webel 2014, p. 7). Therefore unintended consequences are an illustrative example of what Kuhn saw as anomalies. To solve these anomalies we have to change the context and that means, in no uncertain way, nothing less than a paradigm shift will do.

Negative and positive peace

Peace studies, inspired by the work of the founder of the Peace Research Institute Oslo (PRIO), Johan Galtung (2012a, 2012b), have a comparable focus on the importance of structural change as we found in Merton's theory and Kuhn's theory of paradigms. Galtung differentiates between two contrasting structures for peace: one, peace as absence of violence (negative peace) and two, peace-promoting structures (positive peace).

Negative peace is negative because something undesirable has stopped happening. Galtung (1996) refers to different kinds of violence that is absent in negative peace: nature violence, actor or direct violence, structural or indirect violence. So we can look at negative peace as an absence of conflict or the lack of large-scale human violence. The problem is that the structures leading to conflict and violence are still there even if the direct violence is absent. Since absence of violence is not enough to secure peace in the long run, a shift on the systems level (etiological level) is required.

Positive peace is filled with content that describes and defines the presence of harmony, well-being and social systems that promote values such as equity and fairness. Positive peace focuses on "the establishment of non-exploitative social structures, and a determination to work toward that goal even when a war is not ongoing or imminent" (Barash and Webel 2014, p. 8). Positive peace refers to a social condition in which "exploitation is minimized or eliminated and in which there is neither overt violence nor the more subtle phenomenon of underlying structural violence" (Barash and Webel 2014, p. 7). Positive peace is the best protection against violence.

To illustrate these arguments Galtung draws a link to medicine, where health is defined as the body's positive capability to resist disease (cf. positive peace), not only the absence of negative symptoms (cf. negative peace). Negative and positive peace are to be considered as two independent concepts, where one is possible without the other.

To initiate positive peace Galtung suggests focusing on structural procedures such as egalitarian distribution of power and resources. He recommends more focus on communication, peace education, international cooperation, dispute resolution and practical conflict handling. If the structures prohibit people from actualizing their potential then society is in a state where negative peace can only be obtained through external pressure, such as social and political repression. At the cultural level, values and norms influence the prevalence of violent behavior in a society. Structural and cultural conditions largely explain the occurrence of negative or positive peace in a society.

A peace formula

To delve deeper into the question of peace, Galtung (2012a) introduced the formula shown as Figure 3.2.

This formula should not be interpreted as a theory but rather as a kind of statement summing up some core concepts of peace research (Galtung 2012a). It indicates that the more of the good, Equity × Harmony, and the less of the bad, Trauma × Conflict, the better. Zero is the lower limit and there is no upper limit. To solve conflicts in a sustainable way it is necessary to make incompatible and contradictory goals more compatible. To promote equity and harmony we have to develop fair institutions and authenticity that lead

$$\text{Peace} = \frac{\text{Equity} \times \text{Harmony}}{\text{Trauma} \times \text{Conflict}}$$

Figure 3.2 A peace formula

to compassion and an appreciation of the joy of others and the suffering of others too. Equity involves cooperation to achieve mutual and equal benefits.

It also presupposes working against structural violence, by which we mean the difference between the potential (utopia) and the actual (ideology); typically a justice gap. A violent structure impedes the development of the group and the self through a structure which is generally invisible. For example, cultural violence is very hard to change since it is a deep-rooted phenomenon which legitimizes different forms of inequality, in casual discrimination between sexes and class differences.

To implement positive peace we have to increase the values in the numerator and decrease the values in the denominator of the peace formula. A fruitful concept in peace theory and peace economy is, therefore, joint projects. By putting people together, joint projects invoke strong "I & We" cultures, extending structures based on weak individualist cooperation. The structures can be established through social pacts, contracts or other more or less formal arrangements (Galtung 2012a, p. 42). At a cultural level, increasing the values of the formula can be stimulated by introducing arts, for example, music, theatre, poetry, painting, sculpture in the public space. "Art can lift individuals beyond the ordinary and unite them and creating such unity may be peacebuilding" (Galtung 2012a, p. 162).

If the denominator of the peace formula increases through extensive competition among individuals or economic actors, the chance of joint projects decreases. According to Galtung, "the more pronounced I–culture at individual or collective levels, the less likely positive peace, the more likely direct and structural violence" (Galtung 2012a, p. 42). Galtung's advice is to write simple rules for both negative peace, avoiding violence and positive peace, building peace with nature, in the self, couples, companies, states, nations, regions and civilizations.

Structural change

Movement from negative to positive peace requires, according to Galtung, a change at the personal level in addition to changes at the systems level. There is an A-road and a B-road to positive peace. The A-road is inside the parties, something happens within them, and the B-road is on the outside, something happens between them. "The A-road passes from hatred, antipathy and indifference to sympathy, the B-road passes from violence and indifference to cooperation" (Galtung 2012b, p. 53).

Since values and norms influence the prevalence of violent behavior in a society, cultural conditions largely explain the occurrence of negative and positive peace in a society. If the structure is unfair and the cultural values and norms accept aggressive behavior, the occurrence of direct violence on an individual level will be more likely than in societies where the structural and cultural conditions are different. "Structural peace can be institutionalized around us, cultural peace internalized inside us, direct peace enacted between

---

Box 3.2 Roads A and B to peace

	Negative peace, absence of:	*Positive peace, presence of:*
Road A Within the parties	antipathy indifference	sympathy harmony
Road B Between the parties	violence repression evil	cooperation shared human values shared feeling of humanity

---

us" (Galtung 2014, p. 53). It is important to stress that structural violence stems from violence in the organization of society, "rather than the actor-generated personal and direct violence" (Grewal 2003, p. 2).

Positive peace refers to a social condition in which "exploitation is minimized or eliminated and in which there is neither overt violence nor the more subtle phenomenon of underlying structural violence" (Barash and Webel 2014, p. 7). According to Barash and Webel, ecological well-being is included in positive peace, "the web of life has been fraying; positive peace requires that it be rewoven or, at least, allowed to regenerate on its own" (Barash and Webel 2014, p. 426). They add that ecological well-being cannot be achieved piecemeal. Positive peace denotes the presence of an equitable and just social order as well as ecological harmony. This indicates that peace research should seek to understand conditions for preventing violence.

Since negative peace seeks to keep things the way they are, we can see that negative peace is a conservative goal in harmony with the established ideology. Though negative peace can be useful in the short term, longer-term remedies are only achievable by a positive peace approach. Positive peace is much more radical as its goal is to create a utopia that does not currently exist. Boulding argues that stable peace depends on elements from positive peace such as stable social systems and a fair economy in balance with natural and social systems.

To integrate all these perspectives peace research becomes a transdisciplinary field of science, including, among others, social science, economics, culture, ecology and philosophy. Philosophy and economics are openly related because economic life is influenced by the dominating worldview and the metaphysical beliefs of the people living and working in an economy.

Low- and high-synergy societies

Maslow (1971) discusses the impact the underlying philosophical ideas and values of a society have on individual behavior. He drew a distinction between high- and low-synergy societies. In high-synergy societies the social institutions are set up to transcend the polarity between selfishness and unselfishness, between self-interest and altruism. "The society with high synergy is one in which virtue pays" (Maslow 1971, p. 194). In high-synergy societies the gap between rich and poor is small and wealth tends to be spread around. Low-synergy societies have a structure which promotes mutually opposed and counteractive behavior. Low-synergy societies encourage "the development of jealousy, envy, resentment, distance, and finally a real likelihood of enmity" (Maslow 1971, p. 196).

In accordance with Galtung, Maslow argues that if the structure is unfair and the cultural values and norms accept aggressive behavior, the occurrence of direct violence on an individual level will be more likely than if the structural and cultural conditions are based on fairness and humanistic values. It is also important to stress that structural violence stems from violence in the structure of the society, rather than direct actor-generated violence. According to Maslow "no Utopia can be constructed henceforth by the knowledgeable person without making peace with the concept of synergy" (Maslow 1971, p. 200). To do this it is important to set up social conditions so that one person's advantage would be to another person's advantage rather than to the other person's disadvantage. Any utopia must have as one of its foundations a set of high-synergy institutions that improve both individuals and the whole society.

Even if it is necessary, according to Maslow, to work on both levels simultaneously, structural changes are of the utmost importance. "Even the best individuals placed under poor social and institutional circumstances behave badly" (Maslow 1971, p. 205). To prohibit conflict and violence some of the most successful utopian societies are anchored in decentralized dialogue-based network structures. Kuhn's, Merton's, Galtung's and Maslow's reflections on paradigms, unintended consequences, negative and positive peace, and low- and high-synergy societies, respectively, are of great relevance for understanding the difference between green and ecological economics.

These perspectives have implications on micro, meso and macro levels and the three levels are strongly interrelated. Frustration and despair on one level may lead to aggression on the other levels. From the preceding reflections it is reasonable to expect that the good society is characterized by becoming, an ongoing process driven by opposing forces.

Economy

Based on the preceding paragraphs I suggest that an environmentally responsible economy can be separated into two categories: green economy and a new economic system based on the ideas characterizing ecological economics. As noted earlier, I define green economy as part of the existing paradigm or ideology, while ecological economics represents an alternative paradigm or utopia. The tension between actuality (ideology) and potentiality (utopia) gives energy and direction to the change processes. To capture the most serious problems (anomalies) in the current economy and society, it is necessary to introduce structures that motivate the development of an economy in harmony with both social and ecological systems. As previous chapters have shown, it is necessary to change from a mechanical to an organic worldview. In other words it is not enough to mend the system; it is necessary to change the system.

Since present-day society does "contain the elements of its potential transformation" (Levitas 2013, p. 129), the possibility of radical change is realistic. Realism requires that the utopian aspirations are based on obtainable potentialities. As an example, an increasing number of people accept that it is necessary to decrease the exploitation of nature by reducing both production and consumption in rich countries.

In addition, "ecological footprints imply a collective reduction in consumption, redistribution away from those who have plenty to enable others to survive" (Levitas 2013, p. 170). There is, moreover, evidence to indicate that a redistribution of wealth from rich to poor would have positive effects on everyone's well-being. Many people in economically advanced countries experience "development fatigue" due to materialistic overconsumption, while an increase in production and consumption would have a tremendous positive effect on the well-being of people in poor countries. Giddens concludes that "expectations of continuous economic growth would have to be modified [... and] global redistribution of wealth would be called for" (Giddens 1990, p. 166).

Spash has pointed out that the concept of ecological footprints might have some unintended consequences as well. He argues that ecological footprints are amplifying the existing ideology because "its land theory of value is implicit and its problems seem neglected due to the importance given to achieving political impact" (Spash 2013, p. 14). On a more general level, monetary valuation supports politics based on neo-liberal market ideology.

The main task is to encourage and initiate holistic solutions to the anomalies we are facing in our time. "All of us live in a community, a system of local and mutual interdependence, where our welfare depends on the welfare, cooperation, and activities of our neighbours, locally and globally" (Priddle 1994, p. 57). Today we experience growing pressures for democratic participation and cooperative strategies to resolve conflicts through viable networks instead of formation of mega-sized superstructures. "The organic health of the earth is maintained by decentralized ecological cycles which interact to form a self-sustaining biochemical system" (Giddens 1990, p. 171).

Green economy

In order to understand the creative tension between actuality (the dominating ideology) and potentiality (realistic utopia), I find it relevant to start with a brief description of green economy and ecological economics. As a starting point I accept that both perspectives are based upon a willingness to solve the environmental and social problems embedded in mainstream economics. Inspired by the distinction between negative and positive peace, it is evident

---

Box 3.3 Different interpretations of growth

	Green economy	*Ecological economics*
Short-term perspective	economic growth	de-growth
Long-term perspective	green growth	qualitative development

---

that green economy is based on more or less the same toolkit as used in mainstream economics (ideology) and ecological economics is revising the paradigmatic assumptions of economics (utopia). In other words, green economy focuses on reducing negative symptoms to save the existing neo-classical economic paradigm, while ecological economics claims that the neo-classical economic paradigm based on a mechanical worldview is the problem and has to be substituted with a paradigm anchored in an organic worldview.

Representatives of green economy accept that in a short-term perspective increased growth has the highest priority in order to solve the current crises in economy, ecology and society. In a longer-term perspective they argue that growth should be as green as possible. For ecological economists growth is not part of the solution; indeed, on the contrary, growth is the core problem and they argue that in a short-term perspective it is necessary to implement a de-growth economy. In a long-term perspective the focus ought to turn from quantitative growth to qualitative development.

Green economists often argue that environmental responsibility is closely coupled to green growth, because we need more resources to spend on the different tools to handle the most serious economic and social anomalies. In addition, they argue that greening the economy is an efficient marketing tool to develop a reputation based on ecological and societal responsibility. Hence, green strategy is an effective instrument to increase a company's competitive advantage and its profits.

Hopfenbeck (1992) argues that economic internalization is an effective step in the process of greening the marketing strategies of a company. Within the logic of neo-classical economics it is adequate to quantify the environmental and social costs connected to business activities and measure them in the firm's accounting systems. By doing this the problems connected to externalizing environmental cost will be reduced, based on economic rationality.

The idea is similar in "ecosystems services." By making the environment into a costly commodity, business will be given an economic incentive to develop environmentally friendly products, procedures and use of resources. Following the same line of reasoning, green taxes, laws and regulations are also relevant tools. To break established habits we must see the benefits of the change and contrast it with the cost of following the old track. Only when we clearly discover the downside (unintended consequences) of the existing system will we see that this is the moment to change our habits, our accounting system and our old assumptions about the Earth and what it can sustain.

Ecological economics points to systemic failures connected to the mechanical and linear way of thinking to explain our limited success in reducing the negative and often unintended effects of the dominant economic system. There seems to be a conflict between the physically impossible (continual growth) and the politically impossible (limiting growth) (Daly 2007, p. 10). However, to the ecological economists, this conflict provides the most exciting opportunity for change.

Ecological economics

Contrary to green economy, the focus in ecological economics is on bringing the economic and ecological crisis down to Earth by changing the system. Pearce argues that the failure to address metaphysical questions has led to many of the central errors of conventional economics. Economics needs an internal metaphysical critique. Instead of focusing on physics, quantitative measures and products, economists should turn instead to discuss metaphysics, qualitative values and processes (Pearse 2001). The critique articulated by Pearse is both valid and relevant to understanding the negative symptoms following mainstream economy. The critique is also a powerful argument for the need for ecological economics.

Ecological economics is based on an organic worldview

Just like peace research, ecological economics is a transdisciplinary field of science studying the conflict between the growth of the economy and the destruction and negative modification of the environment from different scientific disciplines. Boulding claimed that "the pursuit of any problem of economics draws me into some other science before I can catch it" (Kerman 1974, p. 6). He was looking for connections between diverse fields of knowledge, economics, social sciences, natural sciences and philosophy. Ecological economics presupposes that economic activities are in constructive interplay with the cultural and natural effects that originate from them.

The Earth is understood as a system comprising closely interacting and interdependent subsystems based upon dissipative structures. Since every system is connected to and dependent on others, everything evolves together over time. Co-evolution is characterized by path-dependency and change is the rule rather than the exception. We have to admit that the Earth itself and all its living and non-living components is a community and that humans are members of this integral community and find their proper role in advancing the well-being of this whole community. Berry concludes as follows: "There can be no sustained well-being of any part of the community that does not relate effectively to the well-being of the total community" (Berry 2007, p. 63).

Box 3.4 Mechanistic vs. organic worldviews

Mechanistic worldview	*Organic worldview*
atoms	relations
instrumental values	inherent values
linearity	circularity
deterministic	co-creation
product	process

Atoms vs. relations

The principle of relativity says that all actual entities are constituted by their relations to other entities and each living entity arises out of its relations and is internally constituted by these relations. One important consequence of accepting the fundamental interrelatedness in reality is that the market is not reducible to atomistic competition between autonomous actors. The market is more like a cooperative web of interrelated economic actors. From this perspective, ecological economics describes the market as consisting of flexible and changing patterns. When the system-perspective is applied it is important to describe the elements, and especially the relationships between the elements. Based on the fact that both social and environmental structures change through succession, it is of great importance that the economic system can also adjust flexibly to this process.

Linearity vs. circularity

One of the vital roles of business is to contribute to an efficient use of resources that meets human needs while being in accordance with sustainable development. A general goal is to introduce systems that lead to increased production combined with decreased extraction of raw material and amounts of waste. At present we find ourselves at the beginning of the search for an assertive and integrated theory and practice of environmental management. To reach this goal it is important to establish efficient systems for recycling.

Redistribution has an essential function in ecological economics and connects consumption and production (the ends in the linear value chain). In Norway, as in most European countries, companies in the field of redistribution are representatives of one of the fastest-expanding sectors in the economy and we find positive signals which indicate solutions in harmony with ecological economics. The strategies to reach the goals of sustainability presuppose products designed for efficient reprocessing and these are combined with the establishment of collective systems for coordinating the companies dealing with redistribution. These systems must be integrated with the production side of the economy if we are to reach optimal results

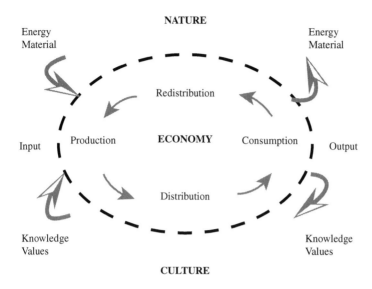

Figure 3.3 Circulation economics
Source: Ingebrigtsen and Jakobsen 2007

Within a linear perspective of the economic value chain, environmental problems connected to the use of resources (input) often appear as separated from environmental problems connected to pollution and waste management (output). The reason is that problems occur at different places, both in time and space, and an important aspect of circular interconnectedness is that efficient utilization of resources presupposes a holistic and dynamic view of resource and waste management.

Instrumental vs. inherent values

It is important to integrate cultural values in economic behavior by being conscious of the fact that business strategies "require adherence to sets of values held in common between people and with the organization" (Welford, 1995, p. 116). But also one can argue that environmental values must have a fundamental place and value in economics. "The debate over what values reside in nature, or what is the value of nature, has highlighted the fact that the core concept is complex and multidimensional" (Turner et al. 2003, p. 494).

Economic activity does not take place in a vacuum and is always situated in an environmental and a social context, so business organizations should also be involved in the development of new social and environmental standards of a more substantial nature (Zsolnai 2004, p. 23). Figure 3.4. shows that nature has an intrinsic value as a necessary condition for life as well as having

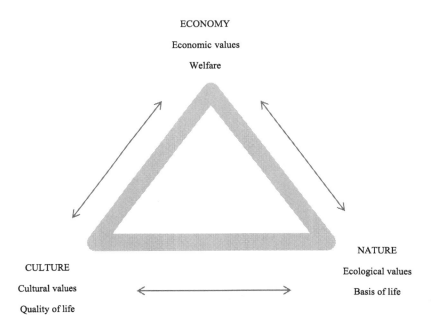

ECONOMY

Economic values

Welfare

CULTURE

Cultural values

Quality of life

NATURE

Ecological values

Basis of life

Figure 3.4 Value triangle

an instrumental value as input in economic activities. Next, culture represents intrinsic value as a context for developing individual and collective identity and life-quality. The output of cultural activities, knowledge and creativity has an instrumental value as input to economic processes. Last, effective and efficient economic processes are essential to human welfare. In addition, work represents an intrinsic value to most human beings. According to Georgescu-Roegen the true economic output is the enjoyment of life (an inherent value), not growth in GNP (instrumental value).

Physical laws vs. co-creation

Boulding argues that it is possible to turn the process of increasing entropy by introducing evolutionary principles. The continuing struggle between evolution and entropy is very important in Boulding's evolutionary economics. Evolution keeps adding "useful, improbable, sometimes beautiful things to our world, while entropy keeps tearing down this improbable organization to its eventual end as a thin brown soup" (Kerman 1974, p. 14). Knowledge is a kind of magic which does not obey the laws of entropy. It does not diminish when it is spent, and, in fact, knowledge often grows in the sharing.

The interplay between economy, nature and culture possesses properties such as dynamism, evolution, integrity and change. Throughput of material and energy affect the integrating structures and processes. The economy has the ability, through human action, to restructure and reform processes in ecosystems and societies of which they are a part. Sustainable economy presupposes that economic activities are in constructive interplay with the cultural and natural effects that originate from them. The exclusion of wisdom from economics, science and technology was something which we could get away with for a little while, as long as we were relatively unsuccessful, but now that we have become successful, the problem of spiritual and moral truth takes center stage.

By their very nature processes are interrelated and interactive. We are in the world and the world is in us. "If we stress the role of the environment, this process is causation," if we, on the other hand, "stress the role of my immediate pattern for active enjoyment, this process is self-creation" (Whitehead 1977, p. 42). Nothing in nature could be what it is, except as an integrated ingredient in nature's dynamic evolving web of life. According to Whitehead's "philosophy of organism," an isolated event is not an event, because every part is a factor in a larger whole and has significance for the process of the whole. The isolation of an entity in thought, when we think of it as a bare "it," has no counterpart in any corresponding isolation in nature. Such isolation is merely part of the procedure of intellectual knowledge.

Product vs. process

If we interpret economics within a mechanistic perspective, we find that the product is described as an isolated item without ethical dimensions. This perspective characterizes the competitive market economy, where values are instrumental only. If we change perspective and look upon the product from the perspective of ecological economics, we find that the product is interpreted as an integrated part of social and environmental systems. In an organic economy, where values are inherent in the processes, the consumers are more conscious of the prominent role they play in the economic network (Ims, Jakobsen and Zsolnai 2015). A first step would be to be less individualistic and more oriented toward the vulnerable sellers and producers, society and nature, and we should always ask "who am I supporting when I buy these commodities?"

Based upon the philosophy of organism, the "product" concept is understood holistically, emphasizing the processes which are necessary parts of the creation, distribution, using and recirculation of a product. Thus we suggest taking a more extended view which encompass the space and time dimensions of the product in terms of when and where it grew, who were the growers, taking in the quantity of (artificial or natural) fertilizer used, asking which means of transportation was used, and what the profit margin in all the different stages of the value chain was.

In much the same way, a number of questions are to be addressed concerning the future of the product. What happens to the product when the basic product is in some sense used by the customer, and how does the used product influence the ecology?

Three questions of special importance arise and have to be addressed: scale, equality and allocation. To handle these challenges, holistic thinking, including adaptability, flexibility and learning, are important. Self-organization and cooperation are important characteristics too in a society described as a living, self-regulating community. Ecological internalization implies that environmental and social responsibilities are integral and integrated parts of business management. Creativity and divergent thinking are essential within ecological economics, because it is more important to discover new questions than to find new answers to the old questions. A strong sense of global citizenship is needed to "generate both thought and action that really engage with the problems of human and environmental flourishing at a global level" (Albritton 2012, p. 154).

First, production and consumption must be sustainable in the long run (and in the short run). Economic growth, as an end in itself, is based upon the highly questionable assumption that "there are no limits to the planet's ability to sustain it" (Pearce 2001, p. 7). Instead, sustainability implies recognition of the fact that natural and social capital are not infinitely substitutable by technology and human capital, and that "there are real biophysical limits to the expansion of the market economy" (Costanza 2008, p. 33). So we can see that a sustainable economy should at some point stop growing, but it need not stop developing, as there is no necessary connection between development and growth, and, quite conceivably, there could be development without growth (Georgescu-Roegen 1975). Instead of firing the engine of capitalism and wealth creation by prioritizing selfishness, individualism and narcissism, the ability to say yes to love, kindness, generosity, sympathy and empathy alleviates the birth pangs for a new world.

Second, the distribution of resources and wealth must be fair. Fairness implies recognition that the distribution of wealth is an important determinant of social capital and quality of life (Costanza 2008, p. 33). We must move from an economy oriented toward the satisfaction of the wants of the rich, to an economy committed to satisfy the basic needs of all human beings. Everybody should have access to the basic necessities that make human flourishing possible, such things as "a good diet, shelter, clothing, health care, education, and sanitation" (Albritton 2012, p. 148). Instead of focusing on economic growth and increasing profits, the global economy must include (possibly for the first time) moral considerations and equity. Lindner (2011) describes how destructive competition must not be chosen at the expense of life-enhancing cooperation. Today, systems biologists have discovered that the healthy function of any living system depends on collaboration. "Most all living organisms exist, thrive, and co-evolve only within living communities engaged in a continuous synergic sharing and exchange that from a big-picture perspective is fundamentally cooperative" (Korten 2015, p. 70).

Third, the allocation of resources must be efficient. Real economic efficiency implies the inclusion of all resources that affect sustainable human well-being in the system of allocation, not just goods and services being on the market. "Our current market allocation system excludes most non-marketed natural and social capital assets and services, which are huge contributors to human well-being" (Costanza 2008, p. 34).

Change along two dimensions

Referring to Lovelock's Gaia hypothesis we can argue that ecological economics recognizes that economy, nature and culture are integrated parts within a great "living" organism (Lovelock 1988). The art of progress is to preserve order amid change (Whitehead 1967a). Figure 3.5. indicates change along two dimensions. First, there must be a change toward the culture of fairness and environmental responsibility. Second, there are arguments for both internationalization and globalization.

Internationalization, on the one hand, is based upon a cooperative network of smaller communities. Boulding argues that international trade is based upon treaties and alliances between different states and nations and these networks consist of members and relationships among its members who form patterns and structures.

Globalization represents direct membership of a global community. There are no national borders and the whole world is one. Free trade presupposes free mobility of goods, capital and people. "We are no longer writing the rules of interaction among separate national economies. We are writing the constitution of a single global economy" (Ruggiero 1966).

Figure 3.5 Values and structure

Teilhard de Chardin argues that the principles of the "creative union" indicate that wherever a genuine union in human relations exists, "persons do not merge into a homogenous collective, but, rather, each enables the others to develop their distinctive uniqueness" (Fabel and St. John 2007, p. 215). Collaboration can enhance human economic survival and advancement, since much mutual cooperation provides great scope and encouragement for individuality and creativity in the cause of evolutionary progress.

Concluding remarks

Some of the key benchmarks to help us to differentiate between green economy and ecological economics are illustrated in Box 3.5. Green economy is anchored in a mechanical paradigm characterized by low synergy, focused on reducing negative symptoms, preserving the dominating ideology. In other words, green economy is happy to save the system by reducing negative symptoms (anomalies) connected to systemic faults. Because creativity is limited to prevailing ideology it enhances status quo.

Ecological economics is anchored in an organic paradigm and characterized by high-synergy solutions based on structures which enhance resilience and development. Since ecological economics describes an economic system very different from the dominating competitive, atomized configuration of the market economy, it is reasonable to characterize ecological economics as utopian. The contrast and force operating between actuality and potentiality stimulate creativity that unfolds the full potentiality in society. According to Eisenstein, what we experience today is a birth crisis, "expelling us from the old world into a new" (Eisenstein 2011, p. xx).

In the following chapters of part II, a number of contributors to the field of ecological economics, broadly defined, are presented. Their contributions give shape and substance to the many different topics integrated in ecological economics. In Part III, I will offer a narrative which gives a full-scale presentation of utopian ecological economics.

Box 3.5 Green economy vs. ecological economics

	Green economy	*Ecological economics*
Paradigm	mechanical	organic
Synergy	low synergy	high synergy
Peace	symptoms	structures
Perspective	ideology	utopia
Process	actuality	potentiality
Creativity	status quo	adventure

Part II

Perspectives on ecological economics

Part II gives a brief overview of some of the most important contributors to ecological economics. The selection of thinkers does not provide a representative account of current scholars in the field; instead I have chosen to present contributions reflecting a variety of backgrounds and intellectual traditions, spread out in time and space. The ideas stem from the beginning of the twentieth century up to today. They come from different parts of the world, both men and women are represented and there is a mixture of theoretical and practical argumentations.

In addition to presenting an overview of the complex history of ecological economics, Part II consists of material for the development of the utopian narratives presented in Part III. In Part I, I gave a brief description of the main differences between mechanical and organic worldviews based on Whitehead's philosophy of organism. Philosophy of organism represents a categorial scheme or worldview for interpreting the different contributions in Part II and the creative process characterized by change and order, connecting past, present and future.

The dynamics of Whitehead's philosophy of organism is based on the tension between actuality and potentiality. The dialectics between ideology and utopia represent a similar idea. Creativity and adventure are of great importance to initiate change processes. In this perspective the task of ecological economics is to create disturbance in the dominating economic ideology by introducing utopian perspectives that make it possible to see our current challenges from outside. We are now in a phase of transition away from the capitalist economic order that has been more or less hegemonic for the last two centuries (Albritton 2012, p. 142).

With the frame of interpretation discussed in Part I alive in our consciousness, we are prepared and ready to jump into Part II with open minds. When reading, try to identify and reflect on these areas, the ideas different contributors have in common, the topics where they differ and try to identify trends or tendencies.

More specifically, are their definitions of problems and suggested solutions in accordance with the existing ideology? Or are they more like utopia? And more important still, are the tensions between ideology and utopia, represented by mainstream economics versus ecological economics, strong enough to make the required changes?

Part II is organized in eight chapters. Four different sources of inspiration for ecological economics are identified in the first chapter. Ensuing chapters focus on different topics, all integrated and mutually dependent. Contributions which focus on ontology (economics as a moral science), epistemology (transdisciplinarity), spirituality (Eastern perspectives), management, institutions and projects with empirical content are presented. Part II concludes with a presentation of some contributors focusing on the future development of ecological economics. To place the different contributions in perspective, each description starts with a biography.

4 Four sources of inspiration

At least four main sources of inspiration can be identified in the historical process leading to ecological economics: thermodynamics, evolutionary theory, anthroposophy and Buddhism. Georgescu-Roegen introduced thermodynamics as fundamental to economics, Boulding argued that economy should be based on evolutionary theory, Holbæk-Hanssen developed a cooperative economy anchored in anthroposophy and Schumacher referred to the influence of Buddhism. Today ecological economics exists as a mosaic of different ingredients.

These four sources of inspiration represent different perspectives on the nature of economics. Thermodynamics is focused on the material world and seeks a physical explanation of reality showing how the world has developed through eternal, immutable physical laws. Darwinism explains the

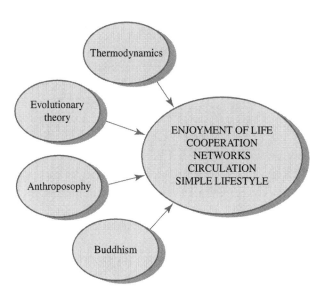

Figure 4.1 Four sources of inspiration behind contemporary ecological economics

development in the living world by reference to nature's universal unity and the existence of natural laws with eternal validity. Anthroposophy introduces a dimension that says that matter can never exist and operate without spirit any more than spirit can operate without matter. Buddhist philosophy begins with humanity's ultimate question: what is the meaning of life? Buddhism refers to dharma, the natural order of things, and as we come to understand the nature of dharma we also discover our own potential and responsibilities.

In the following chapters we will find these ideas in many different guises often blended into one. All perspectives have the process of understanding in common so we will never find a final definition of ecological economics. What we can hope for is to find some fundamental principles which characterize the process.

THERMODYNAMICS

Rudolf Clausius

The algebraic sum of all the transformations occurring in a cyclical process can only be positive, or, as an extreme case, equal to nothing.

Rudolf Clausius

Introduction

In the last decades of the nineteenth century, Clausius, one of the pioneers of thermodynamics, pointed out the ideological connotations of the interconnectedness between energy and economy. He was also interested in the ethical and socio-economic impact of technical change. In 1865 Clausius formulated the first and second law of thermodynamics, saying that the energy of a closed system remains constant, while its entropy strives toward maximum. He argued that since energy did not exist in unlimited amounts in nature, it follows that energy stocks have great importance for the economy.

Biography

Rudolf Clausius (1822–1888) was born in Köslin in Prussia. He studied mathematics and physics at the University of Berlin, where he graduated in 1844. Clausius studied for his doctorate at the University of Halle, researching optical effects in the Earth's atmosphere. Later he was given a chair in physics at the Royal Artillery and Engineering School in Berlin and also worked as *Privatdozent* at the University of Berlin. In 1855 he became a professor at the Swiss Federal Institute of Technology in Zurich, where he stayed until 1867. In 1869 he moved to Bonn.

First and second law of thermodynamics

Thermodynamics is the discovery of the conservation of energy. It states that the total energy involved in a process is constant, that is, it may change its form but none is lost. But, at the same time, "while the total energy involved in a process is constant, the amount of useful energy is diminishing" (Capra and Luisi 2014, p. 33). Clausius reflected on the process of the flow of heat between bodies at different temperatures and recognized that "energy flows as heat spontaneously from a body at a high temperature to one at a lower temperature" (Atkins 2010, p. 42). He introduced the concept of entropy to describe the process. "Entropy" represents a combination of "energy" and "tropos," the Greek word for transformation or evolution.

The specific parts of the universe on which thermodynamics focuses Clausius called a system. "A system may be a block of iron, a beaker of water, an engine, a human body" (Atkins 2010, p. 1). The rest of the universe is called the surroundings. A living thing has very low entropy compared to its surroundings. A system is open if it is possible to add or remove matter or energy to it. Hence, the Earth is not a closed system, since the sun provides the Earth with a constant input of low-entropy energy. Plants use this energy to produce organic material, food for other beings, keeping their low-entropy-dependent life processes running. "A system with a boundary that is impervious to matter is called closed" (Atkins 2010, p. 2). The system together with its surroundings is called the universe.

Clausius argued that evolution is always accompanied by increasing disorder, and a measure of disorder is entropy. Another important discovery is that all natural processes move only in one direction (unidirectional). Van Ness asked an interesting question: "If all real processes are irreversible, why do we spend so much time discussing reversible processes?" (Van Ness 1983, p. 27). Unidirectional processes have dramatic consequences for scientific methods since it is not possible to repeat experiments, because the framework will always change.

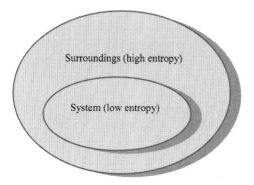

Figure 4.2 The universe

Thermodynamic laws summarize the properties of energy and its transformation from one form to another. Laws that state that a certain property does not change are called conservation laws. The first law of thermodynamics is a conservation law that gives a description, not an explanation, of how nature works. More specifically, the first law of thermodynamics states that the total amount of energy is constant and that energy can neither be created nor destroyed. It can only be transformed into other forms – you can't get something from nothing. "However much energy there was at the start of the universe, so there will be that amount at the end" (Atkins 2010, p. 16).

The second law of thermodynamics states that energy can only be transformed toward increasing entropy and the entropy in the universe increases in the course of spontaneous change. Entropy is a measure of the quality of energy: low entropy means high quality, high entropy means low quality. Heat is a mode of transfer of energy but it is not a form of energy itself. "Heat is the name of a process, not the name of an entity" (Atkins 2010, p. 22). The second law of thermodynamics provides a foundation for understanding why change occurs and is of central importance to our understanding of the universe.

From this line of argument we can conclude that entropy measures the condensed level of energy. Generally speaking, the quality of the energy is reduced when energy is transformed from one state to another. Any increase in entropy means that the accessible energy is reduced. Thermodynamics can be applied to mass as well as energy. Hence, natural and economic processes lead inevitably to a reduction of substances with low entropy. This means that matter does not disappear, rather that the particles will be spread throughout the environment. While all kinds of materials will disintegrate as time goes by the molecules themselves do not disappear.

Thermodynamics and economy

Clausius connects thermodynamics to economy by pointing out that economic processes are not isolated, self-sustaining processes, but are always in a continuous exchange with the environment. Even if the first law of thermodynamics postulates that the amount of non-renewable resources is constant over time, the amounts of available resources are decreasing all the time. Even if we cannot avoid an increase in entropy, we can reduce the process by developing more efficient technical and administrative solutions for the recycling of materials.

Clausius had a long-term perspective on energy and economy. He stated that any use of energy (heat) to produce work is "accompanied by an irrecoverable loss of available energy, to be seen as an increase in entropy" (Martinez-Allier 1987, p. 79). Even if the economy, according to thermodynamics, should be seen as a one-way entropic throughput of energy and mater, Clausius argued that it is possible, at least to some extent, to slow down the growth of entropy by recycling of materials. In order to prolong the use of resources we have to use low-entropy input in the economy as efficiently as possible, that is, we must find recycling solutions throughout all sectors of the economy.

In principle it is important to distinguish between recycling which takes place in a natural cycle, and recycling which happens within economic cycles. In nature organic material is continuously subject to renewal through the addition of biological material composted through photosynthesis and solar energy. The decomposition and transformation of waste substances is a central function in all ecosystems. Resources retrieved in this manner are referred to as "renewable."

Entropy and economy

The first implication of thermodynamics for economics is its establishment of a maximum efficiency for heat engines. More specifically, the first law implies that at least as much energy would be locked up in recycling as was obtained when the material was first used. The second law points to the fact that the entropy in the universe increases during the process of recycling. "That means that during recycling the sum of the energy that has to be degraded and the energy that has to be locked up is strictly greater than the amount of energy which will be obtained from [material] X once it has been reconstituted" (Beard and Lozada 1999, p. 99). In other words, energy can neither be created nor destroyed (the first law), and recycling energy and materials will always be uneconomical (the second law).

Hence, the amount of energy and materials would be degraded regardless of future technological developments. Energy consists of two qualities, free or available and bound or latent. In thermodynamics, freedom refers to the energy's availability to do work, "rather than just tumble out of a system as heat" (Atkins 2010, p. 63). The two qualities represent the limits on the scale: from free energy, capable of being used for work, to bound energy, which cannot be used for work. We are living in a universe of ever-greater entropy, and all economic transformations, regardless of their type, result in increasing entropy. In this perspective of the universe there is always a greater increase in entropy elsewhere than the reduction in entropy in the system. The material universe continuously undergoes a qualitative change, a degradation of energy. The final outcome is a state where all energy is bound, "the heat death as it was called in the earliest thermodynamic theory" (Georgescu-Roegen 1999, p. 129).

Biology

In biology, renewable resources are opposed to non-renewable chemical materials, such as metals, which only exist in limited quantities on Earth. According to this argumentation it is of great importance not to exceed the ecosystems source and sink capacity. The capacity will differ between different ecosystems depending on their productivity and the ability to absorb waste.

All living organisms sustain themselves on a flow of low entropy. Thermodynamics makes it clear that photosynthesis represents the most important production process on Earth and that it is of great importance to secure the best possible conditions for natural renewal. It is not unreasonable to assert that photosynthesis is the only source of absorbing high-quality energy on Earth. Therefore photosynthesis is the process of all renewable resources making up ecological as well as economic systems. Korten states that each and every living organism, from the individual cell to the living Earth, "maintains itself in an internal state of active, adaptive, resilient, creative thermodynamic disequilibrium in seeming violation of the basic principle of entropy – the loss of ordered structure" (Korten 2015, p. 76). Consequently we can argue that "the global ecosystems have developed chains of subsistence, within a complex, interactive network of material cycles and biological/chemical reactions" (Ingebrigtsen and Jakobsen 2007, p 162). The process is not contradicted by the laws of thermodynamics because it depends on importing low-entropy energy from the sun. Energy from the sun is most valuable; it emits an enormous amount of radiation energy.

Concluding remarks

Thermodynamics points out that the total amount of resources are limited and entropy makes energy and materials becomes less available in a closed system. On the one hand this means that all kinds of materials disintegrate. Concerning energy, the Earth is an open system since the sun provides energy to the Earth all the time. On the other hand, through photosynthesis low-entropy energy from the sun is transformed into organic materials.

Nicholas Georgescu-Roegen

> I once asked Georgescu-Roegen why the "MIT–Harvard mafia" (his term) never cited his book. He replied with a Romanian proverb to the effect that, "in the house of the condemned one does not mention the prosecutor."
>
> Herman Daly

Introduction

Nicholas Georgescu-Roegen is often connected to thermodynamics and specifically the second law. He used the concept "entropy" to refer strictly to the amount of unavailable energy in a thermodynamic setting. It is exciting to notice that Georgescu-Roegen argued that the second law of thermodynamics is very special and unlike other physical laws. He states that the law is evolutionary and that it was valid, relevant and illustrative of the inadequacy of the mechanical worldview in economics. If economists accepted thermodynamics they would be free to escape from the mechanical "prison" of their worldview.

Biography

Nicholas Georgescu-Roegen was born in Romania in 1906 and died in the United States in 1994. He began his academic career with studies in mathematical statistics at the University of Bucharest and the Sorbonne in Paris. After meeting Joseph Schumpeter at Harvard he became interested in economics and became a respected critic of neo-classical economic theory. In the book *The Entropy Law and the Economic Process* (1971) Georgescu-Roegen launched bio-economy as an alternative to neo-classical economic theory. Georgescu-Roegen was searching for solutions that offered excitement with the least possible consumption of natural resources. He argued that bio-economy promotes resource efficiency and equitable distribution of economic benefits.

Perspectives

Georgescu-Roegen was critical of economic research that sought regularities that could explain and predict actions in the same way as the laws of classical physics. He argued that thermodynamics was the most economical natural law and it shows that resource scarcity was a reality.

He developed an extensive theoretical framework for bio-economy based on the statement that the amount of energy in a closed system is constant and that input power is transformed to increased entropy. Bio-economy focuses on qualitative change, irreversibility, interdependence and resource scarcity. To secure a viable economy it was, according to Georgescu-Roegen, necessary to develop technological solutions that could sustain themselves with the least possible consumption of non-renewable resources. In addition, it was important to avoid overuse of renewable resources.

To achieve resource efficient solutions, it was vital to ensure that waste was drawn, as a valuable resource, into the economy. Georgescu-Roegen pointed out that waste is as necessary part of economic processes, as are natural resources. He criticized neo-classical economics for overlooking the value of waste.

Bio-economics

There are many reasons for taking the warnings from thermodynamics seriously and for trying to develop an economy which is as resource-effective as possible. Even if the media has a tendency to dramatize global environmental problems linked to CO_2 and changes in climate, humanity faces a host of environmental problems, many of them never heard of before. Therefore it is important to shed light on the gradual degradation occurring in several different ecosystems, such as the depletion of the soil, desertification, the reduction of the groundwater level and life forms becoming extinct and so on. In the long run such changes will not only influence conditions for the sustenance of life (including human beings) in the affected ecosystems, they may have an effect on the development of life on Earth in a wider sense. Bio-economics combines knowledge about biological and social systems with thermodynamics.

An important point in bio-economics is that economic actors always act within a social and natural reality. Economic processes change the natural and social environments while these changes affect the economy. Bio-economic practice should therefore be adapted to regional conditions, because it thus becomes easier to discover and experience how economic processes directly and indirectly affect and are affected by individuals, communities and the environment. If economic theory and practice ignore this, it may cause serious negative and unintended consequences (cf. today's environmental, social and financial crisis).

Georgescu-Roegen argued that both economists and ecologists should study processes as part of "the web of life." If economics is studied separately from social and ecological contexts and that knowledge, expressed through mathematical models of general validity becomes abstract, then economy and life become remote. The basic principles of bio-economics are listed in Box 4.1 (Beard and Lozada 1999, p. 120).

Many global challenges are connected to conflicts that arise from the combination of biological necessity, limited low-entropy materials and man's essential nature. According to Georgescu-Roegen, the only factor that could be changed

---

Box 4.1 Bio-economics

1 Economic activity is an aspect of man's biological existence.
2 Economic activity, and all life processes, require a steady diet of energy and "low-entropy" material from the environment.
3 All economic activities necessarily represent a deficit in entropy terms, and result in a reduction in the stock of useful matter available to sustain the human race.
4 There is a "dictatorship of the present over the future."
5 Humans, unlike animals, use created "exosomatic" tools to gather low entropy, and this circumstance leads to social conflicts.
6 With the exceptions of animal husbandry, fire and heat engines and denoted "promethean" technologies, technology is "parasitic" and cannot form the basis of a viable economic system.
7 The bio economic problems of mankind can be solved only through changes in human values, and such changes would need to be accompanied by significant alterations in politics and economic behavior.

is human beings. "Man can change, but it was pure fantasy, in Georgescu's view, to imagine that technological means would be found to rescue humans from their worst impulses" (Beard and Lozada 1999, p. 123). The purpose of Georgescu-Roegen's environmental advocacy was to change people's minds. "For example his constant criticisms of mechanical analogies in economic theory, and the neo-classical treatments of environmental inputs, were made precisely because he believed such patterns of thought were a substantial barrier to accurate thinking about the future of mankind" (Beard and Lozada 1999, p. 129).

Recycling

According to thermodynamics, recycling will always be imperfect. All human economic activity degrades matter into waste in the sense that utilization results in their dispersion throughout the environment. Consequently, future generations will have fewer low-entropy materials available for them than the current generation. In relation to this statement, Georgescu-Roegen argued that we must alter our behavior to preserve resources for the future inhabitants on the Earth.

He delved into several issues to throw light on these questions. First, he argued that we have a moral obligation to future generations, because there simply is no substitute for natural resources. Second, the existing price system will not prohibit the continued consumption of natural resources. On the contrary, it will result in excessive exploitation of natural resources. Recycling could reduce some of the problems, at least in the short term, but in the long run the amount of bound energy will increase because "recycling itself requires capital equipment made of materials, which are in turn refined and made by equipment made of materials, and so on and so forth" (Beard and Lozada 1999, p. 121). The only logical and ethical consequence is that minimal quantities of natural low-entropy resources should be used up by each generation and any use above this level represented an immoral dictatorship of the present over the future.

Enjoyment of life

Instead of focusing on profitability and utility, as is the case in neo-classical economics, bio-economics gives priority to the quality of life ("enjoyment of life," as Georgescu-Roegen called it). Anything that helps to create the good life has economic value. Moreover, this value cannot be quantified and is not identical to the market price. A necessary condition for offering encouragement is that the basic needs are met through consumption of goods and services. In addition, Georgescu-Roegen made clear that leisure is an important factor for creating quality of life.

The basis for increased interest in the social dimensions of an economy is the intensified awareness that social utility cannot be measured exclusively in terms of money. It is therefore problematic to argue that we should always choose alternatives with the highest monetary value. An economic operation which is resource-intensive and causes pollution can, in many cases, be economically profitable even if it results in negative consequences for both nature and society. Georgescu-Roegen strongly believed that the primary outcome of economic activity should be "enjoyment of life." Every activity that leads to enjoyment of life has value for its own sake.

As mentioned earlier, the productivity of ecosystems does not only presuppose that the input side of the economy is kept within sustainable limits, it is also necessary to ensure that the output side does not damage nature's own capacity for decomposition and recycling. In accordance with thermodynamics, it is therefore necessary to emphasize that resource efficiency is the most interesting relationship with regard to the total extraction of resources. This means that extraction of natural resources only becomes a problem the moment the level exceeds the ecosystem's source and sink capacity.

Fairness

Bio-economics requires that resources are distributed fairly within and between generations. This means that consumption in the rich countries must be reduced if people in poor countries are to be satisfied in their basic needs. Another consequence is that the consumption of the present generation should not undermine the possibilities of enjoyment of life for generations yet unborn.

In his article "Energy and Economic Myths" (1975), Georgescu-Roegen mentions a number of measures that are appropriate for a bio-economic program based on minimal resource consumption. First, all production of armaments should cease, and the resources should be transferred to the enhancement of standards of living in poor countries. Second, waste of energy from "overheating, overcooling, over speeding, over lighting" should be drastically reduced. Finally, the lifespan of products should be extended and it must be more profitable to repair them than to buy new products at an ever-increasing speed.

Concluding remarks

Referring to thermodynamics, Georgescu-Roegen drew a great many interesting conclusions regarding economic theory and practice. First of all, exponential growth in the use of natural resources is logically absurd and practically impossible. To reduce the entropy it is of great importance to establish circular value chains. Waste should be an integrated part of the economy. All economic activity is aimed at the enjoyment of life and not economic growth. To reach this goal the distribution of resources must be based on the principle of fairness.

Even if Georgescu-Roegen's economic vision is inspired by thermodynamics, it includes important biological elements. Evolution is described as an organic process: "Evolution – true change – was, for Georgescu-Roegen, the starting and ending point for the vast majority of his work" (Beard and Lozada 1999, p. 134). He clearly believed that evolutionary laws, especially the entropy law, substantially and materially affect social evolution. We focus on evolutionary theory in the next section.

EVOLUTIONARY THEORY

Charles Darwin

> To kill an error is as good a service as, and sometimes even better than, the establishing of a new truth or fact.
>
> Charles Darwin

Introduction

Darwin's founding idea is that all forms of life have the same origin. A consequence of this understanding is that we are all linked in an extremely complex network. Biological evolution depends, according to Darwin, on the adaptation of organisms to their different environments. The difference between organism and environment depends on the perspective and the context of interpretation. According to Darwin, evolution's direction does not depend on a guiding force.

Biography

Charles Darwin was born in Shrewsbury (England). He studied medicine and theology at Edinburgh and Cambridge. Darwin's friendship with Henslow (a professor of biology), combined with his early interest in nature, led him to neglect his medical studies and instead he helped to investigate marine invertebrates. Afterwards he studied biology at Cambridge (Christ's College). He is regarded as the most important biologist in the nineteenth century, whose work has had far-reaching consequences in different fields of science. His most famous books are *The Origin of Species*, 1859 (1982) and *The Descent of Man*, 1871 (2007). Darwin became internationally famous and his pre-eminence as a scientist was marked by burial in Westminster Abbey. Darwin has been described as one of the most influential figures in human history.

Darwinism

Although Darwin is considered by many to be the "father" of evolutionary thought, he was in fact aided and guided by the works of many scientists before him. Malthus had great influence on Darwin's ideas. Malthus was an economist who tried to understand how populations grow and decline. The botanist Lamarck was one of the first to propose that humans evolved from a lower species through adaptations over time. His works inspired Darwin's ideas of natural selection. The mathematician de Buffon influenced Darwin with his thoughts on how life on Earth originated and changed over time. And last, but not least, Wallace is in a special category because he came up with the idea of natural selection, independently, but at the same time as Darwin.

Darwinism has both a narrow and a broad meaning. In its narrow meaning it is a theory of evolution which claims that all living things, including man, have developed from a few simple life forms. All species on Earth have descended over time from common ancestors. Life's earliest forms seem to have been one-celled organisms like bacteria, while the next step was the development of many-celled organisms beginning with plants. Then the animals came. Darwin explained this process of development through transmutation of species by the principle of natural selection based on the struggle for survival. According to Capra and Luisi, there is nothing more holistic and systemic than this notion of Darwinian biological evolution: "all living creatures are intrinsically linked to each other and form a single family" (Capra and Luisi 2014, p. 182).

Darwin published the theory of evolution with compelling evidence in *On the Origin of Species*. It provides, on the one hand, a sweeping portrait of the history and the biology of living things, while on the other Darwin shows the applicability of his theory to a variety of phenomena. Many years later his theories were accepted by the majority of scientists and laymen. Whitehead, among others, accepted "the major finding of Darwin that the complex structure of living things evolved from forms of minimal complexity" (Eisendrath 1999, p. 195). In other words, Whitehead found good reason to agree with Darwinism's claim that the development of man is the product of a long evolution. Today, in a modified form, Darwin's scientific discovery is established as a unifying theory of the life sciences, explaining both the development and the diversity of life. He observed that there is a certain amount of variation of traits or characteristics among the different individuals belonging to a population.

Darwin described three mechanisms that explain evolution: "natural selection, sexual selection, and the inheritance of characteristics acquired during lifetime of the individual organism" (*Encyclopedia of Philosophy* 1967, p. 296). According to Boulding, "We seem to be able to trace several directionalities here" (Boulding 1981, p. 12). First, the increase in the size of the individual organism; second, the increase in complexity; and third, the development of awareness, consciousness and intelligence.

Natural selection

According to Darwin, the Earth's species have changed and diversified through time under the influence of natural selection. The theory of natural selection can be summarized as follows: populations of animals and plants exhibit variations and some variations provide the organism with an advantage over the rest of the population in the struggle for life. Favorable variants will transmit their advantageous characters to their progeny. Since populations tend to produce more progeny than the environment will support, the proportion of favorable variants will be larger than the proportion of unfavorable variants.

Thus a population may undergo continuous evolutionary change that can result in the origin of new varieties, species or indeed new populations. Darwin himself had no knowledge of genetics and, therefore, his theory of natural selection as an explanation of evolution was based solely on what he observed at his time. Modern understanding of the origins of species is based on the theories of Darwin combined with a knowledge of genetics found in the work of Mendel. In the twentieth century, the development of the science of genetics helped explain the origin of the variation of the traits between individual organisms and the way in which they are passed from generation to generation. This basic model of evolution has since been further refined, and the role of genetic drift and sexual selection in the evolution of populations has been recognized.

In *Descent of Man*, evolution by the inheritance of acquired characteristics and sexual selection play a larger role than in *Origin of Species*. Sexual selection refers to the struggle between males for females. Basically, the advantages given to some individuals influence the probability of having offspring. Some of these traits confer fitness; they allow the individual organism that possesses them to survive in their environment better than other individuals who do not possess them and to leave more offspring. Darwin accepted and adopted the theory of inheritance of acquired characters in his later years. The offspring then inherit the beneficial traits, and over time the adaptive trait spreads through the population.

Social Darwinism

The broad meaning of Darwinism refers to a complex of social theories based on evolutionary theory. The American political economist Sumner described society as the outcome of social struggle in which each man, in pursuing his own good, can succeed only at the expense of others. According to Spencer, those who fit best in human society are "the richer and the better educated." In this social struggle the fittest are the ruthless, the imaginative and the industrious. They climb to the top and it is right that they do so. "These would and should go ahead and survive, whereas the weaker and poor should be left to their fate" (Capra and Luisi 2014, p. 204). They are a product of natural selection, "acting on the whole body of men to pick out those who can meet the requirements of certain work to be done" (*Encyclopedia of Philosophy* 1967, p. 305). This explanation came very close to being tautological, since it defined fitness as success in the struggle for survival and then used it to explain this success.

It is fascinating to notice that this interpretation of Darwinism provided a rationale for Smith's doctrine of the invisible hand (published about a hundred years earlier). Smith pointed out that if every economic actor maximized his or her own profit the common good is the result. Darwin argued that the net result of each organism engaging in a struggle for its own survival was continuous evolution of the species as a whole in the direction of better adaption to its environment. "The political implications of this viewpoint are clear" (*Encyclopedia of Philosophy*, p. 305). While the social Darwinists of the nineteenth century saw only competition in nature, we are now beginning to see continual cooperation and mutual dependence among all life forms as central aspects of evolution. To illuminate this very important point Capra refers to Margulis and Sagan, who ascertain that "Life did not take over the globe by combat, but by networking" (Capra 1997, p. 226).

Some critical comments on social Darwinism

The French philosopher Bergson pointed out and discussed some of the major weaknesses in Darwinism. In Bergson's opinion one of most important difficulties was the lack of any satisfactory explanation for the source of new genetic information from which natural selection could select. Bergson's theory proposed a non-Darwinian mechanism to produce new genetic information that, in turn, allowed well-documented mechanisms, including natural selection, to function. Bergson maintained that evolution of life results from a vital impulse, not from mechanical forces as Darwinism taught. Following the same line of argument, Whitehead argued that the driving force in evolution was to be found in the power of creativity, not in a mechanical elimination of the unfit. According to Darwin, nature creates many possibilities through blind "trial and error" and then lets the process of natural selection decide which species survive. From this point of view, the creative process is the unity of three stages: variation, selection and retention of the best combinations.

According to Boulding, Darwin himself was certainly not a social Darwinist. The principle of "the survival of the fittest" is often interpreted to mean the survival of "an aggressive, macho-type mentality at the expense of the cooperative and accommodating patterns of behaviour" (Boulding 1981, p. 18). A much better phrase would be "the survival of the fitting," that is, the species that fits into a niche in the ecosystem. In biological evolution cooperative behavior very often gives a better result than competition. As an example of cooperation in nature the term "symbiosis" is illuminating. Symbiosis refers to the tendency of different organisms to live in close association with one another. It is interesting to notice that Darwin himself never used the expression "survival of the fittest," instead he talked about "the struggle for existence." "Survival of the fittest" was introduced by Spencer in his interpretation of Darwinism.

Boulding also criticizes the metaphor "struggle for existence." In fact "ecological interaction involves little struggle in the sense of organized and conscious fighting" (Boulding 1981, p. 18). Cooperation is a better strategy for adaption to the environment. According to Capra and Luisi, "cooperation is clearly visible [...] at many levels of living organisms" (Capra and Luisi 2014, p. 202). The evolutionary perspective on society and economics does not deny the existence of dialectical processes, "the view that sees the long processes of the history of the universe as essentially conflicts between mutually hostile and opposing systems, each of which arises out of the contradictions of the other" (Boulding 1981, p. 21)

Concluding remarks

To conclude, despite his critical remarks toward Darwinism, Boulding argues that the evolutionary perspective is extremely relevant to explain the ongoing processes of economic life within the political and social environment. "Economics has rested too long in an essentially Newtonian paradigm of mechanical equilibrium and mechanical dynamics" (Boulding 1981, p. 17).

Kenneth Boulding

> Anyone who believes in indefinite growth in anything physical, on a physically finite planet, is either mad or an economist.
>
> Kenneth E. Boulding

Introduction

Kenneth Boulding connected environmental challenges, social development and economics into a new field of science called evolutionary economics. He pointed out that the basic problem was overconsumption of natural resources combined with increasing amounts of waste. He argued that the economy must harmonize with the evolutionary principles in nature and society. Boulding was primarily concerned about the biophysical limits as a long-term problem to be faced by future generations. To solve the problems he often refers to "evolutionary analogies applied to social and economic systems" (Spash 2013a, p. 15). His efforts in the development of evolutionary economics had great influence on the ecological economics movement.

Biography

Kenneth E. Boulding (1910–1993) was born in England and studied at New College, Oxford. Later he went to the United States and continued his studies at the University of Chicago and Harvard. He was soon noted as a highly gifted intellectual with a special ability to pose pioneering questions from original perspectives to established economic theory and practice. His creativity can be attributed to a broad academic horizon, which in addition to economics encompassed philosophy, ecology, poetry and religion. Boulding's scientific development can be described as a transformation from being a pure economist to becoming a cohesive social philosopher. His professional versatility led to his being nominated for both the Nobel Peace Prize and the Nobel Prize in economics (Bank of Sweden Prize in Economic Science in Memory of Alfred Nobel). In 1968 he served as president of the American Economics Association.

Economics as an ecological science

Boulding criticized economics for trying to develop mechanical models of the business cycle. "On the whole, these have been a failure, mainly because the business cycle itself is a very irregular phenomenon" (Boulding 1970, p. 8). He discovered quite early on that any search for solutions in economics always led him into other disciplines. As a consequence Boulding argued that economists must include knowledge from a variety of other disciplines to discover and understand the dynamic interplay between economy, nature and society. One result of this realization was that he used ecological concepts and models to explain economic theory and practice.

Boulding believed that evolutionary theory is suitable as a basis for developing the new theory of the economy (evolutionary economics). "The principle of ecological interaction is the first foundation of the evolutionary perspective" (Boulding 1981, p. 11). In an ecosystem everything depends on everything else. He supplemented the "second law" of thermodynamics about increasing entropy (disorder) with arguments indicating that it is possible to initiate processes that counteract entropy through the organization of interaction between different economic actors. Biological evolution can only take place in open systems like the Earth, in which energy is imported from the sun. Evolution, Boulding declares, builds increasingly complex castles:

> It keeps adding useful, improbable, sometimes beautiful things to our world, while entropy keeps tearing down this improbable organization to its eventual end as a thin brown soup. Production and organization are similar building up processes while consumption and death are tearing down. But knowledge is a kind of magic which does not obey the laws of entropy but keeps increasing irrepressibly.
>
> (Kerman 1974, p. 14)

Boulding's argument is based on the fundamental recognition that the Earth is regarded as a living organism in constant development. Its ecosystems consist of interaction between different kinds of species. Nature is a system with limited capacity of natural resources and the absorbing of waste. In such a system the goal to minimize resource consumption is fundamental. By integrating social, biological and physical dimensions of the economy, Boulding concluded that recycling is an important precondition for viable communities. Boulding said, quite clearly, that a reduction in production and consumption is consistent with increased well-being (quality of life). He argued that "enjoyment of resources is the good thing, and this is not equivalent to using them up" (Kerman 1974, p. 36). Boulding concluded that it is necessary to replace an environmentally harmful "cowboy economy" (in which it is always possible to conquer new territory when the resources are exhausted) with a "spaceship economy."

Evolutionary theory in society and economy

There are "important differences between societal and biological evolution" (Boulding 1981, p. 15). The development of human consciousness changed the process of evolution. Biological evolution proceeds by nonconscious interaction, while human development is based on conscious interaction. According to Boulding (1981), economic life is a subset of the total human activity on the planet. In accordance with this line of argument economic goods are "part of the general ecosystem of the world" (Boulding 1981, p. 17).

The evolution of human artifacts is of three kinds. The first is material objects (from stone axes to computers), the second is organizations (from tribes to the United Nations) and the third is learning processes (from hunting to computer programming).

Change

Bioevolution is characterized by constant ecological interaction, "which is selection, under conditions of constant change of parameters, which is mutation" (Boulding 1981, p. 18). Although Boulding was most concerned about the deeper underlying problems in the economy he meant that attention to the negative symptoms of the current economy was important to induce change. He pointed out that "there may have been times in the evolutionary process when biological change was very slow and something like a genetic equilibrium seems to have been reached" (Boulding 1981, p. 15). An interesting question is to what extent catastrophes have influenced the process of evolution. In a famous article, "The Economics of the Coming Spaceship Earth" (1966), Boulding argued that the environmental crisis will lead to increased understanding of the necessity and willingness to implement measures that change the underlying structures causing the imbalance between economy and nature.

According to Boulding, the mechanical linear economy, "which extracts fossil fuels and ores at one end and transforms them into commodities and ultimately into waste products which are spewed out the other end into pollutable reservoirs is a process which is inherently suicidal and must eventually come to

---

Box 4.2 Evolution of human artifacts

- Material objects
- Organizations
- Learning processes

an end" (Boulding 1970, p. 147). Based on the argument that the implementation of changes presupposes "slack," Boulding meant that the rich countries should take the lead in efforts to develop and implement evolutionary economic principles. In addition to focusing on the negative environmental effects of the current economy, Boulding was also concerned about the significance of the economic system for the development of freedom and humanistic values.

Economics as a moral science

The development of human consciousness indicates the important differences between social and biological evolution. Biological evolution proceeds on the whole by unconscious interaction and non-dialectical processes, social development is anchored in conscious interacting between human beings. In 1966 he published the article "Economics as a Moral Science," in which he points out that all cultures (including economics) are based on a set of common values. All individuals are guided by values. "No one could live, move, or act without one" (Boulding 1968, p. 227). According to Boulding the history of value systems can be regarded as an evolutionary process. In all societies new ethical standards are proclaimed by different groups all the time. Each new ethical "mutation" "encounters the selective process [...] some may have survival value in the short run and some in the long run" (Boulding 1968, p. 229). He is not claiming that selection is the only test of validity, only that it narrows the field of possibilities.

Boulding argued that ethical relativism must be rejected, just as cultural relativism is not acceptable. Not all ethical answers are equally valid, and we could criticize the value of any culture. Hence, before applying ethical principles to business and the economy, we must take a brief look at systemic preconditions. Boulding argued that society can be understood as a balanced interaction between three types of relationships.

First, a threat system is based on the use of power: "you do something nice to me or I will do something nasty to you." This system has much in common with Galtung's description of negative peace. A threat system is intrinsically unstable according to Boulding. Second, an exchange system is characterized by the following idea: "you do something nice to me and I will do something nice to you." An exchange system is based on promises rather than threats, and is characteristic of business and the economy. In the long run the exchange system is more stable than a system based on threat. Third, an integrative system includes persuasion, teaching, love and trust. "What you want,

---

Box 4.3 Three types of relationships

- Threat system (negative-sum games)
- Exchange system (positive-sum games) and
- Integrative system (games without quantifiable points)

I want." According to Boulding we can find a mixture of all three systems in every organization and society. To survive in the long run it is necessary to develop integrative institutions in both society and economy. Exchange systems in the economy are based on instrumentality and are not capable of developing these kinds of values from within.

In addition to criticizing economic theory as one-dimensionally focused on market-based exchange relations, motivated by egocentric utility maximization ("the economic man"), Boulding argued that the values of self-sacrifice, love and loyalty must have more influence within the economy.

Communication and interaction that connect actors together in organic networks are fundamental in Boulding's evolutionary economy. He emphasizes, therefore, that organization through decentralized, collaborative networks provides better results than what can be achieved through giant globalized organizations based on hierarchical power structures. Large-scale organizations based on hierarchical power structures focus exclusively on economic return and ignoring humanist values and economic environmental responsibility.

Concluding remarks

Boulding points out that economists have, for the most part, failed to understand the consequences of the transition from the open (cowboy economy) to the closed Earth (spaceship economy). In a closed system the outputs from the system are linked to the inputs of the same system. The only way to solve challenges in a closed system is to participate in cooperative interactions. Economic theory presupposes an open system where it is possible to receive input from outside and throw the output out of the system. "Given a capacity to draw upon inputs and to get rid of outputs, an open system [...] can persist indefinitely" (Boulding 1968, p. 276). The question is: "are we able to accept the earth as a closed system and change economics in ways that will make it less pathological?" Boulding describes a realistic utopia by indicating that "the traditional village economy [...] may be more a prototype of the world to come than the economics of the great age of expansion in which we are living now" (Boulding 1970, p. 148). To a large extent, the village was cyclical, it did return all waste back to the Earth, and it did not depend much on imports from outside.

ANTHROPOSOPHY

Rudolf Steiner

> One of the conditions of the social organism's life is that those who can serve the community through their individual abilities should not be deprived of using their free initiative.
>
> Rudolf Steiner

Introduction

"Anthroposophy is a body of knowledge concerning the spiritual in man and in the universe" (Wilkinson 2001, p. 15). Steiner criticized the dualistic world-view of matter and spirit and stated that knowledge about the physical world must be integrated with knowledge of the spiritual world.

According to Griffin, one of the main differences between Rudolf Steiner and Alfred North Whitehead is connected to their fundamental aims. Whitehead was concerned with the truth, while Steiner was interested in truth "primarily for the sake of transformation – of individuals primarily, and through them of the world as a whole" (Griffin 1991, p. 1). Steiner had suggestions which should bring about solutions to the most important problems in the world. He realized that "the natural scientific age and its consequences would bring about the downfall of mankind unless counterbalanced by some other influence" (Wilkinson 2001, p. 11). Anthroposophy exemplifies such a counter-impulse.

Biography

Rudolf Steiner (1861–1925) was born in Kraljevec, Austria, and died in Dornach, Switzerland. He studied at the Technical College of Vienna. His doctoral dissertation "Wahrheit und Wissenschaft" was the precursor of his major work *The Philosophy of Freedom*. Steiner was a keen Goethe researcher and for years he was Germany's leading theosophist. Steiner is known primarily as the founder of anthroposophy. From the basis of anthroposophical philosophy, he made contributions in various fields. Most famous is the Waldorf pedagogy, the educational foundation for Steiner schools. Steiner also developed ideas and principles of biodynamic farming and anthroposophical medicine. He furthermore made important contributions in economics and social sciences.

Anthroposophy

"Is a man in his thinking and acting a spiritually free being, or is he compelled by the iron necessity of purely natural law?" (Steiner 1964, p. 3). This is the first sentence in Steiner's book *The Philosophy of Freedom*. Steiner made thinking a key to freedom and individual responsibility. Freedom, thinking and individuality "interweave in Steiner's work like three strands of a single braid, uniting through their dynamic cooperations the subtle interconnections of a complex and powerful vision" (Hughes 1995, p. xiii). Thinking must never, according to Steiner, be regarded as a merely subjective activity: "Thinking is beyond subject and object" (Steiner 1995, p. 52).

The connection between subject and object is introduced by thinking, not by the subject or the object. Freedom depends on the individual's ability to will what they themselves hold to be right. In addition he links intuition to thinking; the essence of thinking can be grasped through intuition. Intuition is the conscious experience of spiritual essence. "Intuition is to thinking as observation is to perception" (Steiner 1995, p. 88). In other words, intuition and observation are the sources of knowledge. To explain something is to place it into a context; nothing can be cut off from the world as a whole. Thinking is the element through which we participate in the cosmos; feeling is the element through which we withdraw into our own being. "Our thinking unites with the world; our feeling leads us back into ourselves and makes us individuals" (Steiner 1995, p. 101).

The social organism

Steiner asks the following question: "How can we […] hope to cope with the chaotic condition of society if we approach it with a thought process which has no relation to the reality?" (Steiner 1977, p. 10). Observation of the contemporary world indicates that the spiritual life requires free self-administration, while the economy requires associative work. Between them, the political state, as a third function, is necessary. In other words, to develop a healthy society Steiner meant to facilitate a balanced interaction between a free self-organizing culture, a democratic constitutional system and an associative cooperative economic sector. The three functions in the social organism are based on different assumptions and they have different characteristics (Box 4.4.).

Each area can be described with the ideals of the French Revolution: liberty, equality and fraternity. Freedom in the spiritual life enables cultural diversity. Equality in juridical life ensures the individual rights and opportunities. Businesses facilitate efficient resource utilization and equitable distribution of benefits through associative cooperation. If one of these areas becomes dominant the result is a disease. Many of the problems we face in society today indicate that the economy is dominating the society organism.

An important point in Steiner's philosophy is that the social organism is evolving, always unfinished. Therefore it is not possible to prepare ready-made final solutions. What is important is to facilitate processes that help to develop a course for long-term change. Steiner points out that an important prerequisite for change is that we become aware of disease symptoms in the community. To do that we need to develop a practical understanding of how

---

Box 4.4 Three functions of the social organism

- Spiritual life (education, research, arts and culture, religion) – freedom
- Juridical life (politics, law, contractual relationship) – equality
- Economic life (production, distribution and consumption) – fraternity

healthy conditions can be developed. In a healthy social organism the autonomous spiritual sector must function alongside the political and economic sectors. It depends on the freedom of art, science and philosophy. In spiritual life everything is integrated, hence "the freedom of one cannot flourish without the freedom of the other" (Steiner 1977, p. 76). Change is dependent on a sufficient number of people developing a social conception of life, based on practical experience and realistic visions of the future.

Co-creation

Steiner points out that it is not unproblematic to transfer knowledge from biology and ecology to the social organism. An important difference is that biological organisms developed through evolutionary processes, while the social organism is changing through human participation. "It is not possible to consider evolution objectively as regards the social organism. One must activate evolution" (Steiner 1977, p. 124). Because we are co-creators in the process it is not possible to regard social development in the same manner as we observe nature. However, many characteristics are in common, for example, that living beings are always undetermined. In the same way that human beings can make use of their abilities in different ways there are many possibilities for the realization of the potential in a social organism. "In every human mind – for every human mind takes part in the functioning of the social organism – not only in the minds of a few specialists, must be present at least an instinctive knowledge of what the social organism needs" (Steiner 1977, p. 55).

The economy

The economy must constitute an autonomous part within the social organism. Economy is concerned with all aspects of "production, circulation and consumption of commodities" (Steiner 1977, p. 58). Everyone working in a social organism based on the division of labor earns his income through the work of all the participants in the social organism; he never earns it by himself. "One can only work for others, and let others work for oneself. One can no more work for oneself than one can devour oneself" (Steiner 1977, p. 121). Economic activity depends on nature and human labor and legal regulations.

Important conditions for business practice are, on the one hand the condition of the ecosystems, climate, regional geography, natural resources, etc., and on the other hand the juridical conditions that regulate the interaction between the actors in the market and between economy and nature. In this way economy depends on two conditions: the natural base, which we must take for given, and the legal regulations, which should be rooted in a political state independent of economic interests. Seen from this perspective an economic value "is a Nature-product transformed by human Labour" (Steiner 1972, p. 29). An important common feature between organisms and businesses is that the resilience in organizations and businesses is weakened over time in the same manner as in all biological organisms. To maintain a high level of energy, both depend on the ability to be constantly evolving, which is of great importance. This process helps dynamism and constant change in the social organism.

Work, labor and consumption

The task of economy is to ensure that goods are produced, distributed and consumed in such a way that human needs are satisfied without disturbing the ecosystems. A commodity has values through the person who consumes it. According to Steiner we can distinguish between work that transforms nature, and work that modifies processes. Managerial activities must be based on individual abilities. The legal relationships between manager and worker must allow individual abilities to manifest themselves in the best possible manner.

One consequence of division of labor is that an increasingly larger share of what the individual produces is consumed by others, while the individuals own consumption consists of goods produced by others. Through division of labor the economic agents are interdependent. Through active participation the worker should be able "to develop a clear idea of his own involvement in society through his work on the production of commodities" (Steiner 1977, p. 88). It is the essence of a living organism that something is continually being formed and unformed. In any organism there must be a continual production and consumption. In the economic organism "there must be a constant producing and a using-up of what is produced" (Steiner 1972, p. 62).

Referring to interdependence and cooperation toward common goals, Steiner concluded that division of labor counteracted the tendency to selfishness and greed. A healthy economy depends on a balanced interplay between production and consumption. In any organism a combination of constructive and destructive processes takes place in parallel. While production creates values, consumption breaks them down. The two processes must be carefully coordinated, if not they will cause disease and negative symptoms in the social organism. The task for the future is, according to Steiner, to find, "through associations, the kind of production which most accords with the needs of consumption, and the most appropriate channels from the producers to the consumers" (Steiner 1977, p. 112).

Money

According to Steiner, money is nothing but "the externally expressed value which is gained in the economic process through the division of labour and transmitted from one man to another" (Steiner 1972, p. 53). Money is completely abstract in the beginning but it grows more concrete through the economic process. The total number of commodities in the economic organism and money present represent a real interaction. No kind of money in reality could only be an expression of the sum-total of means of production available in a given region. Steiner distinguishes between three types of money (see Box 4.5.).

Purchase money always has a specific value, which corresponds to the product or the service you are exchanging. When I act as a seller, money has a higher value for me than it has for the buyer. On the opposite side, the buyer ascribes the products a higher value than they have for the seller. In other words, the seller demands money, while the buyer demands goods. Steiner argues that the right price implies that the producer receives a payment that is large enough to cover all their needs until he has produced a similar product. Concretely, this means that the time he has spent to produce the commodity is not crucial, the question is how much time he uses to create the next one. On a general level, "money will wear out, just as commodities wear out" (Steiner 1977, p. 120).

The value of loan money is measured in a very different way. It corresponds to the expectations and aspirations of the borrower. Gift money, given to cultural purposes, is crucial to ensuring a viable culture. To ensure that money provides the basis for new value creation it is extremely important that they undergo all three stages, purchase, loan and gift. Money, in a healthy social organism, can be nothing other than "a draft on commodities produced by others, which the holder may claim from the overall social organism because he himself produced and delivered commodities to this sector" (Steiner 1977, p. 117).

Associations

To handle all the tasks bound for the economy in the social organism Steiner advises founding associations that underlie the entire economy. Associations are economic organizations which allow people to unite in cooperative networks based on reciprocal activities. Healthy social development requires an autonomous economy within a political context where the state is able, through the process of law, "to affect economic organizations in such a way that the individual does not feel that his integration in the social organism is in conflict with his rights-awareness" (Steiner 1977, p. 71).

Box 4.5 Three kinds of money

- Purchase money
- Loan money
- Gift money

Through associative cooperation between people with different experiences and perspectives, it is possible to develop a comprehensive insight that helps them understand economic realities from within. From the perspective of associations it is possible to discover the true meaning of economic life. Exchange processes connected to supply and demand are economic realities. When somebody brings commodities to the market and offers them for a price it is usually called "supply," but, according to Steiner, it is no such thing. Rather it is a demand for money. If a man brings commodities onto the market and wants to sell them, it is, unquestionably, a demand for money. "Supply of commodities is demand for money and supply of money is demand for commodities" (Steiner 1972, p. 98).

Cooperation between producers, distributors and customers also helps to develop the necessary comprehensive understanding that ensures that commodities and money circulate optimally. Associations are independent, self-governing cooperative bodies in economic life. Associations can be regional, horizontally or vertically oriented. Within an association, it is possible to clarify conflicts of interest before they develop into a battle of interests. Mutual trust between the members of an association is necessary for cooperation to work. The task of the future is to find, through associations, "the kind of production which most accords with the needs of consumption, and the most appropriate channels from the producers to the consumers" (Steiner 1977, p. 112).

Concluding remarks

It is no surprise that objections are raised from mainstream economists toward the implementation of associative economics. According to Steiner, this is a natural consequence of accepting that real-life processes are characterized by contradictions. Today's resistance toward such ideas will vanish when human beings become conscious of impulses consistent with real life. Steiner's optimism has been, at least in part, confirmed today. Important aspects of his economic insights are beginning to be integrated in contemporary ecological economics. These include the importance of embedding the economy in organic worldviews, economy as integrated into nature and culture, a focus on the real economy, decentralization, coordination through collaborative networking and far more concentration on bottom-up initiatives.

Leif Holbæk-Hanssen

If we don't give people opportunities to release their personal potential we cannot expect them to contribute more than robots soon will do better and cheaper.

Leif Holbæk-Hanssen

Introduction

Holbæk-Hanssen pointed out that competitive market economies are not capable of handling the environmental and social crises that will inevitably arise. He claimed that crises were a symptom of a deeper conflict between the economic worldview and physical and social reality. In economies all things are interconnected. We must think of things as a whole, interconnected with one another.

Biography

Holbæk-Hanssen was born in Christiania in 1917 and died in Oslo in 1991. He studied economics and marketing at Copenhagen Business School in Denmark. In addition to that he studied sociology and social psychology at the University of Oslo and at the University of Michigan, Ann Arbor. Holbæk-Hanssen was appointed as Norway's first full professor of marketing and distribution economics at the Norwegian School of Economics in 1960. He was a key person in the creation of marketing as a scientific discipline in Norway. In addition to publishing academic articles and books he kept in touch with practice through a series of lectures and seminars.

In retrospect Holbæk-Hanssen is best known for having developed economics and marketing within a larger context of thought and cognition. The aim was to lay the foundation for a comprehensive practice-theory based on the idea that economics, politics and culture are in a mutually dependent relationship. This approach, inspired by Steiner's anthroposophical analysis, is evident both in the trilogy *Methods and Models in Marketing* (1973–1976) and in his book *A Society for Human Development* (1984). *Economy and Society: When Man Is of Importance* (2009), is a collection of unpublished speeches and articles that shed light on the three main areas in Holbæk-Hanssen's academic work. To capture the most serious challenges facing economics he argued that it was necessary to effect change in our basic perception of reality, our methods of seeking knowledge and our way of acting.

Ontological criticism

Holbæk-Hanssen was an articulate critic of neo-classical market economy. He believed that many of the ideas that underlie our actions are based on inherited thought patterns that we use more or less unconsciously, often without considering either their validity or their relevance. It turns out all the time that we are only going part of the way when we use mechanistic concepts and explanatory models such as "market forces" and "price mechanisms" to find solutions to issues related to such issues as environmental and poverty crisis. Inflation, currency crises, resource depletion, pollution and centralization are symptoms showing that neo-classical economic theory fails completely to capture the complexity of today's globalized world. In our breathless rush to increase production and consumption, we have forgotten to be aware of ecosystem consequences connected to the extraction of natural resources and energy and the disturbance caused by increasing amounts of waste.

Philosophy of science

Problems can, according Holbæk-Hanssen, be explained by pointing to structural weaknesses in the current economic system. He argued that economic theory and practice have to change from a mechanical to an organic understanding of reality. According to Steiner, organic thinking points out that everything is changeable, unfinished, dynamic and always in a state of flux. A transition to an organic-based economy has major consequences for the understanding of scientific methods and research in general. According to Holbæk-Hanssen, the consequence of unilaterally using analytical methods to identify and describe the smallest parts in various cause–effect chains is that we are left with a fragmented and "lifeless" view of reality where we only have large amounts of bits and pieces about the least human part of the economy and society.

As inspiring alternatives to the empirical-analytical research tradition, Holbæk-Hanssen suggested hermeneutics and phenomenology. Hermeneutics is based on a worldview where everything hangs together in a whole and where knowledge and meaning occur in the interaction between part and whole. Knowledge is validated by eliminating all forms of embedded inconsistency and shortcomings of logical relationships. The aim is to understand or find meaning in different phenomena with reference to a larger context. The meaningful relationship between part and whole represents the basis for hermeneutics.

Switching between part and whole is fundamental in hermeneutical method. By interpreting the part in the context of the whole and the whole as a totality of integrated parts, we achieve a deeper understanding of how it all fits together in a greater whole. Holbæk-Hansen used the phrase "spiritual bend and stretch program" as a designation for research processes where one alternates between concentration down to details and a stretching upward toward larger wholes. Holbæk-Hanssen argued that researchers should make more use of methods that are geared toward interpretation of how phenomena relate to each other. The main task is to find concepts, or, rather, stories, that help to understand economic life from the inside.

Phenomenology

Phenomenology emphasizes observations and intuitive experience in concrete reality. Holbæk-Hanssen focused on a combination between observation in concrete reality and adaptation of empirical material in a process of thinking. However, he emphasized thinking more than is normally found in traditional scientific methods by trying to isolate thinking from emotions and the will-impulses that often control most of our thoughts in general. It is furthermore important to do the observations without any preconditions. Key concepts in the phenomenological research tradition are imagination, inspiration and intuition.

Holbæk-Hanssen defined imagination as the ability suddenly "to see the entire pattern." It is, in other words, a creative process that consists of finding a pattern or creates a pattern where the individual elements, joined together, are synthesized as a whole. This represents more than the sum of its elements, and the patterns are essential. Inspiration is connected to the ability to experience that something is in conformity with reality. The experience is part of the living reality and will therefore help to create direction of development. It is precisely this experience that is significant in a social context; the experience can change our living conditions. New knowledge is tested in a confrontation between ideas and reality.

Intuition

Even if the logical content is often vague, Holbæk-Hanssen based the phenomenological method on intuitive insight. When it comes to conclusions or judgments about the relationships between phenomena, we have to trust the intuitive experience of these connections. Exercise and training are significant in developing intuitive competence. Intuition is defined as the conviction that it is right or good to implement new ideas in practical contexts. Through the use of intuition, it is possible to find solutions to how practical tasks should be resolved or handled.

These conclusions can only be tested by a confrontation with reality. Holbæk-Hanssen points out that people working in practical business are very often in favor of the phenomenological research procedure since they are used to making judgments and decisions based on intuition.

Specifically, this approach to knowledge states that issues related to economic activities are given a far deeper meaning if they are illustrated by long-term social and ecological contexts. If, for example introducing technologies that damage the natural world to increase short-term profitability, then long-term environmental and social interests could well be harmed. Based on a comprehensive understanding of how things hang together, we can use our creative abilities to develop and implement new and better solutions.

Box 4.6 Key concepts in phenomenology

- Imagination
- Inspiration
- Intuition

Associations

Along with Whitehead and Steiner, Holbæk-Hanssen explains creativity as a phenomenon that occurs in the field of tension between "actuality" and "potentiality." To give a direction to creativity it is necessary that we continually make up our mind about the values we want to prioritize. In accordance with Holbæk-Hanssen's democratic ideas we should develop organic structures that initiate constructive cooperation to achieve common goals. It is partly necessary to establish new arenas for dialogue and cooperation between stakeholders with conflicting interests. He suggested (and tried out in practice) various forms of collaborative networks (associations) with representatives from a varied branches of the economic life, production, consumption and circulation.

An important purpose of establishing integrated networks is to contribute to the reduction of tendencies to economic egoism. Holbæk-Hanssen argued that the new organizational structure helped to remove "all the devilry" that could follow in the wake of an established atomized competitive economy. The idea behind networks is that they put people with opposing views together to come up with agreements on difficult tasks. The networks allowed for better coordination between needs and production, more appropriate utilization of labor, as well as the more efficient use of natural resources and technology. In this way, he believed that several of the most urgent anomalies in the contemporary economy could be solved.

In accordance with this mind-set, Holbæk-Hanssen argued that global challenges could be addressed through integrated local and regional networks where creative thinking is combined with practical experimentation. Dialogues in cooperative networks make it possible to open up pluralistic values that exceed the economy's traditional one-dimensional monetary scale. In economics, everything depends on an open-minded consideration of life as a whole. We must gain a clear vision of the whole of life. In the associations the sense of community (community spirit) must be working.

Box 4.7 Associative economics

- It is more important to understand the relationships and the dynamic change processes, than to create static models showing the relationship between quantifiable economic variables.
- Competition between autonomous actors is changed in favor of cooperation between interdependent actors.
- Developing collaborative relationships through the creation of associative networks is more important than removing all obstacles to competition.
- Instead of searching for objective and value-free economic knowledge it is necessary to develop a science where knowledge and values are integrated.

Practice

An important characteristic of Holbæk-Hanssen's research was that he constantly tested his ideas in practical contexts. Since Holbæk-Hanssen claimed that we always have to look upon the cultivation of land as the starting point in any economy, it was not very surprising that his ideas of networking and collaborative solutions fell into good soil within the Helios community. In the 1980s and 90s there were several interesting experiments in Norway with collaborative networks where organic farmers, manufacturers, wholesalers, retailers and consumers participated.

Working with the Helios movement Holbæk-Hansen's concepts were filled with practical content. The guiding principle behind the development of cooperative networks was individual responsibility and autonomy; in addition individual freedom and creativity were central. If we don't give people opportunities to release their personal potential we cannot expect them to contribute more than robots soon will do better and cheaper.

Today lessons from the experiments with Helios are useful in connection with the establishment and development of regional network-based solutions where the objective is to contribute to improved quality of life and sustainable use of resources. In addition, Holbæk-Hanssen was an important source of inspiration behind the establishing of Cultura Bank in Oslo. Today Cultura Bank is a viable bank that has contributed to giving the term "social banking" a concrete and meaningful place in an international context.

Concluding remarks

Anchored in anthroposophy, Holbæk-Hanssen argued that it was impossible to understand the real world from a mechanical perspective by using analytical methods. To capture the life processes in nature and society it is necessary to be conscious about the world as a living organism. A practical consequence of the organic worldview is the necessity to change from atomistic competition to cooperation in associations or integrated networks. In order to understand the world we are living in it is of the greatest importance to complement positivistic research models with hermeneutics and phenomenology.

BUDDHISM

Mahatma Gandhi

First they ignore you, then they laugh at you, then they fight you, then you win.

Mahatma Gandhi

Introduction

Even if Gandhi was a Hindu, he proclaimed himself a Buddhist, saying that Buddhism was rooted in Hinduism and represented its essence. "He saw Buddhism as cleansed Hinduism" (Balachandran 2006). Gandhian development is based on "the same foundations as Buddhist philosophy, for it aims at the reduction of craving, avoidance of violence and development of the spirit" (Sivaraksa 2009, p. 35). Buddhist philosophy is relevant for a deeper understanding of modern science. In Buddhism bifurcation or dualism is non-existent, mind and matter are interconnected. All phenomena arise in mutual dependence and are dependent on contextual causes and conditions. "Things derive their being and nature by mutual dependence and are nothing in themselves" (Capra and Luisi 2014, p. 290). Gandhi required us to think afresh about things we have long taken for granted, and therein lies his greatest contribution and true originality (Parekh 2001).

Biography

Born on October 2, 1869, in Porbandar, India, Mahatma Gandhi grew up in an eclectic religious environment. He studied law in London. He took lessons in dancing, elocution and violin. When he left England, he became an advocate for the rights of Indians, first in South Africa (for twenty-one years) then in India itself. Gandhi became a leader of India's independence movement, organizing boycotts against British institutions in peaceful forms of civil disobedience. He was killed by a fanatic in 1948.

Human nature

According to Gandhi human beings are characterized by three fundamental properties (Box 4.8).

The cosmos is a well-coordinated whole where all parts are linked in a mutual supportive system by the deepest relations (bonds). He also argued, in accordance with Buddhism, that the universe is not material; it is infused with a cosmic spirit. This interconnectedness is expressed in Gandhi's favorite metaphor: "the cosmos was not a pyramid of which the material world was the base and human beings the apex, but a series of ever-widening circles encompassing humankind, the sentient world, the material world, and all including cosmos" (Parekh 2001, p. 50).

Human beings are interdependent and formed an organic whole. Every human being's personality and character is a benefit to others and therefore every human action was both self- and other-regarding. Another consequence of fundamental interconnectedness is that human beings could not hurt other living beings without brutalizing themselves.

Four-dimensional nature

Referring to Box 4.8, human beings have a four-dimensional nature. First, the body is able to maintain its integrity because it is distinct and clearly separated from others. Wants and desires are situated in the body. The body is the force of physical energy. Second, the mind (*manos*) included the stream of consciousness from birth until death. Intelligence, intuition and passions are also part of the mind. Even if the mind is distinct from the body, it is still an integrated part of it. The mind is also the center for the ego. Third, the soul (*atman*) infuses all living beings. The soul is the source of spiritual force or energy. This indicates that the whole living universe has one soul, which everyone is part of. The world soul/spirit is eternal and indestructible, "it is not an entity, a thing or a being, but as force, and active principle, a source of intelligent energy" (Parekh 2001, p. 55). Fourth, human beings have a psychological and moral constitution (*swabhava*).

According to Gandhi, this unique individual nature is ontologically as important as our common human nature. This non-material body (*swabhava*) survives physical death and persists through several lives. Hence, personal character is the product of karma (human action produces inevitable consequences) stemming from the previous lives.

The four noble truths

The truth of suffering is the first noble truth in Buddhism. It states that suffering is an intrinsic part of life and that the only opportunity to put an end to suffering is by fulfilling the human potential for goodness and happiness. Associating with what is unpleasant is suffering, the same counts for disassociation from what is unpleasant. The second noble truth is the thirst for craving which gives rise to a thirst for sensual pleasure, thirst for existence, thirst for non-existence. The third noble truth is cessation of suffering. The simplest means to reach spiritual joy and compassion is to put an end to greed, hatred and delusion. The fourth noble truth is the eightfold path to nirvana and its three divisions (Box 4.9).

Box 4.8 Human beings in nature

- They are an integral part of the cosmos.
- They are interdependent on each other.
- They are four-dimensional beings, made up of:
  - the body
  - the mind (*manos*)
  - the soul/spirit (*atman*) and
  - the psychological and moral constitution (*swabhava*).

Box 4.9 The three divisions to nirvana

1 Wisdom: right understanding (acceptance of Buddhist teachings), right resolve (developing the right attitudes).
2 Morality: right speech (speak in a thoughtful and sensitive way), right action (abstain from killing and stealing), right livelihood (do not engage in actions that harm others).
3 Meditation: right effort (cultivating a positive state of the mind), right mindfulness (cultivating constant awareness) and right meditation (developing deep levels of mental calm and integrating the personality).

The eightfold path is known as the middle way because it steers the way between asceticism and indulgence.

Modern society

Gandhi argued that every society is inspired by a concept of nature and human beings. If the concept is mistaken, as it is in modern society, it corrupts the entire civilization and makes it a force for evil. Since Gandhi was able to see modern society from outside (cf. utopia) he was able to uncover assumptions, contradictions and limitations that were hidden from a Western perspective (cf. ideology). The modern society had achieved knowledge that brought nature under greater human control, but it had not developed a holistic frame of reference for how to use the knowledge. Modern society is characterized by features such as rationalism, secularization, industrialization, the scientific culture, individualism, technological mastery of nature, the drive toward globalization and liberal democracy.

Although Gandhi certainly accepted that there are many positive achievements in modern society, he went on: "it is fundamentally flawed, as was evident in the fact that it was aggressive, imperialist, violent, exploitative, brutal, unhappy, restless, and devoid of a sense of direction and purpose" (Parekh 2001, p. 79). In other words modern society has undermined man's unity with the natural and social environment.

Because modern society is driven by self-interest and self-indulgence it is dominated by materialistic desires and the goal of unrestrained satisfaction of wants. Consumers are manipulated through intensive marketing techniques to desire commodities they don't need and which are not, in any sense, in their long-term interests. Following this line of argument it is not a surprise that the economy, based on profits, conquers both nature and culture. Driven by greed and ruthless competition, the economy has created an ever-increasing gap between the rich and the poor. Gandhi maintains that modern economy has reduced human beings to "helpless and passive spectators and represented a

new form of slavery, more comfortable and invidious and hence more dangerous than the earlier ones" (Parekh 2001, p. 80).

The economic system is anchored in egoism or enlightened self-interest,
not in human dignity (positive freedom) but in a restriction of external con-
straint (negative freedom). In addition, centralization of production has created social and economic problems of national and international magnitudes.

Gandhi concluded that modern society is aggressive against both human
beings and nature. Natural resources are exploited at an ever-increasing speed
and the balance in the ecosystems is disturbed. He also focused on the brutal-
ity toward animals as an example of the violence characterizing the materialistic society. Parekh argues that Gandhi was too critical of modern society
and that he overlooked some of its great achievements and strengths. "It
encourages selfishness and greed, but it also fosters human unity, individuality, equality, liberty, creativity, rationality, intellectual curiosity, and all-round
human development" (Parekh 2001, p. 90).

Non-violent society

According to Gandhi the search for a single model for a future society is both
incoherent and dangerous, because different societies have different histories
and traditions. Instead he wanted to come up with some fundamental principles by which a good society should be governed. How to implement these
principles in practice was up to the people involved.

The good society should be informed by the cosmic spirit, that is, a good
and simple life which does not disturb the integrity, diversity, rhythm and inner
balance in society and nature. The principles follow from accepting that all
human beings are interconnected and mutually interdependent, a good society should institutionalize and stimulate the spirit of love, truthfulness, social
service, cooperation, and solidarity and discourage all forms of exploitation,
domination, injustice and inequality. To reach this goal it is of great importance to stimulate dialogue and creative interplay between human beings. In
addition a good society depends on mutual responsibility, characterized by a
high level of self-discipline and self-restraint. Within this framework a good
society should provide the maximum space for personal autonomy.

A good society should also accept scientific pluralism, that is, it should
appreciate that reason, intuition, faith, traditions, emotions and accumulated
collective wisdom are relevant sources of knowledge which contribute to coping with the complexities in society. A community's resilience and creative
potential increase the more complex, diverse and coherent the connections are.

Peace economy

Gandhi points out some fundamental principles of the new economy. First
of all, nature cannot possibly be privately owned, because nature is common
property. Second, all products are a result of collaboration and nobody has

---

Box 4.10 Principles in the new economy

- Nature is common property
- Products are results of collaboration
- Interaction based on cooperation and dialogue
- More emphasis on spiritualism and frugality

---

an exclusive claim on them. Third, market interaction is based on cooperation and dialogue rather than competition and egoism. Fourth, all reductions in materialism and consumerism are to the benefit of spiritualism and frugality.

Trying to lay out clearly his ideas about economic matters, Gandhi describes a small decentralized economy anchored in the personal character of the members in local societies. Gandhi argued that "each community should become relatively self-sufficient in its basic needs" (Parekh 2001, p. 97). The more self-sufficient the local communities are the more participation is required in making decisions. "Development from the bottom-up emphasizes individual freedom and responsibility" (Sivaraska 2009, p. 32). Beyond the relatively self-sufficient villages, society would be organized in terms of expanding circles. Central authorities should have enough power to organize the nation but not enough to dominate local societies. Work is both a right and a duty, as through work individuals develop self-respect and initiative and counteract the tendency to egocentric behavior. Participation in local production have a bonus effect in developing workers' pride and self-discipline.

Although large-scale industries are of great importance, they should be restricted to a minimum. Competition between large-scale centralized industry and local production is problematic because it could eliminate the fundamentals required for small-scale activities. To support local production, small-scale technology is necessary. Patnaik reasons that "productivity combined with creativity preserves and promotes human identity and dignity which are subdued to the point of elimination by the use of large-scale technology" (Patnaik 1991, p. 118).

In order to reduce the gap between the rich and the poor, the state should define maximum and minimum levels of income. To sum up, decentralized cooperative networks are a prerequisite to develop a "community of communities," "a unity of unities" or a "living organism," not an impersonal machine. To succeed in developing "self-sufficient local communities depending on small-scale production units mostly using local resources in a decentralizing system of economic management" (Patnaik 1991, p. 117), a fusion of mind and heart is required.

The good society

To develop good societies "we need to engage community members to participate in making decisions about the things that affect their lives and livelihoods" (Sivaraska 2009, p. 29). To do this it is important to develop decentralized small-scale economics that promotes human values, limits suffering and where nature's inherent values are respected. Buddhist economics is based on sustainability, where the needs of the people are in harmony with the rhythms of the ecosystems. Human beings are an integrated part of nature, not nature's master. Interdependence is the source of our shared humanity. From a Buddhist point of view prosperity is not based on income and wealth but on self-reliance and self-dignity.

On a political level, "mindfulness can help in our work against consumerism, sexism, militarism, and the many other isms that undermine the integrity of life" (Sivaraska 2009, 83). Based on Buddhism as practice and experience, Gandhi suggested certain key principles of the good society (Box 4.11).

Concluding remarks

According to Buddhism the universe is both material and spiritual, and economic thinking must take into account both dimensions. One consequence

---

Box 4.11 Principles for a good society

1 The good society should be informed by the spirit of cosmic piety.
2 Since human beings are interdependent, the good society should discourage all forms of exploitation, domination and injustice. Inequality, which necessarily coarsens human sensibilities and depends on falsehood for its continued existence, should find ways of institutionalizing and nurturing the spirit of love, truthfulness, social service, cooperation and solidarity
3 Since human beings are spiritual in nature, the good society should help them develop their moral and spiritual powers and create the conditions for self-rule or autonomy.
4 The good society should cherish epistemological pluralism. It should appreciate that reason, intuition, faith, traditions, intergenerationally accumulated wisdom and emotions are all valuable sources of knowledge, and make their own distinct contributions to understanding and coping with the complexities of human life.
5 The good society should encourage a dialogue, a creative interplay between them, and not allow one of them to acquire a hegemonic role or become the arbiter of all others.
6 Since each individual has a distinct moral and psychological constitution and comes to terms with life in his or her own unique way, the good society should provide the maximum space for personal autonomy.

(Parekh 2001, pp. 93–94)

is that material consumption should be minimized to the benefit of spiritualism. People are at the center of Gandhi's economic framework. "Human welfare and social progress cannot afford to ignore the moral and spiritual dimensions" (Patnaik 1991, p. 118). Gandhi was an advocate for small-scale farming and micro-sized industry for local markets, and the idea that local societies should be self-sufficient as far as basic needs are concerned. Buddhism's essence is "to overcome selfishness and transform greed into generosity, hatred into loving kindness, and ignorance into wisdom" (Sivaraska 2009, p. 92). Simplicity and non-violence are closely related in the framework of economics.

E. F. Schumacher

Any intelligent fool can make things bigger and more complex [...]. It takes a touch of genius – and a lot of courage – to move in the opposite direction.

E. F. Schumacher

Introduction

One way of looking at the world as a whole is by means of a map, said Schumacher, who was one of the first holistic thinkers in economics. He was also a great synthesizer, who brought many different perspectives into the economic frame of reference. He was well aware of one of the most fundamental explanations behind the challenges in modern society – that modern man does not see himself as a part of nature but as an outside force destined to dominate and conquer it. "He even talks about a battle with nature, forgetting that, if he won the battle, he would find himself on the losing side" (Schumacher 1993, p. 3). To handle the problems in modern society we have to be creative and start coming to terms with alternative futures (utopia). Even just to talk about the future can be the start of concrete action.

Biography

Ernst Friedrich Schumacher was born in Germany in 1911 and emigrated to the UK in 1936 and died in Switzerland in 1977. He was trained as an economist and achieved wide recognition through cooperation with, among others, Keynes and Galbraith. He began to question the Western economy's one-sided emphasis on material growth, efficiency and profitability. In his book *Small is Beautiful: A Study of Economics as if People Mattered* (1973) he presented Buddhist economics rooted in long-term perspectives, equality, reduced consumption and increased quality of life. *The Times* has placed it among the 100 most influential books published after 1945. The Schumacher Society has been an important driving force in the effort to translate *Small is Beautiful* into practical action.

Buddhist inspiration

Schumacher refers to Gandhi when he argues that the goal is to describe a system so perfect that no one needs to be good. A peaceful society could not be built on prosperity in the modern sense, because it is attainable only by cultivating such drives in human nature as greed and envy, "which destroy intelligence, happiness, serenity, and thereby the peacefulness of man" (Schumacher 1993, p. 19).

Based on inspiration from Buddhism, Schumacher argues that we have to develop a peaceful society based on organic agriculture in harmony with the ecosystem, small-scale, non-violent technology and wisdom. We have to learn how to live peacefully in society and with nature, and, above all, "with those Higher Powers which have made nature and have made us" (Schumacher 1993, p. 9).

Buddhist economics

Having been an advisor to the governments of India and Burma in the 1950s, Schumacher developed a platform for a Buddhist economy based on the "middle way" between materialism and pure spirituality. Schumacher was particularly concerned by the growing conflict between economic growth and the ecosystem's natural limitations. He believed that science's almost one-sided emphasis on instrumental knowledge, which gives people power over nature, had resulted in great damage to many ecosystems caused by massive pressure on all kinds of natural resources. Combined with institutionalized individualism in the competitive market economy, neither buyer nor seller is responsible for anything but themselves. The idea of unlimited growth must be questioned on at least two grounds, according to Schumacher, "the availability of basic resources and alternatively or additionally, the capacity of the environment to cope with the degree of interference implied" (Schumacher 1993, p. 17).

Prioritization of cleverness over wisdom has led to a monster economy destroying the world. A new economic theory and practice must, according to Schumacher, be rooted in wisdom, that is, the objective and value-free economy must be filled with spirituality and values. The exclusion of wisdom from

---

Box 4.12 Indicators of happiness

- The degree of trust, social capital, cultural continuity and social solidarity.
- The general level of spiritual development and emotional intelligence.
- The degree to which basic needs are satisfied.
- Access to and the ability to benefit from health care and education.
- The level of environmental integrity, including species loss or gain, pollution and environmental degradation.

Box 4.13 Small-scale technology

- Cheap enough to be accessible to virtually everyone
- Suitable for small-scale application
- Compatible with man's need for creativity

---

economics, science and technology was something which we could perhaps get away with for a little while, as long as we were relatively unsuccessful, "but now that we have become very successful, the problem of spiritual and moral truth moves into the central position" (Schumacher 1993, p. 20).

Buddhist economics aims to create viable communities through small-scale production and customized technology. What we need today is methods and equipment which satisfy different needs (Box 4.13). Buddhist economics has an influence on economic development in many poor countries (micro-credit). In the shadows of the environmental and financial crisis, Schumacher's ideas become more relevant even in rich countries.

Minimize consumption

Right livelihood is one of the requirements of Buddhism. Buddhist economics sees the essence of civilization in the purification of human character, not in multiplication of wants. "But Buddhism is 'the middle way' and therefore in no way antagonistic to physical well-being" (Schumacher 1993, p. 41). The ideals of simplicity and non-violence have fundamental consequences for the economy. Instead of maximizing the use of natural resources, Schumacher argued that we should explore opportunities to minimize consumption while we pave the way for a society based on improved quality of life.

To reduce economic growth it is necessary to introduce a simpler lifestyle where material consumption needs are downplayed. Schumacher refers to Gandhi's famous statement "Earth provides enough to satisfy every man's need, but not for every man's greed." The aim is to obtain maximum well-being with minimum consumption.

In his book *A Guide for the Perplexed* (1978) Schumacher elaborates on the assertion that one consequence of the modern economy, based on a materialistic worldview, is that we have lost contact with basic human needs and values. The quest for profit and technological development has led to both environmental degradation and cultural dissolution.

Work

The Buddhist point of view has a particular focus on the function of work, which is of great importance in Schumacher's economic model. He argues, on the one hand, that firms often consider human labor as a cost-driving factor that they want to replace with more productive machines. On the other hand, the workers often experience work as a necessary evil in order to earn money to live.

In contrast to this negative attitude to work, Schumacher argued that work gives people opportunities to develop and make use of their abilities and skills. The progression from passivity to activity is closely connected to the progression from necessity to freedom. In addition, working together with others to help to develop social understanding reduces the selfish tendencies. The third positive feature of work is that the individual helps to produce goods and services that meet the community's needs for these.

According to Schumacher, all jobs should contribute to develop each individual's creativity and moral character. In line with this reasoning, he argued that boring, meaningless and hazardous workplaces are very much unwanted. Customized technology means that solutions must be rooted in an organic, decentralized, non-violent (to both humans and nature) and aesthetic basic attitude where human development is in focus. In this way we are compensated for potentially lower productivity through more meaningful jobs.

Local communities

An important point in Buddhist economics is that local and regional small-scale solutions are better than giant globalized businesses. The challenges consist in finding an appropriate size for communities and to develop a customized small-scale technology. According to Schumacher, we need both freedom and order. "We need freedom of lots and lots of small, autonomous units, and at the same time, the orderliness of large-scale, possibly global, unity and co-ordination" (Schumacher 1993, p. 48).

Local communities, in this context, could be small villages or neighborhoods in big cities. For the economy to function it should be organized through networks of smaller units. We must learn to think in terms of a network-based structure that can cope with the multiplicity of many interrelated small-scale units. Schumacher suggests some propositions to establish healthy economic activity (Box 4.14).

Schumacher's ideas on increased utilization of local resources through small-scale production are currently implemented in many poor countries

---

Box 4.14 Propositions for a healthy economy

- Workplaces have to be created in the areas where people are living.
- Workplaces must be cheap enough to be created in large numbers.
- Production methods must be relatively simple.
- Production should be mainly from local materials and mainly for local use.

through, for example, micro-credit. In recent years many countries in the rich parts of the world have started doing experiments based on Schumacher's thoughts and ideas.

In addition to environmental benefits caused by reduced need for transportation, the resurgence of local jobs has strengthened cultural vitality in many regions.

Concluding remarks

According to Sivaraska, "It took a British Catholic, E. F. Schumacher, to remind us that Buddhist economics could serve as an example for those who regard human beings more highly than money" (Sivaraska 2009, p. 30). The ideas that fill our mind represent the context of how we interpret the world. "At present, there can be little doubt that the whole of mankind is in mortal danger, not because we are short of scientific and technological know-how, but because we tend to use it destructively, without wisdom" (Schumacher 1993, p. 63). Schumacher criticizes the modern acceptance of "competition, natural selection, and the survival of the fittest" (Schumacher 1993, p. 69) as natural laws, and not as a set of observations among others. What we need is a society where people collaborate to find the best solutions for individuals, society and nature. Therefore it is of great importance to describe and discuss the view of nature and society that underlies present-day economic theory and practice. "There are no final solutions [...] there is only a living solution achieved day by day on a basis of a clear recognition" (Schumacher 1993, p. 218).

5   A transdisciplinary perspective

Nobody can be a great economist who is only an economist. I am tempted to add that a pure economist is a worry if not a real danger.

F. A. Hayek

Herman Daly (USA), Johan Galtung (Norway) and Peter Söderbaum (Sweden) are thought-provoking representatives of ecological economics anchored in interdisiplinarity, transdiciplinarity or multi-paradigmatic approaches.

All of them are influenced by the same experience as Boulding when he became aware that in his search for solutions in economics he always found himself led into other disciplines. As a consequence he claimed that economists must include knowledge from a variety of disciplines to discover and understand the dynamic interplay between economy, nature and society.

Today most contributors in ecological economics agree that economics must be linked to, or even stronger, interconnected to natural sciences, social sciences and humanistic science. Economics isolated from, for example, biology, ecology, sociology, psychology, history and philosophy is lifeless and mechanistic. A living economy is integrated in the web of life. For economics to become a force in the progressive movement toward social and environmental renewal, diversity in scientific perspectives (paradigms) is a necessary condition.

HERMAN DALY

Future progress simply must be made in terms of the things that really count rather than the things that are merely countable.

Herman Daly

Introduction

Herman Daly is an important contributor in establishing and developing ecological economics as an academic discipline. Daly has a special interest in the efficient use of resources, equitable distribution of goods and services and sustainable consumption of renewable and non-renewable natural resources.

Biography

Daly (b. 1938) wrote his doctoral thesis in economics at Vanderbilt University in 1967. There he met Georgescu-Roegen and became interested in the fundamental importance of thermodynamics in economic theory. Daly was hired by Louisiana State University in 1968. In 1973 he was appointed professor at the same university. From 1988 to 1994 he was Senior Advisor at the Environmental Department of the World Bank. Then he went back to teaching and research and became full professor at the University of Maryland, where he developed ecological economics into an academic discipline. Daly was one of the initiators of the International Society of Ecological Economics (ISEE) in 1988. He was also co-editor from its launch in 1989 of the scientific journal *Ecological Economics*. Daly has achieved international recognition for his pioneering work in ecological economics. He has received numerous awards, among others the Heineken Prize for Environmental Science (Royal Academy of Arts and Sciences, the Netherlands), Sophie Prize (Norway) and Leontief Prize. Herman Daly was elected Man of the Year in 2008 by *Adbusters* magazine.

Thermodynamics

Daly began his efforts to revise economic growth theory at the beginning of the 1970s. He was motivated by thermodynamics, which explicitly postulates that exponential growth in the exploitation and consumption of natural resources is physically impossible. According to Daly the first and second laws of thermodynamics should also be the first and second laws of economics. After some years, he admitted, however, that it was difficult to reach the goal of zero-growth economy within the established financial institutions based on the neo-classical economic paradigm. Therefore he engaged in establishing a new economic paradigm, "ecological economics."

In 1989 Daly, together with Cobb Jr., published the pioneering book *For the Common Good*. In this book Daly and Cobb Jr. pointed out a number of weaknesses with the mainstream economy. They argued that it is almost impossible to cope with problems related to overuse of natural resources and equitable sharing of benefits within the dominant economic paradigm. They also criticized the use of GDP as an instrument to measure economic success and pointed out the incorrectness of the economy's image of man, *homo economicus*. *Homo economicus* is more like a mechanism than a flourishing human being, they said.

Daly and Cobb Jr. also explained some basic principles for a new economic paradigm. To capture complex issues in a dynamic reality they claimed that ecological economics had to be a multidisciplinary project.

Organic thinking

On several occasions Daly and Cobb Jr. have mentioned that ecological economics is inspired by Whitehead's organic philosophy ("philosophy of organism"). Among other subjects, they refer to the fallacy of misplaced concreteness and state that this fallacy flourishes because of the disciplinary organization of knowledge, which requires a high level of abstraction. They maintained that the more successfully a discipline fulfills the criteria established for it, "the higher is the level of abstraction involved" (Daly and Cobb Jr. 1994, p. 25).

When these abstractions are applied to the real world without recognizing the level of abstraction involved, the negative (unintended) consequences could be serious. Understanding the economy as an integrated part of nature and society are lost and the outcomes for society and nature become invisible to economists. "The frequency of appeal to externalities is a good index of the overall problem of misplaced concreteness in economic theory" (Daly and Cobb Jr. 1994, p. 37). The fallacy of misplaced concreteness could be minimized by getting back to the concrete and by avoiding excessive specialization. Through specialization the whole is lost in focusing on the parts.

A significant feature of organic philosophy is that everything (including the market) is linked through dynamic relationships. Another characteristic is that reality is constantly changing. That is, relationships are more important than objects and becoming is more relevant than being. According to Whitehead, creativity is the driving force of all change processes. Daly and Cobb Jr. argued that the mechanical worldview is an ultimate precondition in mainstream economics and that it had to be replaced with an organic understanding of reality. This means that man-in-community takes over the idea of economic man. One consequence of this change is that network-based interaction is more important than competition between autonomous actors in the market. *For the Common Good* has a central position among Daly's extensive publications in ecological economics.

Beyond Growth (1996)

In his book *Beyond Growth* (1996), Daly focused on the objective of sustainable development. He discussed sustainable development in different contexts and perspectives. Among other topics he was concerned about the extensive use of GDP. If information about the negative (and positive) environmental and social consequences of economic activity was to be included in reports, he argued that criteria and principles must change. According to Daly, the current practice is characterized by defining many of the serious side-effects on nature and society as externalities which are thus excluded from the reports.

In addition, activities related to repair after accidents and environmental disasters have to be removed from the positive side of the accounts. The rule has been that all activities, both positive and negative, are evaluated positively in GDP. To handle environmental problems and to reduce the gap between rich and poor, Daly argued that the World Bank policy had to be changed in several significant respects. He was critical of solutions based on the idea that the global challenges with regard to poverty and the environment should be addressed through reinforced growth in the rich part of the world.

Daly also justified why it is necessary to revise the target of material growth toward more focus on quality of life. The aim was to change the economy in a direction where it was possible to create high quality of life without material growth. Daly often uses metaphors taken from ecology when he explains economic processes. Resource flows in the economy are, for example, compared with organic metabolism.

On the one hand this indicates that all kinds of economic activity require input of matter and energy and economic activity necessarily entails waste products on the output side. The consequence is that the solution to problems connected to increasing amounts of waste cannot be handled without changes on the input side of economic processes. It is important to notice that even if Daly points out that material growth must terminate, he is very positive that we have to intensify efforts to create qualitative development.

Ecological economics

In *Ecological Economics and Sustainable Development* (2007) Daly discussed several challenges, for example, economic growth, sustainable development, peak oil, globalization, that the existing economic paradigm is unable to handle properly. A prominent argument in several of the chapters in the book is that the global economy has become so large that it cannot grow more without causing dramatic ecological and social consequences.

Daly uses the term "full-world economics" to illustrate the need for fundamental changes in economic theory and practice if we are to avoid reduced welfare and ecological disaster in the future. As a suggestion to solve the problems, Daly defines ecological economics as an academic discipline focused on developing a theoretical framework that makes it possible to handle these issues and to stimulate further development of the subject.

Box 5.1 Three questions to be answered

- Allocation: determining efficient allocation of available resources in various product groups.
- Distribution: determining fair distribution of goods and services nationally and globally.
- Scale: determining sustainable total size of consumption of natural resources (source) and the amount of waste that is recycled ecosystems (sink).

Concluding remarks

To avoid the fallacy of misplaced concreteness Daly argues that it is necessary to extend the scientific perspectives of mainstream economics. Economics has to connect to the real world by integrating knowledge from natural, social and human sciences. Daly's interpretation of ecological economics is a fusion of significant ideas in thermodynamics (Georgescu-Roegen) and evolutionary theory (Boulding), respectively.

In addition to being one of the most influential contributors in ecological economics as an academic subject, Daly also defined some interdisciplinary research questions in ecological economics: allocation, distribution and scale.

JOHAN GALTUNG

> We have the economy and the economists we deserve given our social and global structures, our culture and our history.
>
> Johan Galtung

Introduction

Johan Galtung has provided significant scientific contributions within peace research. In addition, he has written influential articles and books in several other disciplines. According to Galtung, the development of a peace-making economy presupposes structural changes, and it is not sufficient to moderate the negative symptoms within the framework of the existing system.

Biography

Johan Galtung was born in Oslo in 1930. He studied mathematics and sociology at the University of Oslo. In 1959 he founded the Peace Research Institute Oslo (PRIO) and established the *Journal of Peace Research* (1964). In 1969 he was appointed the world's first full professor of peace studies. Galtung has received a number of awards for his scientific work, among others the Right Livelihood Award (1987). He was appointed Professor of Peace at the University of Hawaii in 1993. Until recently Galtung lived in Kuala Lumpur in Malaysia; today he lives in Spain. He is director of the international Transcend network for peace and development. He has published scientific articles and books within – and across – a variety of disciplines, including economics, history, anthropology and theology. In addition to being an active and respected scientist, he is a committed participant in public debate.

Peace economics

Galtung is known for his well-developed talent and capability to move between and across different disciplines. His contributions to peace economics demonstrate the necessity to transcend disciplinary boundaries. He is also well known for his many unconventional viewpoints and partly utopian proposals.

The preface to *Peace Economics: From a Killing to a Living Economy* begins with the following acknowledgment: "When a nature so generous as ours, and a humankind working so hard, share a world with so much environmental degradation, insults to human needs, inequity, inequality, and economic crises, simply something basic must be wrong" (Galtung 2012b, p. 7). Galtung emphasizes that it is not only economic practices that should be criticized; he tracks the causes to problems with basic theories and models in economics.

Seven trends

Galtung mentions seven trends that underlie the severe challenges the current economy and society are facing (Box 5.2). The increasing economization in modern society is rooted in a (tacit) acceptance of some key assumptions in the current market economy. First, market mechanisms (the market's invisible hand) ensure that egocentric advantage is transformed into common benefit. Second, there is no upper limit to economic growth.

When a resource is expended the market ensures that another takes over. Third, it is possible to calculate, with mathematical accuracy, what kind of action provides the best solutions. The conclusion is therefore simple: we live in the best possible world, if we let market forces rule the economy.

It turns out, however, that the introduction of (abstract) economic concepts, theories and models in new areas (health, education, culture) leads to increasing alienation.

The result of this alienation is that the economy is left in a state of conflict with both society and environment.

Three structural changes

Galtung laid the foundation for a peace-promoting economy through structural changes. He mentions that the requirement for growth must be removed,

---

Box 5.2 Seven trends in modern society

- Economism (all values are converted to cash)
- Globalization (loss of overview)
- Mass production (local small producers are being replaced by centralized mass producers)
- Privatization (holistic common solutions crumble)
- Shareholders (profits trickle upwards to the owners)
- Productivity (increased productivity reduces the number of jobs)

Box 5.3 Consequences of economization

- Nature is atomized and reduced to an economic resource.
- Humans are reduced to producers and consumers.
- The community is reduced to a market for the sale of commodities.
- The world is reduced to a global market.
- The time horizon is reduced both backward and forward.
- Culture is reduced to marketable products.

---

and in its place we have to introduce principles of fair trade and a balance must be created between financial and real economy.

First, the objective of exponential economic growth is the cause of both ecological and social crises. Overuse of resources combined with increasing waste volumes has resulted in disturbance in many ecosystems, leading to vulnerability and risk of severe problems. Unilateral focus on economic growth has led to a situation where luxury needs in the rich part of the world are prioritized above basic needs of the poor majority. Economic growth must therefore be replaced by an economy that prioritizes human development and quality of life. Specifically, this means that we have to abandon the objective of growth in GDP and instead focus on measures that register the development of HDI (Human Development Index). Our predominant goal must be to satisfy the needs for water, food, clothing, housing and other necessary goods for all humans.

Second, the growing gap between rich and poor (global and national) leads to serious conflicts of interest. To deal with the difficulties it is necessary to make profound structural changes that ensure equitable conditions for the exchange of goods. As it is now, there are some who get too much and even more who get too little. Market forces reinforce the distance between rich and poor for the reason that profit maximization is given priority over the satisfaction of basic needs of people who lack purchasing power.

Third, the consequences of a financial economy living its own life, regardless of the real economic conditions, is that economics has lost touch with physical and social reality. Today's globalized financial economy represents a form of "casino capitalism" which, according to Galtung, is much worse than what happens in a regular casino because the gamblers are staking other people's money. They put rewards in their own pockets, while losses are transferred to others.

Characteristics of peace economy

Galtung uses the term "living economy" as a concept for a peace-making economy. A vibrant economy is characterized by structures that promote local self-sufficiency through local production and local consumption. Much of what is produced goes to local consumption and what is consumed is produced locally. As an example he mentions that food should be prepared from

---

Box 5.4 Principles for a vibrant economy

- Production for need, not for greed (quality of life)
- Circular value chains (eco-cycles)
- Production will replace what is consumed (steady-state economy)
- Encourage the development of local markets (slow food)
- No companies/organizations must be too large (human scale)

---

scratch, based on local ingredients. As a means for promoting increased production and consumption of local goods and services Galtung calls for local currencies and exchange of time coupons. The vibrant economy is based on five basic principles (Box 5.4).

We can thus say that a peace-making economy is rooted in partnership with nature. Economic objectives and instruments must be coordinated with environmental conditions and social and cultural goals and values. Altruistic values are more important than egocentric utility maximization. Cooperating networks connecting actors in the market help to find common solutions to the benefit of all involved. The economy is decentralized so that local communities become the center of planning. To counteract economism, spiritual needs must acquire a more prominent position in society.

Concluding remarks

The main premise for a peace economy is fair distribution of resources, securing the basic needs for all human beings. Substantial parts of the economy are decentralized so that local communities, regions and nations, as far as possible, are self-sufficient in food. Proximity between production and consumption increases accountability among manufacturers and the willingness of customers. When the connection between economy and environmental and social consequences becomes accepted among economists, mutual responsibility will increase. To reach this goal interdisciplinary cooperation is an unquestionable precondition.

PETER SÖDERBAUM

It is more important to protect the environment than to protect the neoclassical paradigm.

Peter Söderbaum

Introduction

Involvement in environmental issues contributed to the Swedish economist Söderbaum's critical approach to neo-classical economic theory. He introduced new perspectives on economics in his teaching in business schools and universities. He argued that even if neo-classical economics was usable for some purposes, it was insufficient to meet the demands for sustainable development.

Biography

Peter Söderbaum (b. 1937) wrote his doctorate in business administration at Uppsala University in 1973. After that he started his career as teacher and researcher in environmental and resource economics. Söderbaum got a position as full professor in ecological economics at Mälardalen University in Västerås, where in 1995 he developed a comprehensive program of study in ecological economics. Söderbaum has written numerous books and articles in which he elaborates the need to break the dominance of neo-classical economics. Today Söderbaum is professor emeritus at Mälardalen University and is still active as researcher, writer and lecturer.

Problem understanding

According to Söderbaum it is difficult to understand the conflict between traditional economics and ecological economics without examining the paradigmatic assumptions. Questions related to paradigms and worldviews are therefore central to his research. Söderbaum is critical of the almost dominant position neo-classical economic theory has in higher education. He also questions the increasing specialization of science, because it leads to a situation where we no longer experience how things hang together in larger wholes.

In several books and articles, including *Ekologisk ekonomi* (1993), he argues that multidimensional and irreversible environmental problems can, to a limited extent, be solved within the framework of modified neo-classical environmental economics. In *Ecological Economics* (2000) he formulated a dynamic definition of "a problem" that is highly relevant when it comes to the handling of environmental challenges within economy. According to Söderbaum problems arise when development is off-track concerning the values we want to prioritize. When we choose the most profitable alternatives for action the (unintended) consequence could be that fundamental values like justice and environmental responsibility are set aside.

Paradigmatic pluralism

Instead of arguing that the established economic paradigm has to be replaced by a new paradigm that is fundamentally different, Söderbaum is an advocate of paradigmatic pluralism. A variety of economic models may be reasonable depending on the challenges we face. In other words, he believes that the modern world is totally dominated by neo-classical economics. He insists that the situation would not be better under an authoritarian economic paradigm. Söderbaum argues that democratic values will suffer if one single economic system displaces all the other options. In addition, he maintains, along with Whitehead, that diversity contributes to creativity. Interdisciplinary cooperation and dialogue between science and practice contribute not only to the finding of new solutions, but also to asking new and exciting ground-breaking questions.

The political economic person

The neo-classical description of "economic man" as an autonomous rational being who is only concerned with maximizing his or her own utility is not suitable for understanding economic practices nor for dealing with the current environmental and social challenges. Söderbaum proposes that "economic man" is replaced by "the political economic person (PEP)." From this perspective, the economic actor is a socially integrated, reflective human being. Identity, lifestyle, worldview and ideological orientation are thus essential characteristics of economic actors. According to this approach everyone has the opportunity to influence economic and social developments and at the same time everyone becomes co-responsible for economic action.

Well-being

With his richer and broader definition of man, Söderbaum states that it is no longer relevant to equate increase in well-being in a country with growth in GDP (the total production of goods and services in one country expressed in money). In a holistic perspective, well-being includes more than production and consumption. Qualitative values such as public health, cultural situation and access to nutritious and environmentally responsible food are important elements in a country's welfare. A major consequence is that critical questions must be raised about expressing the total welfare of a country in terms of one single number.

Actor-network model

Söderbaum launched the idea that all economic actors are embedded in a network of mutual dependence. All are affected by others, while the individual actors influence the development throughout networks. Social and emotional aspects of network relationships are important when it comes to relations between actors in the market. Relations in social reality can be characterized by both trust and distrust. It is therefore necessary to use ethical values and ideological assessments to orient ourselves toward practical reality. Söderbaum points out that the financial networks must be seen in an extended socio-cultural context in which laws and regulations are essential ingredients. Characteristics of ecosystems also constitute an important part of the economic context.

Need for innovation

Neo-classical economics developed during the eighteenth century and today it represents the dominant paradigm in most universities, not only in the Western world. Neo-classical economists were inspired by the success of Descartes' analytical method, Newtonian mechanics and the language of physics and mathematics. Transferred to economics, the result was an abstract theory, detached from reality. The market was reduced to a game controlled by (market) forces and (price) mechanisms, where human relationships, values and attitudes were swept away.

According to Söderbaum, a profound change is needed within economics and business administration, especially when these fields of social science have such a central position in current societies. Most business students enroll in institutions that create the illusion that there is no alternative to neo-classical economic theory. It is therefore, without any doubt, essential to find ways to break this monopoly and find new paradigms.

Institutional economics

Söderbaum launched an institutional interpretation of ecological economics as an alternative to neo-classical theory. Instead of referring to physics and mechanics as ideal sciences, institutional economics is influenced by biological evolution theory. He argues that positivism's "objective and value-neutral" scientific ideals should be supplemented with increased emphasis on subjectivity and commitment.

The rationale is that environmental problems must be understood from an ideological grounding, and it is therefore of vital importance to understand the context of interpretation by different actors before it is possible to come up with solutions for the common good.

As a supplement to the neo-classical paradigm, Söderbaum offers some requirements for ecological economics that require policy changes at community level. First, questions concerning environment and survival are focused on very closely. If long-term sustainability is to be the overarching goal, it is not enough to make marginal changes or merely to reduce the negative effects of economic activity. This indicates that it is not sufficient to reduce the negative symptoms; instead, fundamental changes are required to deal with challenges such as reduced biodiversity and climate change. Second, we need scientific pluralism, which offers openness to different paradigms in

---

Box 5.5 Changes at community level

- Long-term sustainability
- Scientific pluralism
- Ethical pluralism
- Multi paradigmatic approach

economics combined with multidisciplinary perspectives. To understand and manage complex problems a pluralistic scientific approach is required. Third, openness concerning values that allow various ethical and ideological perspectives is required. Economic science must take into account, and accept, that environmental challenges are understood differently depending on the ideological frame of reference. Fourth, we must get away from the idea that positivism is the only scientific ideal in economics. Researchers in ecological economics should be encouraged to make value-based commitments.

Concluding remarks

Söderbaum argues that diversity and integration are important in all walks of scientific life. He introduces a multi-paradigmatic approach to ecological economics and he sets it in terms of the political economic person (PEP) and the extended definition of well-being as representing something much more life-enhancing than mere quantitative consumption levels.

To reach the goals of sustainable development, fundamental changes are required on several levels; instead of describing the market as an atomized, competitive arena populated with utility maximizing actors, Söderbaum argues that the solutions to the problems we are facing today depend on our willingness and ability to discover the market as a living system of interconnected political economic persons. Companies are integrated in networks, characterized by cooperation and shared responsibility. Söderbaum mentions the fair-trade movement as an example of how change toward fair pricing of goods and services could be arranged in practice. Instead of prioritizing profit maximization, the actors are more concerned about increasing social benefits and sustainability.

6 Economics as a moral science

In this chapter we focus on questions concerning ontology and ethics. The authors considered here discuss how values inherent in society and the economy have an influence on decision making, and how ethical considerations influence the interplay between the actors in the market.

Amitai Etzioni (Germany/Israel), Amartya Sen (India) and Laszlo Zsolnai (Hungary) argue that economics is a moral science. These three contributors share the communitarian approach which accepts the interrelatedness between all actors. Even if their main focus is on ethical questions concerning fairness and trust they also discuss ethics in relation to nature and ecology.

They argue that neo-classical economics' definition of the economic man as rational represents a serious problem. They would instead argue that the economic actor is a moral man and not a selfish, utility maximizing robot.

The consequence of this line of argument is to accept the necessity of a fundamental change in economic theory and practice away from one-dimensional egocentrism to mutual responsibility within cooperative networks.

AMITAI ETZIONI

> Changing the normative culture would shift public perceptions to view these changes as an opportunity to abandon consumerism.
>
> Amitai Etzioni

Introduction

Etzioni has a central position in the development of socio-economics. Socio-economics differs from neo-classical economics in several ways, including a stronger emphasis on the importance of culture as a factor in explaining and increased attention to ethical principles and multidisciplinary perspectives. Etzioni is well known for his efforts to develop socio-economics based on a communitarian social understanding. Etzioni authored the communitarian manifesto.

Biography

Amitai Etzioni was born in Germany in 1929 and grew up in Athens and Palestine. In 1951 he started his studies at the Hebrew University in Jerusalem, where he focused on music and sociology. Afterwards he went to the USA, where in 1958 he wrote a doctorate in sociology at the University of California, Berkeley. He was professor of sociology at Columbia University for more than twenty years. In 1980 he was appointed professor at George Washington University, where today he is director of the Institute for Political Studies. He was visiting professor at Harvard Business School from 1987 to 1990.

Lack of belonging

The social context is an integral part of the individual's existence: "We are members of one another." The individual and society create one another and presuppose each other at the same time. The economy is a sub-system of the social system. In line with this reasoning Etzioni argues that changes in the market can be understood as a reaction to more fundamental changes in culture. Western society has long moved in the direction of increasing instrumentalism and selfishness at the expense of fundamental values such as trust and belonging. These phenomena are not captured and recognized by neo-classical economic theory. To the extent that such phenomena are even mentioned, they are reduced to a subset of rational market behavior.

When neo-classical economists argue that market competition serves individual preferences, they ignore the fact that preferences are largely socially shaped and reflect society's values, culture and power structures.

Etzioni criticizes neo-classical economic theory for vastly overestimating the benefits of competition and neglecting more or less entirely the value of cooperation. He emphasizes that cooperation between enterprises is necessary to find solutions to many of the serious challenges related to both environmental and social responsibility.

According to Etzioni it is not sufficient to appeal to individual responsibility as it is also necessary to consider the societal element. The development of socio-economics is an important contribution leading to a communitarian economy. In line with communitarianism, far more than a mere change in human "hearts and minds" is required; changes in economic, social and political structures are also necessary if we are to understand and handle the serious challenges we face in today's society.

Given this communitarian social understanding Etzioni criticized neo-classical economic theory for its assumption that economic actors are solely focused on maximizing their own benefit and that they rationally choose the instruments that serve these egocentric objectives.

Box 6.1   Fundamental paradigmatic changes

- From individuals to social and cultural structures
- From instrumentality to ethical principles
- From specialization to multidisciplinarity

Proposed changes

In *The Moral Dimension: Toward a New Economy* (1988) Etzioni argues that the neo-classical paradigm is too limited, fails to capture essential aspects of reality and to understand the complexity of economic issues. In his article "Towards a New Socio-Economic Paradigm" (2002) he justifies the necessity of a paradigm shift in economics to give us a radical and basic change in perspective and proposes three fundamental changes. First, a transition from a focus on the individual to greater emphasis on social and cultural structures (from individualism to communitarianism). This means that economic actions are affected by phenomena at community level and the consequence of this change of perspective is that the rise in individual consumption is explained by looking at the changing values and structures of today's society.

Second, decision models based on instrumental rationality should be replaced with models that clearly indicate that decisions are affected by ethical principles as well. This means that an economic actor, in addition to assessing the utility of various alternatives of action, also emphasizes (internalized) culturally determined norms and values. The result is that ethical dilemmas often occur in situations where the actor has to choose between the desire to increase his or her utility (happiness, pleasure or consumption) and ethical obligations toward other people (justice, trust and austerity). In other words a conflict arises between what we want to do (weak evaluations) and what we should do (strong evaluations). Third, socio-economics is described as a many-faceted field that builds bridges between different scientific disciplines. The need for a multidisciplinary approach is justified by the fact that decisions and actions within economics will always be influenced by non-economic factors related to the social and cultural context.

Economy as a societal subcategory

Socio-economics argues that the economy is a subcategory of overriding social or societal systems. Socio-economics argues that all economic activity takes place within a social context that cannot be reduced to the sum of individual actions. Humans have not established communities to reach certain goals – they have always existed.

Box 6.2 A communitarian approach

- Society is built on a set of common values that everyone recognizes.
- Actions in the world community come from below (bottom-up) – not from the state (top-down).
- Values in the community are based upon history and tradition.

Etzioni is more concerned with the norms and values that govern the behavior of participants in the market than the economy's impact on nature and ecosystems. In the article "A Crisis of Consumerism" (2009) Etzioni questions the fundamental values held dear in our consumer society. He refers to Maslow's humanistic psychology, where human needs are categorized on various levels, from the most basic physical needs to the highest – the need for self-actualization. Etzioni is critical of the existence of any positive connection between increased consumption and development of self-esteem and self-actualization. He argues that the good life cannot be seen in isolation from the development of the good society.

To describe the interaction between individual and society Etzioni used the concept of the "I & We" paradigm. The individual is made responsible by engaging in social networks. The culture is deeply rooted in human relationships. In recent years common values have been reduced in favor of egocentrism and self-centered pragmatism. The explanation behind this change is, according to Etzioni, that internalized values and external authority have had reduced influence on human behavior. Although Etzioni accepts that more detailed regulations, more inspectors and increased security may be required to mitigate negative symptoms, he argues that they do not guarantee that financial transactions comply with laws and regulations. To develop self-regulating socio-economic practices changes are required on a cultural level. Etzioni notes that such changes are always a result of bottom-up initiatives rooted in social movements and NGOs.

Concluding remarks

Etzioni points out two of the most essential elements in ecological economics: the importance of structure and multi-disciplinarity. Etzioni argues that a change toward an "I & We" economy depends on changes at a structural level and individual changes in consciousness are not enough. In addition, economic science has to bridge the gap between different sciences to relate adequately to the cultural context. The good life cannot be separated from the good society. The communitarian manifesto is an important characteristic of socio-economics, dividing it from neo-classical economics based on libertarian ideology.

AMARTYA SEN

> It would definitely be strange if we were deeply concerned about how it would go with future, still unborn generations, while ignoring the situation of the poor today.
>
> Amartya Sen

Introduction

Amartya Sen attended an elementary school where the teachers put more emphasis on developing the pupils' hunger for knowledge than on achieving good grades. These ideals characterized his attitude to knowledge and research all through his life. Today Sen is well known for important contributions concerning questions of poverty, development theory, welfare economics and political liberalism.

Sen conceptualizes development as freedom both as the primary end and as the principal means. He defines the goal as wider than a calculated measure of GNP. It is worth noting that Sen was the first graduate from Asia who became Master of a Cambridge college.

Biography

Amartya Sen was born in 1933 in Santiniketan, British India. Sen studied at Presidency College, Calcutta before going to the UK to continue his economics studies at Trinity College, Cambridge, where he wrote his doctoral degree in 1959.

In the following years Sen taught economics at a number of universities in India, the UK and the USA, among others the University of Calcutta, Jadavpur University, Delhi, Oxford University, the London School of Economics and Harvard University. In 1998, he was awarded the Bank of Sweden Prize in Economics in Memory of Alfred Nobel for his scientific contribution within "social choice" theory.

Contributions

Sen argues that an economy must be anchored in responsible actors, social norms and cooperation and questions whether it is possible to solve the global poverty and environmental crises without making profound changes in the economic system. More focus must be directed to justice, quality of life and sustainable development than competition and economic growth.

Although Sen has made important contributions in the development of environmentally and socially responsible economics, he was criticized for being a "middle of the road" economist. Sen answered his critics by accepting that it might well be where he is located, but he was moving along a far different road than the traditional market economists.

Economics as moral science

Sen points out that economics, from Aristotle to Adam Smith, was an integral part of practical philosophy, where ethical issues relating to "the good" and "the right" were central. Later Smith's ethical considerations were displaced in favor of more abstract theories and models. One consequence of disposing of ethics as a cornerstone in economics was that the gap between economics and practical realities increased dramatically. The one-dimensional image of the economic man is an illuminating example of abstraction. Even if Sen agreed with Adam Smith that self-interest is an important motivating factor in the economy, he argued that ethical values and moral behavior are necessary to understand and explain economic decisions and actions.

He is critical of the precondition that economic rationality is juxtaposed with maximization of self-interest. In opposition to that, Sen said that economic actors are influenced by social values and norms. According to him, selfless acts represent an important factor behind the economic progress of Asia. He cites the Japanese ethos, Confucian ethics and Samurai codes of honor as examples of cultural values that have a decisive influence on economic activities. In addition, he notes that in Western culture selfless behavior plays an important role in democratic access to public goods (e.g. healthcare) and in communities' management of negative side-effects of economic activity (e.g. pollution). To carry out such social tasks cultural values and norms must be strong enough to hold selfishness in check. Sen finds support for these ideas in Adam Smith's pointing out that "Man ought to regard himself, not as something separated and detached, but as a citizen of the world, a member of the commonwealth of nature, and to the interest of this great community, he ought at all times to be willing that his own little interest should be sacrificed" (Sen 1987).

Poverty

Within neo-classical economics resource allocation is Pareto optimal if it is impossible to improve the condition of any single individual without harming the condition of another individual. A Pareto improvement has taken place if a change in the distribution of goods or resources results in at least one individual being better off than before and the change has not made any other individual worse off. Consequently it follows that we cannot transfer resources from rich to poor because it will reduce the wealth of the rich. Our sole opportunity to improve the conditions for the poorest is to ensure overall growth through efficiency and rationalization. So we can see that the distribution principles at work in mainstream economies are, in other words, no more than a pure efficiency measure with little if any regard for fairness or other ethical values. In accordance with this principle, it is not a surprise that politicians have trouble implementing measures involving higher taxes for the wealthiest and that they see growth in the rich part of the world as a necessary

precondition for solving the global problem of poverty. Sen is unhappy about
the use of Pareto optimality and argues that justice must come to be valued
far more highly than efficiency as a fundamental principle in the economy.

Welfare

Sen criticizes dominant economic thinking for focusing solely on measuring
individual welfare, where society's welfare is the aggregate of individual welfare. Instead, he argues that individual welfare is not independent of how
relationships between people in the society are organized. Sen is concerned
about freedom and democracy and he believes that freedom in the sense of
positive freedom to express values, attitudes and political opinions represents
a fundamental prerequisite for welfare in a society. According to Sen, freedom cannot be reduced to "the ability to meet crucially important economic
needs," and in addition freedom must include the possibility of "expanding
political participation and broadening social opportunities."

Sustainable development

Sen argues that the objective of sustainable development requires a clarifica-
tion of what is to be preserved. One of the strongest arguments for protecting
the environment is our ethical responsibility to ensure future generations the
same opportunities for self-expression that our generation enjoys. But there is
something fundamentally wrong if the responsibility for sustainable development means that we forget our responsibility to improve the living conditions
of the poorest people who live today.

Sustainable development, in time and space, presupposes, in other words,
that the economy's image of man as a consumer (consumerist patients) is
replaced by an image of an ecological man, characterized by holistic understanding and social responsibility. In the article "Why We Should Preserve the
Spotted Owl" Sen argues that we are not only accountable to other people, we
also have a responsibility to safeguard biodiversity in nature, not because it is
important for human welfare, but because all life forms have intrinsic value.

Sen points out that global cooperation is an essential prerequisite if we
are to achieve the goal of equitable distribution of resources and sustainable
development. A necessary condition to establish a binding global cooperation
is that people are given the freedom to think, evaluate and act as responsible
actors. In short, the relevance of citizenship and of social participation is not
just instrumental. They are integral parts of what we have reason to preserve.

Concluding remarks

Sen reasons along the same line as Etzioni, but he extends the ethical position
toward an eco-centric position. According to Sen, freedom and democracy
are of great importance in the new economy. We are responsible for the whole
ecosystem, not only because we as humans depend on sustainable nature,

but primarily because all forms of life have intrinsic value. In harmony with Whitehead's philosophy of organism, Sen points out the necessity of focusing on relations more than objects. Ethics is concerned with relations, including our relations to animals and plants. Buddhist philosophy is embedded in Sen's ethical reflections.

LASZLO ZSOLNAI

> My strategy is to help business students and practitioners to work with alternatives. Not to cooperate with mainstream guys who are the problem, but to develop an alternative business sector.
>
> Laszlo Zsolnai

Introduction

Laszlo Zsolnai has made substantial contributions in business ethics and Buddhist economics. Inspired by Buddhism, Western science and philosophy, Zsolnai maintains that responsible management is required in today's business culture. Mainstream management practices are self-centered, both in an individual and collective sense.

Serious negative consequences arise for nature, future generations and society from the dominant business model. According to Zsolnai, social and environmental responsibility requires leaders to consider all the relevant value dimensions of the choice situation, and evaluate the alternatives and block compromises among non-substitutable values.

Biography

Laszlo Zsolnai was born on May 5, 1958, in Hungary. He holds a major in economics and finance and a minor in sociology from Budapest University of Economic Sciences. In 1994 he submitted his PhD dissertation, "The Challenge of Alternative Economics," to the Hungarian Academy of Sciences. In 1993 Zsolnai established the Business Ethics Center at the Corvinus University of Budapest together with Professor Jozsef Kindler.

Today Laszlo Zsolnai is a professor at Corvinus University, Budapest. He is chairman of the Business Ethics Faculty Group of the CEMS, and he is president at the SPES Forum in Leuven, Belgium. Zsolnai has written and edited a great number of articles and books. Zsolnai serves as editor of the book series "Frontiers of Business Ethics" (Peter Lang).

Ethics in the economy

Capitalism's moral foundation has to be re-examined. Modern capitalism has become disembedded from the social and cultural norms of society and creates a deep financial, ecological and social crisis. Competition is the dominant ideology of today's business and economic policy. Companies, regions and national economies seek to improve their productivity and gain competitive advantage. But these efforts often produce negative effects on various stakeholders nationally and globally. Competition involves focus on self-interest and materialism.

Zsolnai presents a non-instrumental approach to business ethics, and he argues that genuine eco-centric ethical motivation is necessary to improve the overall quality of economic activities. Ecology and ethics provide limits for business. Deep ecology and Buddhist philosophy point out that highlighting individuality and promoting the greatest fulfillment of the desires of the individual together and separately lead to destruction. We need to find new ways of doing business which respect the ecological and ethical limits of business activities.

By transgressing ecological and ethical limits business activities become both destructive and self-defeating. The dominating business model is based on and cultivates narrow self-centeredness. Buddhist philosophy and deep ecology imply simplicity and non-violence both in lifestyle and production.

Moral economic man

Zsolnai argues that economic behavior is multidimensional and context-dependent. In mainstream economics the economic man is described as an agent who is perfectly rational and a self-interest-maximizing individual. To understand economic behavior a more complex and dynamic framework is needed. Zsolnai refers to Etzioni's "I & We" paradigm to underline his claim that the economic actor is a socially integrated person and not an isolated or autonomous person.

Economic behavior is co-determined by utility calculations and moral considerations. Two major factors can explain the ethicality of economic behavior and they are the moral character of the agents and the relative cost of ethical behavior. This means that in situations where large amounts of money are involved it is hard to behave ethically. Economic agents are moral beings but the ethical fabric of the economy determines which face of the Moral Economic Man predominates in the struggle.

Spirituality in management

"Spiritual" refers to a search for meaning that transcends material well-being. It is a focus on basic and deep-rooted human values and on a relationship with a universal source, power or divinity. In Zsolnai's view management has an undeniable existential-spiritual dimension. "Metaphysics of management" is

$$\frac{\text{Moral character}}{\text{Relative cost of ethical behavior}} \implies \text{Ethical Behavior}$$

Figure 6.1 Ethical decision model

a crucial term in leadership and refers to existential concerns, spirituality and recovery. Spirituality in organizational perspective extends traditional reflections on corporate purpose and focuses on a self-referential organizational-existential search for meaning, identity and success.

SPES

SPES (Spirituality in Economic and Social Life) defines spirituality in broad and pluralistic terms so that the forum attracts people from different spiritual backgrounds and traditions whether they be Christians, Buddhists, Jews, Muslims or others. Spirituality represents a multiform search for a transcendent or deep meaning of life that connects people to each other and brings them in touch with the "Ultimate Reality."

As president of the European SPES Forum Zsolnai has made a significant contribution to the development of an alternative to scientific, political and religious fundamentalism, which is spiritual humanism. By focusing on experience-based spirituality he makes a connection between day-to-day activities and the inner and pluriform quest for meaning.

Frugality

Frugality as a conception of the good life has deep philosophical and religious roots both in the East and the West. Monks and religious people all over the world practice it in different forms of asceticism, self-restriction or voluntary simplicity. Frugality is emphasized by philosophers in the tradition of Epicureanism or Stoicism, which emphasize that simplicity and lasting enjoyment of life go hand in hand. In religious ethics frugality is a spiritual virtue, while in profane ethics it is a rational virtue for enhancing happiness.

Frugality has been honored by Adam Smith and supported by Max Weber as the Protestant driver of early capitalism. In an instrumental interpretation frugality represents a way to increase material welfare, related to savings and to investments to enhance future welfare. Zsolnai points out that this interpretation of frugality leads to an erosion of the intrinsic and spiritual meaning of frugality. Paradoxically it ends in consumerism and material greed, which is the precise opposite of frugality.

Business ethics based on frugality, deep ecology, trust, reciprocity, responsibility for future generation, and authenticity make it necessary to find fundamental changes in thinking to dismiss economics profits and growth as no longer the ultimate aims but components of a broader set of values. Similarly, cost–benefit calculations are no longer the essence of the practice of management but reduced to a way to reach more fundamental ends.

Practical consequences

Frugality as an end in itself involves practical consequences, and the first is to make drastic changes to mankind's present unsustainable lifestyle.

A Western-style competitive market economy has resulted in global climate change, dramatic ecosystem degradation and huge biodiversity loss. It has also caused massive unhappiness and emptiness in rich countries and social disintegration worldwide. Second, the interests of nature, society and future generations demand a considerable reduction of material throughput of the economy and a reorientation of our economic activities. This could become possible by employing a more spiritual approach to life and the economy. Third, by rational choice we can develop a more frugal and yet sufficient way of life.

Material temptations can always overwrite our ecological, social and ethical considerations, but the spiritual case for frugality is strong enough to counteract this tendency. Spiritually based frugal practices may lead to rational outcomes such as reducing ecological destruction and social disintegration as well as the exploitation of future generations.

No-self

Zsolnai points out that the most fascinating thing in Buddhism is the concept of no-self (*anatta*). It is difficult to imagine a bigger challenge for the Western mind-set. *Anatta* specifies the absence of a supposedly permanent and unchanging self of any empirical existence. According to Buddhism, what is normally thought of as the "self" is an accumulation of constantly changing physical and mental constituents.

Anatta as a doctrine encourages us to detach ourselves from clinging to what is mistakenly regarded as self, and from such detachment, aided by moral living and meditation, the way to liberation or nirvana can be successfully found. According to Zsolnai, modern neuroscience supports the Buddhist view of the self. Neuroscientists have discovered that the selfless self, a coherent global pattern, is essential as a context of interaction.

Concluding remarks

Buddhism's basic tenets are happiness, peace and permanence. It is not material wealth but the quality of social relationships that determines happiness. People make people happy, not "things" or money. Peace can be achieved in non-violent ways. Wanting less can substantially contribute to this endeavor. A change such as this represents a positive opportunity for humanity to reduce suffering. Zsolnai refers to Buddhism's claim that emphasis on individuality and promotion of the greatest fulfillment of the materialistic desires of the individual lead to destruction. Permanence, or ecological sustainability, requires that the present level of global consumption and production be decreased and this should not be seen as an inconvenient exercise in self-sacrifice.

7   Eastern perspective

The Eastern perspective is strongly influenced by Buddhist philosophy and Gandhian peace economics. The following thinkers are presented in this section: P. A. Payutto (Thailand), Vandana Shiva (India) and Peter Pruzan (Denmark).

They all argue that the economy is a means to reach other more fundamental and deeper ends. Among other things this means that work has inherent value. Work should contribute to personal development through mutually binding collaboration with others. They also express the idea that to focus closely on materialistic consumption reduces the possibility of creating real values like quality of life and well-being.

On an ontological level they share the Buddhist insight that everything in nature and society is interconnected, everything is in an endless process of transformation and moderation is the prerequisite for happiness. Spirituality and mindfulness are not instruments for increased profits and growth.

P. A. PAYUTTO

> The forces of greed, exploitation and overconsumption seem to have overwhelmed our economies in recent time.
>
> P. A. Payutto

Introduction

Payutto is one of the most famous and influential representatives of Buddhist economics. In his book *Buddhist Economics: A Middle Way for the Market Place* Payutto argues that, if we are to deal with the challenges of our time, a mentality change within the economy is necessary. Payutto criticizes the Western economy's one-sided focus on material consumption and pleasure. He proposes an alternative where economy is a means to promote individual and collective well-being. Well-being is based on moderation in consumption of material goods and increased focus on the development of co-responsibility for all life.

Biography

P. A. Payutto was born in 1939 in Suphanburi province in Thailand. After many years of teaching Buddhism, he was ordained as a Thai Buddhist monk in 1961. He continued his studies at various universities in Thailand and received university degrees in Buddhism (1962) and a higher certificate in education (1963). After that he went to the United States and taught at several universities, including the University of Pennsylvania and Harvard. Payutto has written numerous books and articles in different areas based on Buddhist philosophy. In 1994 he received the UNESCO prize for peace-promoting teaching. In *Buddhist Economics* he explains some of the basic characteristics of Buddhist economics.

Criticism

First, Payutto argues that the Western economy lacks an ethical foundation and is therefore unsuitable to handle the problems which confront the world today. Greed, overconsumption of natural resources connected to escalating production and consumption of goods and services bring about negative effects on nature, individuals and society. These problems cannot be tackled without an increased emphasis on ethical values. Second, Payutto wants the boundaries of economics to be expanded so that social and environmental issues actively are drawn into both theory and practice. Third, it is necessary to balance the economy's impact on society against other disciplines that help to promote individual, social and ecological well-being. Today economics has a dominating position in practical politics.

Mentality change

Unlike Western economics Buddhist economics is not focused on developing new models and theories, but more on, as Payutto requires, changes in individual mentality. According to Payutto, ethics constitutes the connection between inner and outer reality. He highlights wisdom, empathy and moderation as important characteristics of an economy that promotes individual and social development within the framework of sustainable nature. Payutto explains Buddhist economics based on the concepts of tanhã and chanda. Tanhã indicates a selfish lifestyle searching for ever-increasing satisfaction and materialistic enjoyment. As the needs are endless, they often lead to greed, hatred and selfishness. Chanda represents wisdom and ethical values that are central to the quest for true happiness and quality of life. The road to chanda goes through reflection on life experiences. According to Payutto we will eventually discover that mental state, moral conduct and economy are linked through a stream of actions. The aim is to develop a holistic understanding that changes conflicts of interest into an experience of common interest between individuals, society and nature.

Box 7.1 Tanhã and chanda

Tanhã	Chanda
knowledge	wisdom
selfish lifestyle	reflection on life experiences
artificial value	true value
dependent happiness	independent happiness
extreme materialism	apathy toward reality

True and artificial values

Based on the distinction between tanhã and chanda, Payutto discusses concepts such as value, consumption, employment, production, competition and happiness. In connection to economic value he distinguishes between true value (chanda) leading to well-being and artificial value (tanhã), which leads only to satisfaction of superficial consumption needs. On the one hand, he believes that moderation is a prerequisite for the development of well-being. Since overuse of goods and services may have a negative effect on the individual, Payutto claims that non-consumption in many cases may be the best solution to achieve true happiness and quality of life. On the other hand, he warns against excessive emphasis on chanda, quality of life and well-being, because it can lead to complacency and apathy toward physical reality. Consumption and non-consumption are both means to achieve the overall goal. It is therefore important to find a balance between tanhã and chanda.

Payutto distinguishes between dependent happiness, independent happiness and harmonious happiness. Dependent happiness is linked to external objects and is thus dependent on things in the material world. Independent happiness is linked to internal states such as peace of mind. Independent happiness is more stable than happiness which depends on the presence of external commodities. Harmonic happiness is based on an altruistic attitude whose goal is to help other people's well-being. Harmonic happiness is linked with the Buddhist objective to cultivate the experience of the relationship between "I" and "we" through the "the extended self." Trust and solidarity (with all living beings) are indicators of true happiness. Public benefit is more related to the absence of poverty than to maximization of production and consumption.

The dark side of wealth

Payutto emphasizes several times in his book that material prosperity is a necessary prerequisite for chanda. However, there are many hazards related to wealth. Payutto warns against making use of unethical methods to search for wealth. One must not be concerned with wealth as a goal in itself. He also clarifies that one must not use wealth in such a way that harms oneself or others. A significant difference between Western and Buddhist economics is that whereas the former states that maximum consumption provides maximum satisfaction, the latter states that moderate consumption leads to true happiness and quality of life.

Work has intrinsic value in Buddhist economics because it seeks common goals through collaboration with other people and contributes to personal development while counteracting selfishness (chanda). When work is reduced to nothing more than a means to raise money for consumption of goods and services it is motivated by tanhã. It means that we want to reduce our working hours as much as possible and at the same time consume as much as possible. At this point Payutto also recommends an imperative balance between extremes so that all tasks contain elements of both tanhã and chanda. We cooperate with others to solve problems rather than competing to win happiness.

What is useful?

Production in Buddhist economics is defined as a change in which energy and matter pass from one state to another. In other words production shouldn't be seen as a question of creating something new in a real sense but rather as referring to processes that create change. So, to determine whether production is useful or not, it is first necessary to determine whether the value of what is produced is greater than the value of what has to be broken down. In situations where nature becomes damaged due to overuse of resources, nonproduction is the better option. Payutto argues that competition is an effective means to maximize production and consumption of goods and services (tanhã). When economic actors collaborate to achieve greater market power, he uses the term "artificial cooperation."

If the goal is to promote development that leads toward the common good then he recommends genuine cooperation which occurs as a result of the insight that everything is interconnected and is motivated by chanda. Payutto argues that change toward Buddhist economics begins with a change in the individual's mentality. "The golden mean" represents the basic idea in Buddhist economics and it is always necessary to strengthen the influence of chanda.

Concluding remarks

In contrast to many of the Western contributors to ecological economics who give priority to systemic change, Payutto, on the other hand, argues in line with Buddhist philosophy that all change starts with the individual. If we change ourselves first then the system will change and the economy will change. Based on the diverging concepts of chanda and tanhã, Payutto gives the change process a solid base. Payutto relates to oneness rather than talking about holism as connections between different entities and experiencing oneness depends on our ability to extend the self. The extended self includes other living entities in our ego. When the ego includes the whole universe we could be egoists all the time.

VANDANA SHIVA

The bigger war is the war against the planet. This war has its roots in an economy that fails to respect ecological and ethical limits.

Vandana Shiva

Introduction

With her basis in Indian culture, Vandana Shiva embodies her own approach to the challenges of an environmental and socially responsible economy. She points out that the problems in the Indian economy and society are to a large extent caused by Europeans' introduction of mechanical models and an atomized competitive economy. She asserts that the economy must be rooted in an organic worldview to relate adequately to reality.

Shiva is engaged in the global ecofeminist movement. She suggests that a more sustainable and productive approach to agriculture can be achieved through reinstating a system of farming more centered on engaging women. A woman-focused system would change the current system in an extremely positive manner.

Biography

Vandana Shiva was born in India in 1952. She is known for her strong commitment to organic farming, equitable distribution of resources, democracy, peace and ecofeminism. She studied in Canada and took her master's in physics at the University of Guelph (1977) and was awarded a PhD at the University of Western Ontario (1978). She continued with interdisciplinary studies in science, technology and environmental policy at the Indian Institute of Management in Bangalore. She had a central function in connection with the establishment of the Research Foundation for Science, Technology and Ecology. In 2004 she started, in collaboration with Schumacher College in England, an international college for sustainable communities in India's Doon Valley. Shiva has written more than twenty books and 500 articles. She has received numerous awards for her international commitment to the environment, justice and peace.

Science and ethics

Science as an objective and value-free discipline is an illusion that arose in Europe in the Enlightenment. According to Shiva, knowledge can never be value-free as all forms of science reflect their cultural value foundation.

Because values and norms are inherent characteristics of our cultural identity, it is impossible to establish a science that is independent of values. The biggest challenge today is to get economists, technologists and politicians to understand that the values underlying current policies are out of step with reality. Rooted in Indian philosophy, Shiva argues that economic policy must be based on understanding the community as a constantly changing living organism. This means that local democracy and decentralized solutions must replace globalized power structures.

Organic farming

For Shiva access to clean and nutritious food is fundamental to sustainable development. Industrial agriculture which measures productivity in return per area of cropland does not take serious negative side-effects into account. She points out that industrial agriculture requires much more land than what emerges in productivity goals. Agriculture in Europe is dependent on imports from other parts of the world that make up seven times the area under cultivation in Europe. Chemical pesticides and fertilizers in industrial agriculture have negative consequences for soil and water. Industrial agriculture is an inefficient and capital-intensive system which is based on high consumption of chemicals and fossil energy.

She refers to studies from Cornell University which show that industrial agriculture uses ten units of energy to produce one unit of energy in the form of food. Further, the quality of products is reduced and that in turn creates health problems in the population as the food is no healthier than the soil it is grown in.

As an alternative she argues that small-scale ecological agriculture based on local inputs, local distribution and local consumption is the best solution for food and nutrition security. In those areas of India where small-scale farming still exists the farmers produce enough food for the population. The conclusion is that the most reasonable solution is organic farming that contributes both to good biodiversity and good health in humus and humans.

Economy

Shiva points out that the globalized economy defines people as poor if they consume the food they have produced themselves rather than buying commercial "junk food." The same applies to people who produce their own clothes from local materials instead of buying mass-produced clothing. In mass-production, synthetic substances are used that can be harmful to both humans and nature. Consequently it is not correct to draw the conclusion that societies defined as poor in the West are necessarily characterized by low material standards or low quality of life. On the contrary, she claims that access to healthy food and clean water, sustainable nature, strong social and cultural identity contribute to viable communities with high individual well-being.

The biggest problem facing many poor countries is that the ownership of land and water is acquired by multinational companies who sell their "products" to locals. This also happens when Western companies take out patents on seed. When natural resources that were previously freely accessible are traded on the market then farmers will get into more debt than they can handle in the long run.

Shiva states that the result of this kind of global capitalism is that Europe and the United States have accumulated wealth that is largely based on resources drawn from countries in Africa, Asia and South America. Shiva concludes that resources move from the poor to the rich, and pollution moves from the rich to the poor. She also points out that free world trade has eliminated the basis for locally produced food and that the result is famine in poor districts that previously had enough food.

Farmers in poor countries like India cannot compete with a heavily subsidized Western agriculture that dumps its products on the global market. To reverse this trend it is necessary for measures other than increasing world trade. Increased exports of agricultural products are not a good solution for poor countries because food production for their own population suffers when production is adapted to consumer demand in the rich part of the world. Shiva points out that a change toward local farmers producing flowers and vegetables for export is simultaneously the basis for increased local food shortages. She concludes that it is not possible to solve the problems with more of the same measures that created the problems in the first place.

Democracy

Shiva is actively involved in the movement Earth Democracy, which assumes that we have a duty to safeguard the living conditions for all forms of life. The rationale is that the web of life is a continuum where biodiversity and diversity have intrinsic value. A vibrant democracy is thus a guarantee that the ecosystems we depend on are protected. Shiva argues that democracy must be developed from below and that is done by creating enthusiasm among people. Decentralized decision making helps to strengthen people's experience of responsibility. Therefore, she has been the initiator to many dialogue-based movements in many parts of the world.

Peace

According to Shiva the "war" against nature is the most serious of our time. The war is rooted in an economic system that does not respect ecological and ethical limits – limits to inequality, injustice, greed and power concentration. She claims that the Earth's resources today are controlled by a handful of multinational corporations and nations that are trying to transform the planet into a gigantic supermarket where everything is for sale. They will commercialize water, genes, cells, organs, knowledge, culture and the whole future.

As more areas of life and culture are being commercialized it becomes more and more expensive to live and the gap between rich and poor will continue to increase.

Concluding remarks

Shiva points out that people without much money can have good social relationships, live in beautiful homes and have clothes and nutritious and good food, if they have access to fertile soil, rivers with clean water and rich cultural traditions. To live in harmony with nature has always been an imperative in Indian philosophy. Today it is also an imperative for man to survive as a species. Shiva appeals to us to ask ourselves the question: "Do we want to be something more than 'money-making' and 'resource-guzzling' machines, or are there more important goals to aim for?"

Shiva points to systemic characteristics when she explains the most urgent problems facing poor countries. To solve the problems she calls for a change at both the individual and systemic levels.

PETER PRUZAN

> What is missing is a paradigm of leadership that looks upon social responsibility, ethical behavior and concern for the environment not simply as instruments for wealth creation and protecting the corporate license to operate, but fundamental principles and values in their own right.
>
> Peter Pruzan

Introduction

Through his interest in Indian philosophy and culture, Peter Pruzan developed an interesting, relevant and forward-looking management education at Copenhagen Business School. Spiritual leadership represents a deeper understanding of business environment and social responsibility.

Biography

Peter Pruzan was born in 1936 in New York, became a Danish citizen in 1972 and is known for his pioneering work within business ethics, ethical accounting and value-based management. Pruzan holds a PhD in Operations Research from Case Western Reserve University, USA (1964) and Dr. Polit University of Copenhagen (1982). In recent years, he has contributed to actualize spirituality as a factor for a wider understanding in economics and management. Pruzan is currently professor emeritus at the Copenhagen Business School.

A pioneer

Pruzan is an original and pioneering theorist and practitioner in social sciences, management and leadership. His influence on the development of these fields of social science is important in an international context. Pruzan's academic development can be divided into three different phases. First, he has developed a practical system for ethical accounting. Second, he has made a significant contribution to the development of value-based leadership. Third, he has put forward a very interesting basis for spiritual leadership. Pruzan's contributions to spiritual leadership are inspired by his many visits to India and his deep interest in Indian philosophy, religion and culture. An important motivation in Pruzan's work has been his contribution to the development of a humanistic, democratic and sustainable foundation for economics, management and leadership.

Ethical accounting

When Pruzan launched the idea of ethical accounting, it was something completely new in economics and business administration. Until then accountants had exclusively developed systems for obtaining an overview of the financial flows (revenues and expenses), with a main focus on maximizing profits. Pruzan pointed out that traditional accounting methods were incomplete because mathematical calculations did not affect the fundamental issues related to ethical values. Through the development of ethical accounting, firms got a method that gave room for measuring other values in the formal of a financial management system. According to Pruzan the need for ethical accounting arises when the monetary language becomes too narrow and merely observes describes and assesses company performance. Ethical accounting is organized as a dialogue process where communication between management and stakeholders is the key issue. The process is a bottom-up model for participation, management support and value diversity. Ethical accounting has to come up with answers concerning the extent to which organizations live up to their defined ethical norms and values.

Today, business ethics, ethical accounting and corporate social responsibility are largely accepted in business (at least theoretically). The problem is that many companies use ethics instrumentally as a means to enhance corporate reputation rather than implementing ethical reflection as an integral part of corporate activities. Focus on values and ethics is often considered as a set of new competitive tools incorporated in established models. According to Pruzan, it is a prerequisite for environmentally and socially responsible economies for the focus in corporate accounting to expand to include ethical values.

Value-based leadership

Larger companies, in combination with increasing globalization, have, according to Pruzan, led to more focus on the ethical dimension in corporate management and leadership. When contact with local communities and culture is reduced the temptation to forget anything but profits and growth becomes dominant. This trend explains many of the serious challenges we face today in connection with the environment, poverty and financial crisis. Pruzan points out that it is possible to reverse the trend in a positive direction.

The point of departure for Pruzan is an understanding indicating that decisions taking into account only the interests of the owners and focusing exclusively on monetary goals lead to an oversimplification of reality. When this oversimplified management strategy is combined with demands for increased bureaucratic control and reporting, the results become negative for people, society and nature. Another explanation of the system's tendency to be ineffective is that there is little focus on the needs of the employees for respect, acceptance and participation. Enlightened, creative, motivated, responsible employees seek meaningful work and personal development and seek out, mostly in vain, some conformity between the company's ethics and their own.

Many feel that an economy which focuses on efficiency, growth, power, reputation and prestige is in conflict with their personal ethical values, including, for example, love, satisfaction, beauty and peace of mind. To achieve such a change leaders must abandon their position of power and instead open up for dialogue and cooperation with both employees and external stakeholders. In other words, value-based management involves, according to Pruzan, dialogue, responsibility and ethical reflection. Dialogue and cooperation are, therefore, characteristics of organizations anchored in value-based leadership. This kind of leadership presupposes a common language and methods that make it possible to reflect on practice and to decide whether the decisions taken are in accordance with the interests of the company and the social and natural environment. One important instrument is to secure measures which lead to decentralization and increased autonomy for internal and external stakeholders. An important prerequisite for value-based leadership is an acceptance of the fact that ethical norms and values are more than instruments for increased profits.

Spiritual leadership

Pruzan found the inspiration for the development of spiritual leadership in Eastern philosophy, and especially in Buddhism. In his article "Spirituality as the Context of Leadership" (2011) Pruzan states that leadership with a spiritual grounding provides the best guarantee for not reducing corporate objectives to increasing profits and efficiency. The term spiritual leadership refers to the spiritual essence of our existence, our nature and our true enduring identity. Spiritual leadership is, therefore, based on an understanding of the need to find a deeper rooting for the organization's values, ethics and accountability. Pruzan has, through interviews with a number of managers, identified that most spiritual leaders refer to an internal perspective on the meaning of life and on governance. The inner spiritual perspective forms the basis for their decisions and actions in the outer world. Managers who work within such a context are characterized by integrity, empathy and holistic understanding. To implement spiritual leadership it is necessary to develop management systems that combine "internal" and "external" values. Today there are several universities offering management education inspired by Eastern philosophy whose goal is to help to develop a deeper spiritual awareness setting out clearly the visions and values necessary for handling the challenges of current society, locally and globally.

Concluding remarks

Ethical accounting, value-based leadership and spiritual leadership are motivated by the need to develop environmentally and socially responsible businesses and organizations that provide employees with meaningful work, contribute to personal and organizational development and provide connection between individual and organizational values. Spiritual leadership helps to give values a deep inner anchoring which reduces the chances that ethics becomes an instrument for achieving external goals. Responsibility is connected to an acceptance of the fact that we (i.e. all human beings) are co-responsible, "co-creators" of development.

Pruzan has focused on and gives priority to the development of new models and practices for business and leadership. In accordance with Buddhist culture he argues that our inner spiritual life forms decisions and actions in the material world.

8 Management perspective

In this chapter ecological economics is set out clearly on a business level. I have chosen Archie Carroll (USA), Waldemar Hopfenbeck (Germany) and Richard Welford (England) to speak for the management perspective in ecological economics. They have offered influential inputs such as stakeholder theory, CSR, partnership approach and cooperation between integrated actors.

Even if their sources of inspiration are different they come up with quite similar solutions to the challenges in business strategy and marketing. Carroll focuses on the interconnection between economy, law and ethics. Hopfenbeck is inspired by communicative rationality in the interpretation of the Frankfurt School in philosophy and Welford is strongly influenced by Buddhism. Their diversity provides a very exciting mixture in the field of management theory and widely defined practice.

ARCHIE B. CARROLL

> The total corporate social responsibility of business entails the simultaneous fulfillment of the firm's economic, legal, ethical, and philanthropic responsibilities.
>
> Archie B. Carroll

Introduction

Archie B. Carroll has a prominent role in the efforts to introduce ethics and social responsibility into the curriculum of business schools and universities worldwide. Carroll is especially known for pioneering contributions to the development of corporate social responsibility, stakeholder theory and ethical leadership

Biography

Archie B. Carroll was born in Jacksonville, Florida in 1941. He holds a doctorate in business administration from the College of Business at Florida

State University. In 1972 Carroll was appointed full professor in management at the University of Georgia. Today he is professor emeritus at Terry College of Business. From 1997 to 2001 he was on the boards of the International Association for Business and Society (IAB) and the Society for Business Ethics. Carroll has published numerous textbooks and articles which influenced teaching and research at business schools and universities worldwide. He is still an active researcher, author and lecturer.

Economic responsibility

Carroll's most important contributions are in the three areas of CSR (Corporate Social Responsibility), stakeholder theory and ethical leadership. For more than thirty years, Carroll argued that companies have a responsibility toward all stakeholders that goes beyond maximizing profits. At the time it represented a dramatic break with established business theory and practice. Friedman, who at that time had a dominant position in economics and business administration in the United States, was a spokesman for the view that the main (and only) task in business was to ensure maximum return on invested capital. The slogan was "The business of business is business."

Carroll claimed that corporate responsibility included, in addition to economics, law, ethics and philanthropy. Economic responsibility means, according to Carroll, that company leaders manage available resources so that profits are generated within a context of legal, ethical and philanthropic responsibility. Profitability justifies objectives that are higher in the hierarchy of responsibility. Carroll claims that prioritizing shareholder profitability, rather than the higher levels of responsibility, causes many of the challenges we face today.

Legal responsibility

Legal responsibility means that companies are obliged to comply with laws and regulations approved by government. The rationale is that the authorities define rules that ensure that the interests of the community are safeguarded, which will not happen if the economic actors take decisions based solely on short-term profitability considerations. In other words, Carroll is critical of established economics' view that market "mechanisms" themselves are capable of providing optimal results for society as a whole.

Ethical responsibility

Ethical responsibility implies that companies should do more than the law requires. They should also follow society's accepted ethical norms and values. Carroll points out that there is an important distinction between ethics (the theory of moral behavior) and morality (practice). He argued that ethically responsible business leaders unite the two approaches through the practice of Aristotle's virtue ethics.

Figure 8.1 Responsibility pyramid

It is thus not sufficient to choose actions that increase the total utility or benefit for a defined group of people (utilitarianism), or to follow valid ethical principles (deontological ethics), it is also necessary to develop moral character among business leaders (virtue ethics).

Philanthropy

Carroll puts philanthropic responsibility at the highest level, that is, companies are encouraged to contribute to positive social development in (local) society. Philanthropic responsibility may be to support various cultural or social activities. By putting into practice high moral standards and proactively supporting philanthropic projects, firms create positive relationships with their local society, which, in the long run, will benefit the business's economic interests. Some years ago, Carroll eliminated the philanthropic level from the responsibility pyramid because of problems related to separating philanthropy from ordinary sponsor activities.

Cooperation

In addition to criticizing the one-dimensional emphasis on economic responsibility within the established economy, Carroll also questions the description of the market as an aggregate of autonomous competing actors. Instead of describing the companies as competitors in an atomized market Carroll changed focus and realized that the market was a network of integrated actors where customers, suppliers, competitors, communities and other stakeholders depend on each other.

When the market is understood as a network of interdependent actors then corporate responsibility is extended from only including shareholders to also including all stakeholders. A stakeholder is defined as an actor who is, in one way or another, affected by business activities, or affects the activities in the business. Business leaders must, for that reason, answer two questions: first, they must decide which stakeholders to prioritize in various decision-making situations, and second, they must decide which values should be prioritized.

Box 8.1 Stakeholder–responsibility matrix

	Economic	*Legal*	*Ethical*	*Philanthropic*
Shareholders				
Customers				
Employees				
Community				
Competitors				
Suppliers				

To make the decision situation more transparent Carroll constructed the stakeholder–responsibility matrix in which the various stakeholder groups are described in conjunction with the four areas of responsibility. The point is that the interests of shareholders, customers, employees, communities, competitors and suppliers must be evaluated in connection to economic, legal, ethical and philanthropic values. Carroll maintained that performing such an analytical process would in itself help to increase the decision makers' ethical consciousness (moral character). By these means, they will develop an ability to recognize, analyze and draw overall value-based conclusions.

Four types of management

Based on his reflections on stakeholders and ethical responsibility Carroll has outlined four alternative management strategies.

1   Reactive: Management denies any liability beyond economic responsibility. Laws and regulations are perceived as obstacles which create difficulties for companies. Government regulations should, as far as possible, be eliminated.
2   Defense: The leaders are not aware that their actions have ethical dimensions that can influence other actors. They believe in principle that ethics and economics have nothing to do with each other. Anyway, they admit (reluctantly) that they should take into account certain ethical considerations to avoid damaging the company's reputation.
3   Constructive: Leaders accept ethical responsibility and follow the well-founded values and norms in society. They acknowledge that they have a moral responsibility toward all stakeholders.
4   Proactive: Management takes its own initiatives, and extends further than expected in the exercise of social responsibility. This applies on the economic, legal, ethical and philanthropic level.

Carroll states that the different levels of responsibility in the pyramid should not be fulfilled sequentially, but simultaneously. "When this is done by a significant portion of the business community, the stakeholder environment of the twenty-first century will flourish" (Carroll 1998, p. 7).

Concluding remarks

Inspired by communitarian philosophy, Carroll outlines a strategy for implementing environmental and social responsibility in business organizations. He argues against the dominating theories and practices in business strategy and marketing, claiming that the main goal is to increase the firm's profits. As an alternative Carroll takes the view that economic responsibility is a prerequisite for the higher-level goals. In addition to the responsibility hierarchy, Carroll's description of stakeholder analysis was an important contribution to the development of meso-level ecological economics.

WALDEMAR HOPFENBECK

> Although it is perhaps too soon to speak of a new philosophy, radically new ways of thinking are necessary if we are to find innovative solutions to the crises of our environment.
>
> Waldemar Hopfenbeck

Introduction

Waldemar Hopfenbeck was one of the first European academics in marketing to develop a comprehensive theory for environmentally and socially responsible marketing management. His theory is based on a holistic view of academics where interdisciplinary collaboration is central. He also argues that neither a Marxist planned economy nor liberalistic market economy is suited to solve today's complex challenges.

What we need is a third option based on partnership agreements. Concerning concrete business practice, Hopfenbeck introduces the establishment of retro-distribution as a new function in the value chain to facilitate circular chains of materials connecting consumption and production.

Biography

Waldemar Hopfenbeck (b. 1944) grew up in Gumbinnen in Germany. He studied business administration and submitted his PhD dissertation at Ludwig-Maximilians-University, Munich in 1977. He has worked in the Department of Business Administration at the University of Applied Sciences in Munich since 1984.

Environmental excellence

Hopfenbeck was one of the first in Europe to develop a comprehensive theoretical framework covering environmental and socially responsible marketing management. He expanded the business management approach to include political, economic and ecological dimensions. In order to integrate the different perspectives, Hopfenbeck argued that it was necessary to study the different fields of economics from a holistic approach. The implication of introducing a holistic worldview in academic study was to give increased focus on the necessity of interdisciplinary cooperation. In *Umweltsorientiertes Management und Marketing* Hopfenbeck stated that an increasing number of economists and business leaders are aware that "our limited, linear way of thinking and decision making, which fails to take account of this web of contexts, can bring about unintended and undesirable effects" (Hopfenbeck 1992).

When his book was translated into English and published by an American publishing house (1992) it was included in the curriculum plans of business schools all over Europe. His numerous publications calling for environmentally responsible management and marketing gave him the 1997 BAUM Environmental Science Award for outstanding achievements from the (then) German Environment Minister Angela Merkel.

Holism and cooperation

In the following paragraphs I focus on some of the most original, interesting and significant theoretical contributions from Hopfenbeck concerning the development of an environmentally and socially responsible economy. To do this I consider three areas:

1 holistic science
2 partnership approach
3 circular value chains.

Holistic science

In order to capture the relationships between economy, environment and society (Figure 8.2) there is a need for a holistic science that transcends the traditional boundaries between disciplines. Hopfenbeck argued that marketing management must be studied as an integral part of larger social and ecological networks where all issues are enlightened from multiple perspectives. It is not sufficient to consider the economic consequences of the various action options.

Holism includes, according to Hopfenbeck, adaptation, flexibility, learning, development, self-regulation and self-organization. Network thinking links economic, technological, scientific and humanistic knowledge so that it contributes to holistic and long-term solutions that are difficult to detect

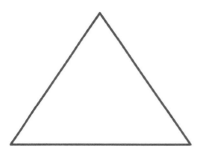

The economic dimension

The social dimension   The ecological dimension

Figure 8.2 Extended management context

within the perspective of traditional economics based on a linear, analytical scientific tradition. By observing the market from a holistic perspective, he includes fundamental values like trust and responsibility in economic theory and practice.

Partnership approach

To deal with the environmental problems, it is necessary to transcend solutions based on an authoritarian planned economy or free market economy. As a relevant alternative or supplement to the established economy, Hopfenbeck suggests a partnership approach based on voluntary agreements and binding cooperation between the actors in the market. Authorities provide comprehensive educational programs that lay the foundations for environmentally responsible production, distribution and consumption.

Through partnership agreements the actors themselves take the initiative to find holistic solutions that are not possible within the context of an atomized competitive market economy.

As an extension of this argument, Hopfenbeck points out that companies that cause environmental problems have a primary responsibility to resolve them (ecological internalization). Ecological internalization differs from the traditional economy's emphasis on economic internalization which says that all environmental costs should be included in the company's accounts. The result of ecological internalization is that companies cannot create problems without being obliged to solve them.

Circular value chains

Increased consumption of natural resources combined with increasing amounts of waste is a massive burden on any ecosystem. To reduce an

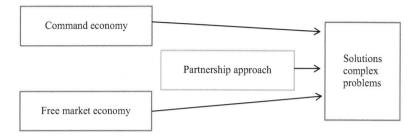

Figure 8.3 Approaches to environmental challenges

Box 8.2 Economic and ecological internalization

- Economic internalization: all environmental costs are included in the company's accounts.
- Ecological internalization: all kinds of economic activity are based on ecological principles.

---

economy's negative impact on the ecosystem, Hopfenbeck suggests that consumption and production should be linked through retro-distribution. Retro-distribution consists of several sub-functions: collecting, sorting and recycling of various materials. By establishing circular value chains (Figure 8.4) it is possible to reduce both the consumption of virgin raw materials from nature and the amount of waste that goes back to nature. The arguments for circular value chains are today accepted within the EU, where efforts to develop functional circular value chains for different materials have been given a high priority.

Collaboration between governments, manufacturers, distributors, consumers and various NGOs is required if efficient material cycles are to be established in practice. By introducing retro-distribution as an integral part of the economy Hopfenbeck has contributed to a general acceptance that waste is not worthless junk but a valuable resource. Business strategy based on the idea of circularity has expanded the linear perspective from "cradle to grave" to a circular perspective from "cradle to cradle."

Hopfenbeck warns that circular value chains could be an alibi for the economic growth ideology, where the aim is to increase production and consumption. To reduce the growth spiral he appeals for responsibility and moderation among both businesses and consumers.

Acceptance of ethical principles including responsibility and respect for the inherent value in human beings and nature is basic to Hopfenbeck's argument. He refers to Hans Jonas' duty ethical principle, "always act in such a way that the effects of your actions are compatible with the continuance

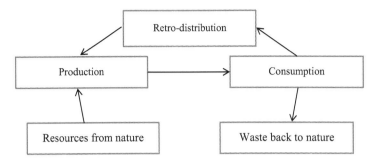

Figure 8.4 Product lifecycle (simplified)

of human life on Earth." The main thing is that environmental and social responsibility are integrated as corporate values and not just instruments to achieve a better reputation in the market in order to make bigger profits.

Concluding remarks

Hopfenbeck is one of the most pioneering contributors in the development of ecological economics with relevance for business practice. He introduced the partnership approach as an alternative to the dominant economic system. The partnership approach describes the market as a collaborative network of integrated actors. Since it is not possible to understand these complex processes within the context of specialized scientific methods, Hopfenbeck calls for a holistic science.

On a practical level Hopfenbeck introduced circular value chains where matter and energy were recycled at an optimal level. Hopfenbeck's distinction between economic and ecological internalization represents one of the most clear-cut criteria for discriminating between green and ecological economics on a business level.

RICHARD WELFORD

> The challenge of the next fifty years must be to develop a humane culture and an associated economic model, which will save the Earth rather than destroy it.
>
> Richard Welford

Introduction

For more than twenty years, Richard Welford's thoughts and ideas have had great influence on teaching and research in environmental and socially responsible business strategy. He argues for the necessity of profound changes in the fundamental principles and values in economic theory and practice. Instead of waiting for national and international regulations, Welford predicts that the fundamental changes will come through local initiatives based on cooperation and shared responsibility.

Biography

Welford (b. 1960) holds a PhD in economics from the University of Warwick (England). For several years he was full professor in environmental management at the University of Huddersfield. Today he is director of the Corporate Environmental Governance Programme at the University of Hong Kong. For more than twenty years Welford has been an important driving force in the development of environmentally and socially responsible business management theory and practice.

He has written fifteen books and over 100 articles within environmental management and corporate social responsibility (CSR). As a consultant for a number of large enterprises Welford had the opportunity to develop concepts, theories and models in close cooperation with business practice. In the early 1990s he was one of the pioneers behind the development of new principles of environmental accounting and environmental reporting in cooperation with, among others, The Body Shop and IBM. In recent years, Welford has been a consultant for the Samsung Corporation and British Telecom.

Profitability is not sufficient

Welford has criticized researchers who consider environmental and social responsibility as a competitive means to strengthen a company's commercial position in the market. In his opinion it is not sufficient to focus on profitable investments in connection with environmentally friendly technological solutions. The consequence of such an instrumental approach could easily be that environmental and social responsibility end up as no more than balancing items in corporate budgets. The consequence could well be that projects which fail to maximize profits will be abandoned, even if they have a high score in other dimensions.

In *Environmental Management and Business Strategy* (1993) Welford argues that the obligation to contribute to sustainable development should be incorporated in the business baseline. According to Welford, sustainable development demands more than merely reducing the negative impact on nature. Equally important measures are contributing to fairness and reducing the gap between rich and poor. He is critical of the practice in Western companies to pay low prices for raw materials and labor from poor countries in order to keep prices down and profits up.

Such practices reinforce the differences between rich and poor countries. He is far from optimistic when it comes to the possibility of implementing the necessary changes within the framework of established economic theory and practice. He argues that it is as unlikely that environmental and social responsibility can be developed within mainstream economies as it is that lions will become vegetarians. Welford mentions several areas where fundamental changes in attitudes and actions are required.

Quality of life

The first area is that the objective of economic growth is replaced by a goal of improved quality of life. It means that an economy goes from being the goal in itself to being an instrument for realizing the good life in the good society. In his article "Examining, Discussing and Suggesting the Possible Contribution and role of Buddhist Economics for Corporate Social Responsibility" (2007) Welford points out that climate change, overuse of resources, pollution and unbridled growth in consumption are inextricably linked with the objective of growth through free trade and globalization in mainstream economics.

Welford stresses that the ideals that underlie Buddhist economics allow for many of the necessary changes. While traditional economics emphasizes egocentric interest and growth in consumption, Buddhist economics is more concerned about the community and inner individual growth. The primary goal in businesses will be, in this perspective, to produce and to offer goods and services that meet basic human needs instead of focusing on luxury consumption demands in the rich part of the world. Firms can also stimulate human development by facilitating work tasks that make it possible to use and develop individual skills and abilities for the common good.

Cooperation

Second, the principle of competition between autonomous actors is swapped for a principle of cooperation between integrated actors. In *Corporate Environmental Management* (2000) Welford delves deeper into this issue and argues that it is inappropriate to talk about a single business as "sustainable." The reason is that all businesses are integrated into social and ecological networks. The challenge therefore consists in finding new forms of interaction that allow solutions within a larger ecological and social context.

Responsibility

Third, Welford is critical of Friedman's argument that a company's only concern is to ensure that shareholders get the greatest possible return on invested capital. An important point in Welford's argument is that companies have a responsibility toward all stakeholders. Stakeholders include, according to Welford, anyone who is either affected by or affects the decisions of the company. The stakeholder category includes, among others, consumers, competitors, suppliers, communities, nature and future generations.

Inspired by Buddhism, Welford stresses that any change starts with the individual (individual human being or business). The transition toward an environmentally and socially responsible economy requires that we get started with bottom-up processes, rather than expect the changes to be made through top-down national and international regulations. Each one of us is therefore jointly responsible for implementing the required change processes which initiate an environmentally and socially responsible development.

Concluding remarks

Welford argues along the same lines as Carroll and Hopfenbeck concerning the need in business to change from viewing profit as an end in itself to becoming instead a way to reach goals connected to quality of life and well-being. In connection with this argument, Welford points to how business could contribute to reducing the gap between rich and poor, on a global level. In harmony with the Buddhist tradition he argued that all change starts with the individual, in other words bottom-up processes are more relevant than changes initiated from the leaders in politics and business.

9 Concepts and projects

The distinguished scholars in ecological economics presented in this chapter have founded their theoretical contributions on extensive empirical projects. From their research many concepts with a special potency have been developed, such as "triple bottom line," John Elkington (England); "prosperity without growth," Tim Jackson (England); "the threshold point," Manfred Max-Neef (Chile); and "ecological footprints," Willian Rees (Canada).

They have all put forward strong arguments in favor of deep changes in order to cope with the massive social and ecological challenges. Greening the economy is not enough because it usually functions as an instrument to increase growth or profits within the existing system. First of all we have to dispel the myth of growth. Second, network-based cooperation is essential in their argumentation for the new economy. Third, transdisciplinarity is needed to grasp the essence of the real world.

JOHN ELKINGTON

> Systems thinking tell us that sustainability cannot be defined for a single corporation. Instead, it must be defined for a complete economic-social-ecological system, and not for its component parts.
>
> John Elkington

Introduction

John Elkington is well known for having developed the concept of the triple bottom line. The triple bottom line refers to the relationship between economic prosperity, environmental quality and social justice. In *Cannibals with Forks* (1997) he explores several global trends that contribute to growing emphasis on social and ecological values on behalf of short-term profitability and economic growth. Elkington gives concrete examples of how the objective of sustainable development has the potential to change economic theory and practice.

Biography

John Elkington was born in 1949 in Padworth (England). He holds bachelor's degrees in sociology and social psychology from the University of Essex (1970) and a master's in urban and regional planning from University College London (1974). In 1987 he founded (along with Julia Hailes) the consultancy SustainAbility, which is a think-tank and a consultancy that helps businesses to contribute to economic, social and environmental sustainability (sustainability.com). In 2008, he established Volans, an organization that prepares solutions to some of the major environmental and social challenges facing the world community. In addition to being director of Volans, Elkington is visiting professor at the Doughty Centre for Corporate Responsibility at Cranfield School of Management.

Elkington is author or co-author of seventeen books, including *The Green Capitalists* (1987), *The Green Consumer* (1993) and *Cannibals with Forks: The Triple Bottom Line of 21st Century Business* (1997). As the titles indicate, he is concerned with the interaction between economics, business and personal finance. Elkington has achieved massive recognition for his work, including the UN's Global 500 Roll of Honour in 1989.

The triple bottom line

Elkington is well known for having developed the triple bottom line concept. The concept is currently assimilated within academic research as well as in business administration and entrepreneurship. The triple bottom line states that corporate responsibility is not only related to economic values, but includes contributions to ecological sustainability and social justice as well. Elkington's understanding of economics and business is based on a systems theoretical perspective. Within this context of interpretation, economic, ecological and social challenges can only be solved through integrated interaction between the actors in the market.

In *The Green Consumer*, Elkington points out that green consumption is an important and necessary condition for solving many serious environmental problems. To help consumers in choosing between different products, Elkington describes and justifies a number of criteria. Generally, the products must not be harmful to either humans or animals. They must not at any stage in the lifecycle (production, distribution, consumption or reprocessing) be harmful to the environment. It means that products should not be allowed to consume large amounts of energy or raw materials, creating a lot of waste, inflicting (unnecessary) animal disorders or making use of resources that are detrimental to endangered ecosystems or plant or animal species. He also points out that consumers should choose products that can be reused or reprocessed. Although Elkington argues that consumers are liable to reduce the overall environmental impact, he is also aware that many environmental problems are too complex to be solved through green consumer choice alone.

Changes

In *Cannibals with Forks* Elkington describes and comments on different examples indicating that there are changes going on in society. These changes will lead to more focus on environmental and social responsibility as important competitive factors in the future. This means that companies that successfully incorporate the triple bottom line will strengthen their competitive position in the market.

Elkington strongly warns against using the triple bottom line only as a means to enhance corporate reputation. An instrumental approach means that firms adapt to changes in customer preferences instead of following their own wishes. The private sector has an important role as a driving force in the ongoing processes of change. Elkington distinguishes between seven different trends that appear to be mutually reinforcing.

First, a competitive market economy will change from unilateral focus on products to become more oriented toward development of cooperative integrated networks. The rationale is that sustainable development only makes sense within an economic-social-ecological systems perspective.

Second, the focus of technological development expands from improving eco-efficiency to also emphasizing social values. Values such as social justice, responsibility and confidence will increase in importance.

Third, the development of more open information systems leads to more democratic decision making. When the flow of information between the actors (stakeholders) in the market improves, the consequence is more stakeholder (customers, suppliers, environmental organizations, banks, communities, etc.) influence in the decision-making processes.

Fourth, corporate responsibility is expanded to include the entire product lifecycle. It means among other things that technology that improves the environmental impact of the products offered on the market, from raw material stage to recycling (cradle to cradle) will be given priority. The aim is to reduce the product's overall environmental, social and economic costs.

Fifth, companies extend the perspective of only emphasizing the shareholders' interests to increasingly involving consideration of all stakeholders. The result is that market participants will eventually experience one another as interdependent partners. Elkington launches "co-opetition" as a concept characterizing a new market situation where firms will "listen to customers, work with suppliers, create teams, establish strategic partnerships – even with competitors."

Sixth, the economy's current short-term perspective is supplemented or replaced by increased emphasis on long-term effects. The explanation is that sustainable development makes little sense within the short-term time horizon of mainstream economics.

The seventh and final change process is, according to Elkington, that corporate governance in the future will be more open to diversity. To create stronger connections between stakeholders it is necessary to facilitate network-based communicative interaction.

Concluding remarks

Elkington's contribution to sustainable economics with a practical content is based on a systems theory perspective. Unlike the traditional actor perspective in economics, he introduces a network perspective to describe the transactions in the market. To achieve the objective of sustainable development it is necessary to break down the barriers between the macro level (economics) and the meso level (business). In addition Elkington introduces the micro level (private economy) as an integral part of economy in practice. Most importantly, decisions (on all levels) must be anchored in the triple bottom line. That economic prosperity, environmental quality and social justice must be incorporated as mandatory values in all decisions. To implement the changes, a venue for multiway active dialogue is required, where the various actors are given the opportunity to develop and coordinate their activities.

TIM JACKSON

> People are not greedy by nature, it is the system that promotes the most primitive characteristics of humans.
>
> Tim Jackson

Introduction

Tim Jackson introduced simplicity and qualitative development as replacements for economic growth. To succeed in this change process we have to rewrite the materialistic myths that our culture is built upon. It is of great importance to re-establish the close connection between individuals and society and between human beings and nature. Jackson maintains that the different levels in the economy – macro (economics), meso (business), and micro (consumers) – have to be integrated.

Biography

In 2000, Tim Jackson, became the UK's first professor of sustainable development, at the University of Surrey. His radical and pioneering contribution is partly inspired by the cooperation with Friends of the Earth and the New Economics Foundation. Jackson has in the last twenty years been studying the relationship between lifestyle, values and the environment by participating in a number of interdisciplinary research groups. He led among others the efforts to develop Surrey Environmental Lifestyle Mapping (SELMA), a model used to estimate the carbon footprint of various forms of economic activity. Today Jackson is well known as the head of the Commission for Sustainable Development (2004–2011) and as the author of the controversial report *Prosperity without Growth? A Transition to a Sustainable Economy* (2009). The report was later published as a book which *Le Monde* described as "One of the most outstanding books in environmental economics in recent years."

Prosperity without Growth

In *Prosperity without Growth: Economics for a Finite Planet* (2011), Jackson stated that all societies are based on one or another myth that says something about reality (ontology) and about the most important values (ethics). He argues that modern society is rooted in the idea of economic growth as a primary goal and value. According to Jackson, the growth ideology is the cause behind many of the most serious ecological and social problems. The result of one-sided focus on economic growth is that the world economy has quintupled over the last fifty years.

On a commercial level, growth is stimulated through product development and constant changes of models, combined with low prices and massive advertising. Consumers are chasing the latest models and the latest fashions in an increasing number of product groups. The combination of corporate and private incentives is driving economic growth toward new heights. Easy access to loans has been an important instrument to stimulate further growth. Jackson refers to Belk, who claims that our relationship to material commodities has gone so far that they currently exist as part of our "extended self." The result is that we are all trapped in consumerism's iron cage.

Energy and food security and increasing differences between rich and poor are today among the most pressing challenges facing the global community. Within the established economic paradigm problems connected with, for example, unemployment and social insecurity are explained by referring to slow economic growth. According to Jackson, this myth, telling us that the problems must and can only be solved through continued economic growth, is to a small extent being questioned.

The acceleration of economic growth has led to overuse of a variety of resources coupled with increasing amounts of waste. The results of reduced biodiversity and climate change are unbalanced ecosystems and low resilience. CO_2 emissions have increased by 40 percent since the Kyoto agreement was signed; this is a serious indication showing that it is difficult to do anything about the problems within the established economic model. It is not sufficient to have good intentions from the world's leaders, more fundamental change is required.

Qualitative development

To deal with the challenges Jackson argues that it is absolutely necessary to develop a new economic system that is oriented toward qualitative development ("prosperity") rather than quantitative growth. According to Jackson these changes must take place primarily at the systems level because it is the economic system that promotes greed. To initiate the necessary changes far-reaching measures in several areas are needed. In addition to advocating changes in the direction of greater emphasis on qualitative development, Jackson is keen to find new environmentally friendly solutions for the production and distribution of goods and services. He distinguishes between (1) technological changes based on improved resource efficiency, renewable energy and clean technology and (2) basic social changes, such as more emphasis on public goods, fair distribution of benefits and reduced materialism.

Technological changes

Jackson reasons that technological development is necessary to develop a sustainable steady-state economy that contributes to human development and global justice. Although he believes that it is impossible to decouple the negative side-effects of economic growth by using improved technology it is possible to reduce many of the environmental problems arising from current economic practice. He illustrates the importance of technology by recalling Ehrlich's equation for environmental impact. Ehrlich describes how growing populations, affluence and technology contribute to environmental impact. The equation indicates that in order to reduce the negative environmental impact, improved technology is necessary in addition to a reduction in population and consumption.

Social changes

Jackson claims that development of "prosperity" does not depend on increasing material prosperity. He justifies this assertion by referring to statistics that show that happiness in wealthy Western countries has been stable (or downward) over decades despite increased consumption. He reinforces the argument by drawing a distinction between "prosperity" and happiness. In line with Schumacher and Payutto, Jackson argues that qualitative individual and social development is associated with the facilitation of opportunities to develop human potential and to realize the importance of inherent values outside the individual. To reach these goals it is necessary to develop positive integrative relationships between people and between

$I = P \times A \times T$
I = Human impact on the environment
P = Population
A = Affluence
T = Technology

Figure 9.1 Ehrlich's equation for environmental impact

people and nature. These connection lines are essential for qualitative individual and social development (prosperity). Key instruments in Jackson's change program are measures to facilitate increased participation in social life.

Simplicity

Jackson is an optimist and he argues that government has a unique opportunity to focus on quality of life. If the economy on a macro level is freed from the myth of growth, then authorities will have greater room for maneuver which makes it possible to focus on goals related to the environment and society.

Jackson refers to studies showing that people with strong intrinsic values are more satisfied and exhibit greater environmental responsibility than people with an exclusive focus on material values. Voluntary simplicity is a philosophy that is central to "prosperity." Life becomes more satisfactory if one engages in meaningful activities rather than having an exclusive focus on increasing the consumption of goods and services traded on the market. Jackson refers to the changes in social structures necessary to influence people's attitudes and behavior toward reduced consumption. Increased investment in public goods will, according to Jackson, give a substantial contribution to increased "prosperity." Prosperity without growth is, in other words, no longer a utopian dream, it is an economic and ecological necessity.

Concrete action

A. Sustainable macroeconomics
   -   investing in public goods and infrastructure
   -   financial prudence
   -   changes in society's accounting systems.
B. Human development
   -   share the necessary working tasks and improve the balance between work and leisure
   -   find appropriate ways to measure qualitative development
   -   more emphasis on human values and less emphasis on material consumption.
C. Respecting ecological limits
   -   introduce defined boundaries for resource use and pollutant emissions
   -   implement taxes which promote sustainable solutions
   -   contribute to the development of environmentally friendly technologies made available to all.

As stated in the proposals for change, any qualitative development is inextricably associated with the development of environmentally friendly technologies. Measures at community level have implications at the individual level, while individual change leads to system changes. If we are to initiate changes in the direction of "prosperity without growth" then the development of new instruments that exceed current registration systems for profitability and GDP goals is required. An important prerequisite for translating measures into practical action is the ability and willingness to cooperate.

Concluding remarks

Jackson argues that a change in the economy from growth in material production and consumption toward qualitative development depends on our ability to rewrite the myth that our society is built upon. The current dominant myth indicates that economic growth is the solution to almost every problem. We need growth in consumption to be happy, we need growth to reduce the gap between rich and poor, and we need growth to innovate technology to solve the environmental problems.

On the contrary, Jackson states that the solutions are connected to our willingness to change focus from materialistic welfare to qualitative individual and social development based on simplicity. Responsible consumers are an important factor in the change process. Jackson argues that we need a systemic change combined with new technology and simplicity to cope with the current challenges.

MANFRED MAX-NEEF

> We have reached a point in our evolution as human beings, in which we know very much, but understand very little.
>
> Manfred Max-Neef

Introduction

Manfred Max-Neef states that current economic theory and practice are unable to properly capture and handle the most important questions in today's society. He argues that a change from an atomized scientific practice toward transdiciplinarity is of great importance. We are not only facing a serious environmental and financial crisis but also a crisis that affects all of humanity. For the first time in history the problems are so interwoven that they cannot be solved from any one particular professional perspective.

Biography

Manfred Max-Neef was born in Valparasio in Chile in 1932. He has been guest lecturer at a number of American, European and Latin American Universities. In the 1960s he taught at Berkeley. In 1981 he established

CEPAUR (Centre for Alternative Development). One year later he was awarded "the Right Livelihood Award" (alternative Nobel Prize) for his efforts to improve the living conditions of the poor. From 1993 to 2001, Max-Neef was principal of the Universidad Austral de Chile, where he is currently director at the Department of Economics. Max-Neef has written numerous books and articles concerning the need for a new economy. He is best known for *From the Outside Looking In: Experiences in Barefoot Economics* (1981) and *Economics Unmasked: From Power and Greed to Compassion and the Common Good* (2011).

Multidisciplinarity

At the beginning of the twenty-first century mankind faces complex challenges in relation to access to clean water, increasing flows of refugees, poverty, terrorism, climate change, financial crisis, debt crisis, etc. Max-Neef argues that these crises are largely due to the fact that the dominant economy is on a collision course with reality. To deal with the problems, a new economy based on comprehensive understanding and interdisciplinarity is required. It takes a transdisciplinary approach, that is, working within a holistic science that captures the contexts and relationships in a complex reality. Given that most universities have a tradition of specialization and the cultivation of scientific monocultures, it is obvious that Max-Neef's proposals involve a substantial change in both research and teaching.

Max-Neef draws a demarcation line between weak and strong transdisciplinarity. On the one hand, weak transdisciplinarity means that representatives of different disciplines work together to solve complex problems. In other words, weak transdisciplinarity is a practical way of dealing with complex issues that does not require any fundamental change in perception of reality by the universities. This need for dialogue across disciplines is becoming accepted.

On the other hand, strong transdisciplinarity presupposes a change from a mechanical to an organic worldview. Within an organic worldview reality can only be understood through holistic science, where disciplines are unclear. Strong transdisciplinarity is based on a holistic approach to reality, which includes a spiritual dimension consisting of, among other things, emotion, imagination and intuition. In this context, Max-Neef refers to Goethe's philosophy of science, where observation consists of both rational and relational aspects of reality. Max-Neef argues that universities must take a leading position in the change process toward strong transdisciplinarity, and has pointed out that the change is underway at several academic institutions.

Problem understanding

Today, the increase in man-made climate change has consequences for people and ecosystems in a large part of the globe. We are beginning to notice a shortage of vital natural resources used in the production of key welfare commodities. This applies not only to cheap fossil energy but also fresh water, forests, fish stocks, soil and various metals. The speculative financial economy which today is fifty times bigger than the real economy brings with it many problems. According to Max-Neef, the problems are to a large extent caused by the dominant economic paradigm based on economic growth at any cost.

Another explanation for the accelerating overconsumption of natural resources is the assumption that increasing consumption leads to increased human happiness. The prevalence of the consumption culture has led to reduction in the austerity values inherent in most traditional cultures. Such values are often based on an understanding of the relationship between man and nature. The prevalence of the consumption culture is that economy is more or less decoupled from nature's limits. The consequences include global warming leading to loss of productive land, storms, rising sea levels and desertification. Economic and social problems, especially in the poorest parts of the globe, generally increase with environmental problems.

When raw materials, including oil and gas, become more expensive, it creates major problems for the existing social structure. In many countries, according to Max-Neef, environmental problems have led to increasing corruption and the development of individual greed.

Max-Neef refers to a number of myths that do not apply in today's reality in order to explain the problems connected to the established economy.

Solutions

Max-Neef argues that the serious negative consequences caused by the fundamental imbalance between economic models and reality cannot be resolved within the established economic paradigm. It requires new economic models that accept limits to the use of natural resources. The economy must abandon the goal of the highest possible consumption level in favor of a goal of sufficient material wealth. In this way, Max-Neef states, it is possible to reduce the enormous differences between rich and poor. He argues that justice is a necessary precondition for peaceful development. In short we must replace greed, competition and growth with solidarity, cooperation and compassion. The challenge we face could be described as a question of how we can change course so that it becomes possible to reduce production and consumption without creating major social problems. Max-Neef summarizes the changes in five postulates for the new economy.

The threshold hypothesis

In every society there is a period when economic growth contributes to improved quality of life, but only up to a certain level, the threshold level, and after reaching this level continued economic growth leads to reduced quality of life. Max-Neef raised questions about how the economy should work up to

---

Box 9.1 Max-Neef rejects all the following myths

- Globalization is the only effective direction of development.
- Globalization of the economy benefits the poor.
- Ricardo's theory of comparative advantage provides the best solutions for the future.
- Globalization creates more jobs.
- The WTO is democratic and reliable.
- Globalization is inevitable.

Box 9.2 Postulates for the new economy

- The economy must serve people, it is not people who should serve the economy.
- Development is about people, not (physical) objects.
- Growth is not the same as development and development does not presuppose growth.
- All forms of economy presuppose vigorous ecosystems.
- Because the economy exists within the biosphere, which is a finite system, (exponential) growth impossible.

---

the threshold level and how it should work after reaching the threshold level. He gives the following answer: in poor countries, far below the threshold level, it is necessary to stimulate growth in production and consumption. After the threshold level, the negative side-effects of growth gradually become dominant so that a steady-state economy is the best solution. Max-Neef concludes that while the pre-threshold-level economy is focused on quantitative values, the post-threshold economy is focused on qualitative values.

Concluding remarks

We have to accept that we live on a finite planet and that we are required to develop an economy that unites zero growth with opportunities for high quality of life. Max-Neef refers to Boulding's statement that "Those who believe that economic growth can go on forever on a finite planet are either mad or are economists." Max-Neef concludes that no economic interests may be given priority over life itself. He goes a step further and argues that the economy must move from an anthropocentric to an eco-centric perspective so that solidarity, cooperation and compassion are extended to all forms of life.

WILLIAM REES

> Perhaps for the first time in human history, individual and national self-interest has converged with humanity's collective interests.
>
> William Rees

Introduction

William Rees is known for a well-founded criticism of established growth economy and original contributions in ecological economics and human ecology. However, he is probably best known for having co-developed the analytical tool, "ecological footprint."

Biography

William Rees (b. 1943) gained his PhD in population ecology at the University of Toronto in 1973. He has been a professor at the University of British Columbia (UBC) since 1969. During the 1990s Rees was director of the School of Community and Regional Planning at UBC. He has also been president of the Canadian Society for Ecological Economics. Rees was an important contributor in the Global Integrity Project. Rees has received several international awards for his extensive research, including the Senior Killam Research Prize (1997), Trudeau Fellowship Prize (2007) and the Blue Planet Prize (2012). Rees' research has resulted in over 130 scientific publications and many articles in the general press.

Worldview

Despite the fact that the globalized economy is in the process of draining the Earth's natural resources, economists working with the established paradigm, according to Rees, are still not willing to revise their abstract models, which have no grounding in ecological realities. Rees explains the lack of comprehensive understanding by referring to Descartes' dualistic philosophy and Newton's mechanical worldview. Today we can observe the negative consequences of economic activity that exceeds the ecosystem's source and sink capacity.

To make a necessary change toward a sustainable society we must free ourselves from habitual frameworks of understanding and become aware of the biophysical and cultural conditions for economics. Rees states that a transition toward an organic worldview is required to solve the environmental challenges we face today.

Ecological footprint

In *Our Ecological Footprint: Reducing Human Impact on the Earth* (1996), Rees and Wackernagel present a method to calculate the size of the ecosystem required to produce the resources and assimilate the waste that stems from a specific level of consumption in a population. The ecological footprint depends on four factors: population size, material standard of living, ecosystem productivity and efficiency in the exploitation of natural resources. Calculations show that the average footprint for the Earth's population is approximately 2.7 gha (global average hectares) per person, while the available acreage is about 1.7 gha. In other words, we are using far too many resources in modern consumption-focused societies.

The current huge overuse of natural resources must come to an end. In addition the analysis uncovers huge differences between the "richest" countries, with more than 8 gha, and the "poorest" countries, with much less than 1 gha. Today, the "ecological footprint" method is the accepted approach to measuring the conflict between economy and ecology and it is widely used by governments in many countries, NGOs and researchers in various fields of science.

Memes and paradigms

Rees points out that the context of understanding (paradigm) used in, for example, economic theory and practice is culturally determined. It consists of assumptions about how reality is constructed and functions, in addition to values and norms, for social interaction. The paradigmatic preconditions determine to a large extent what we look for, what contexts are used for interpretation and which methods are accepted as valid for scientific research. Because it does not fit the established paradigm, new knowledge, showing that the established economy is on a collision course with the ecological framework, is overlooked by economists and politicians.

To explain how the current dominant paradigm has evolved Rees refers to Dawkins' theory of "memes." Memes function as carriers of cultural information, attitudes, values and behavior patterns. The information is transmitted (unconsciously) from generation to generation. Reason and intelligence have little impact on this process. A paradigm is composed of various memes. Such complexes of memes have a major impact on human interpretation of information and behavior.

According to Rees, problems connected to environment and poverty can be explained by reference to meme complexes leading to ego-centered utility

$EF = P + SL + EP + TE$

EF = Ecological footprints
P = Population size
SL = Standard of living
EP = Ecosystem productivity
TE = Technological efficiency

Figure 9.2 Ecological footprints

maximization materialized by the goals of growth in production and consumption. To deal with the environmental challenges, it is therefore necessary to change the meme complexes through increased awareness of the underlying assumptions influencing our more or less unconscious behavior.

Paradigm shift

Rees states that the ecosystems can be considered a complex of self-organizing nexus. The ecosystems consist of integrated interaction between millions of different forms of life. Humans are integral parts of the ecosystems. A consequence of transition toward an organic worldview is that the economy must adapt to ecological limits and principles. The idea that research should come up with knowledge that gives human beings power over nature must therefore be replaced by a new approach to science. The aim should be to develop knowledge that teaches us how we can adapt to the principles found in nature. The consequence of accepting this paradigm shift is revolutionary: nature is superior to the economy – not vice versa.

Rees questions the established positive correlation between increase of production and consumption and improved welfare. He refers to research showing that high levels of welfare include more than access to material goods. Prosperity is also dependent on a vigorous nature, stable societies, safe communities, social justice, belonging and many other social and spiritual qualities.

Green economy

Rees reasons that a green economy has scarcely helped to solve the major environmental challenges we face in today's global society. Instead, green economy has contributed to concealing the real problems behind a veil of green words and concepts (e.g. green marketing or green growth). He also argues that the green economy in many cases has reinforced environmental problems. The explanation is that "green" efficiency measures release resources that lead to an increase in the overall consumption of natural resources. Rees also doubts that it is possible to create sustainable economic growth through technological innovations such as hybrid cars, green buildings and green consumption. According to Rees, every increase in consumption represents a reinforcement of the environmental problems. He uses the load capacity of a boat as example. If the load capacity is exceeded the boat will sink when it meets severe weather, regardless of whether the load is conventionally produced goods or "green" products.

Ecological economics

To achieve the objectives of sustainable ecosystems and equitable distribution of resources, deep changes are required, according to Rees. When the mechanistic paradigm is replaced by concepts, theories and models that are rooted in an organic worldview the consequences for economic understanding

and action are massive. The change entails a change from atomistic competition toward emphasis on network-based cooperative solutions. Rees points
out that "green cities" are impossible as long as the population is dependent
on capital goods and services from outside (external networks) in conflict with
ecological and humanistic values.

Ecological economics is dynamic and assumes continuous development
without increased consumption of natural resources. Development dictates
that companies and entire industries disappear and new ones, more consistent
with ecological principles, take over.

The major changes needed to implement ecological economics in practical reality is, according to Rees, a transition from competition to cooperation; from ego-centered utility maximization to generosity; and from
focus on materialistic consumption to quality of life. To reach these goals
politicians must show vigor and courage in the process of implementing
well-functioning networks based on mutually binding cooperation. Rees
believes such a change is possible because, for the first time in history; it is
obvious that individual self-interest coincides with humanity's long-term
collective interests.

Concluding remarks

Rees uses the results from ecological footprint analyses as a strong argument for a forthcoming paradigm shift in economics. Greening the economy
with tools in the mechanistic ideology is not only inadequate, it is a danger,
because it hides the real problems behind a green-washed vocabulary. To
explain the stability in attitudes and values in a culture, Rees refers to memes.
Information is transferred from generation to generation through memes.
What we need is a deep cultural change toward cooperation, generosity and
quality of life in place of competition, egocentricity and materialism.

10 Institutions, law and money

In this chapter I focus on the contributions from Ross Jackson (Canada, Denmark), who focuses on institutional change; Polly Higgins (Scotland), who argues for the necessity of new laws; Margrit Kennedy (Germany), who is a representative of new monetary systems; Bernard Lietaer (Belgium), who argues that it is time to rethink money; and Malcolm Torry (England), who gives reasons for a general implementation of citizen's income.

These five contributors argue, based on practical experience that we have to make changes on a deeper level if we are to solve the global crises concerning social and environmental breakdown. Their contribution is to establish a global network of decentralized societies. To succeed in the change process, we have to develop interconnected small communities (eco-villages), each with its own complementary local currency. In addition, to prevent ecocide, strict international regulations are required.

ROSS JACKSON

The current global structure is dysfunctional, undemocratic, corrupt and exploitative of the environment, the developing countries and even the citizens of the wealthiest nations.

Ross Jackson

Introduction

Ross Jackson announces a new economy based on an exciting combination of experiences from the international financial world and spiritual experiences with Indian gurus and Western mystics. He gives a thorough analysis of the shortcomings of neo-liberal economics combined with visionary solutions based on the experiences of the establishment and development of networks of eco-villages worldwide.

Biography

Ross Jackson was born in Canada in 1938, he moved to Denmark in 1964 and became a Danish citizen in 1972. He holds a master's in industrial management from Purdue University and he was awarded a PhD in operations research at Case Western University (USA). In 1966 Jackson established a consultancy in collaboration with Peter Pruzan. Jackson has long and varied experience of international finance and of various NGOs. Of particular interest is his involvement (as chairman) in Gaia Trust, an organization that aims to contribute to a sustainable and spiritual world. He is also active within the Global Ecovillage Network.

A road map for reform

Jackson's contribution to the development of a new economy is based on experience from international finance coupled with involvement in several NGOs focusing on environmental responsibility, human rights and social welfare. After several years as a leader in international finance, Jackson concluded that the neo-liberal economic system had so many inherent weaknesses that it had to be replaced by a new economy based on ecological principles. Recognizing that the neo-liberal economy was about to extinguish both the natural environment and social communities around the world was a powerful stimulus to Jackson, who increased his efforts to develop and implement ecological economics locally, nationally and globally.

In recent years, environmental responsibility and spirituality have dominated Jackson's field of interest. He has published three books that show a profound understanding of the problem and an exceptional ability to think comprehensively in finding practical solutions. In his first book, *Kali Yuga Odyssey: A Spiritual Journey* (2000), he describes and explains his own spiritual journey visiting Indian gurus and Western mystics. In his second book, *And We ARE Doing It: Building an Ecovillage Future* (2000), Jackson gives an insightful picture of how ecological economics could be rooted in a network of eco-villages. To fund these projects he established a finance institution, Gaia Trust. The third book, *Occupy World Street: A Road Map for Radical Economic and Political Reform* (2012), is a detailed description of how problems can be solved through development of decentralized communities combined with new institutions for international cooperation.

A spiritual journey

Jackson was searching for alternative explanations for the increasingly serious conflict between economy and natural and cultural environments. His interest stretched from Grof's transpersonal psychology to the Indian guru Swami Muktanda. He was in contact with clairvoyants in London and members of the New Age movement in the eco-village at The Park within the Findhorn

Community in Scotland. The inspiration from the Christian mystic Daskalos and the Indian spiritual leader Sai Baba should also be taken into account to show Jackson's openness to new explanations of relationships and meaning. His spiritual experiences led him into conflict with prevailing mechanistic scientific explanatory models. Efforts to incorporate spiritual insights in economics and environmentally responsible business leadership culminated with the creation of Gaia Trust in 1987. The foundation was intended to support people and projects that helped to develop communities in a sustainable direction.

Eco-villages

Jackson's combination of global finance and Gaia Trust represents an impressive balancing act. It is not unusual that profit-maximizing financiers use a portion of the profits on philanthropic projects to decorate the facade and to contribute to positive reputation building. Jackson differs from this dominant trend and instead uses financial institutions to create social change.

Jackson criticizes neo-liberal economics for prioritizing short-term profits at the expense of environmental and social responsibility. He is concerned that the cost of such a destructive economy will be pushed over onto society and future generations. Institutions such as the WTO and the World Bank actively promote an environmentally destructive and unjust economic order. The solution, according to Jackson, is, ironically, a new protectionism, that is, to protect people and nature against the consequences of globalized free trade.

The best way to establish viable communities within the framework of sustainable nature is to initiate change in the direction of decentralized eco-villages. Based on experience with the creation and development of eco-villages (many with support from Gaia Trust) worldwide, Jackson gives a realistic representation of the challenges that must be overcome on the way to creating a global network of eco-villages.

The Gaian world order

In *Occupy World Street* Jackson presents a proposal for how "the Gaian world order" could be implemented by establishing new economic and political institutions. He mentions eight global institutions that are all rooted in the requirement that ecological sustainability is superior to all other objectives. The new institutions would replace, among others, the World Trade Organization, the World Bank and the International Monetary Fund, all of which are fine servants of neo-liberal ideals. In addition, it is necessary to establish a collaborative network of smaller, self-controlled, independent states that are rooted in a fundamental responsibility for nature. To get started with the process it is necessary to establish a Gaian League consisting of small nations who are willing to go ahead to show the way. Jackson suggests a combination of top-down changes through the establishment of international institutions and bottom-up initiatives driven by engaged and motivated people in various NGOs. Change processes are driven by establishing dialogue-based integrated and collaborative networks at different levels. The alternative to success with the Gaian world order is, according to Jackson, disaster: the collapse of ecological and social systems through overloading ecosystems, overpopulation, extinction of plant and animal species and a dramatic reduction in access to natural resources, including oil and gas.

Ecological economics

According to Jackson, the relationship between economy and ecology is turned upside-down within the Gaian world order. The economy is still an instrument for the most efficient use of resources but always within nature's source and sink capacity. Business leaders have a personal responsibility to address social interests in the broad sense. The goal of economic activity is to contribute to quality of life and well-being, rather than growth in production and consumption. Jackson mentions seven main areas of ecological economics that are particularly important, shown in Box 10.1.

Concluding remarks

The main challenge today is to implement measures that help to realize ecological economics within the Gaian world order. Ecological sustainability and respect for human rights have absolute priority over the values that dominate the current neo-liberal economic system, such as economic growth, competition and productivity. If we fail to initiate such a process of transformation the result could well be that "we may not survive." So, the choice should be easy. According to Jackson: "a bold initiative is necessary to shake up the

---

Box 10.1 Areas of change

- The total consumption of natural resources must be kept within critical levels.
- More emphasis is needed on development (quality of life) than growth (in consumption).
- Strong sustainability implies that natural values cannot be replaced by human-made capital.
- Transition from goods to services does not solve problems related to overuse of resources (can expose problems).
- All economic activity depends on access to natural capital.
- International agreements set limits for the use of natural capital.
- Management based on a combination of bottom-up (personal responsibility) and top-down principles (international treaties).

logjam that is preventing global solutions from emerging in our contemporary world" (Jackson 2012, p. 297).

POLLY HIGGINS

> Corporations are the ones gambling our planet away and our Governments are running the casino – they are taking huge risks on our planet's future.
>
> Polly Higgins

Introduction

Polly Higgins states that the introduction of laws that criminalize all forms of environmental hostile practices (ecocide) is an effective tool for solving many of the serious challenges facing the world community.

Biography

Polly Higgins was born in Scotland in 1968. After studying law in London she practiced as a lawyer for many years. Higgins is well known for her efforts to introduce international laws and regulations that protect ecosystems against all forms of environmentally harmful activities. She has presented "The Universal Declaration of the Rights of Mother Earth" in the UN, where it is determined that the Earth is a living organism that is entitled to legal protection. She has received several international awards (including The Planet's Lawyer 2010 and Campaigner of the Year 2012) for her strong commitment to the protection of the environment. Her two books, *Eradicating Ecocide: Exposing the Corporate and Political Practices Destroying the Planet and Proposing the Laws Needed to Eradicate Ecocide* (2010) and *Earth is Our Business – Changing the Rules of the Game* (2012), have been very well received. *Eradicating Ecocide* was awarded The People's Book Prize in 2011.

Legislation

Higgins' strong environmental commitment stems from meeting, as a young student, the multitalented Austrian architect and ecologist Friedensreich Hundertwasser. He was a committed environmentalist, arguing that the ecosystems are integrated networks consisting of innumerable forms of life. He explains the serious environmental problems we are facing today by referring to our civilization's abstract idea about the Earth as a lifeless economic resource. To solve environmental challenges, it is, according to Hundertwasser, necessary to treat the Earth's ecosystems with respect and dignity.

Inspired by Hundertwasser's ideas, Higgins has drafted a world declaration to safeguard nature's rights. To ensure that we care for all life on the planet the legislation is based on an eco-centric worldview – that law should prevent actions that are harmful to animals, humans and ecosystems in a global, long-term perspective.

Ecocide

Through her work as lawyer Higgins became aware that legal regulations have great influence on human behavior. The law influences our mind-set and governs our behavior (Higgins 2010, p. 152). International law can thus help to change the consciousness of business leaders and politicians. By introducing strict environmental laws, she laid the foundation for a new practice that prevents ecocide.

Higgins defines ecocide as destruction, damage to, or loss of ecosystems resilience within a given territory, to such an extent that the living conditions for human beings are greatly reduced. In this way, she links "wellbeing of the ecology of our planet" to human quality of life (Higgins 2010, p. xii). According to Higgins, ecocide symbolizes the antithesis of life because it causes irreversible damage to ecosystems that weaken nature's resilience. In addition, ecocide has become a major cause of war and human suffering. She concludes that ecocide is a crime against humanity. Today we see clearly that the struggle for limited resources can develop into war and there is evidence of this in many different parts of the Earth. Through new and radical international law, which would see environmentally hostile acts as criminal acts, it would be possible to influence multinational companies in various industries, such as energy, mining, agriculture and forestry, to change current practices in a more environmentally responsible and peacemaking direction.

Personal responsibility

An important point in Higgins' argument is that people, not businesses, are legal actors and they are the ones to be made responsible and judged for ecocide. It should not be possible for managers and directors to hide behind impersonal organizations by accepting large fines paid by the company for environmental crimes for which they themselves are responsible. Higgins points out that today it is not difficult for managers in large companies to avoid personal prosecution because responsibility is untraceable through complicated organizational structures.

By linking responsibility directly to specific actions, it should be impossible to avoid punishment by referring to lack of knowledge about the consequences. If there is uncertainty about the environmental impact of different measures, the precautionary principle should be followed. The requirement to follow the principle should be stricter in cases where uncertainty is high or where the negative impacts are believed to be large. The precautionary principle refers to reverse burden of proof, that is, it is the person performing the action who must prove that it has no negative impact on the social or natural environment.

A law prohibiting ecocide can also be used to prosecute "climate deniers," that is, people and organizations that distort scientific facts so that politicians and leaders in business and public administration are led to downgrade action that prevents climate change.

Preventing

Higgins notes that the focus must be "upstream," that is, the goal is to eliminate the causes of environmental problems that arise, not to reduce the negative symptoms of environmentally hostile activities ("downstream"). Because the quality of human life depends on vigorous ecosystems protection, nature must always be given the highest priority. The consequence is that current policies have to be turned upside-down so that the economy becomes the servant of nature and not the master of nature.

An important instrument in such a turnaround is to adopt stricter legislation for banking, particularly in relation to decisions that determine which projects banks should finance. The World Bank has developed criteria for dividing candidates into category A projects, which have serious negative environmental impacts, category B projects, which have moderate effects, and category C projects, which have positive environmental impacts. Through legislation, banks are forced to avoid projects in category A and increasingly prioritize category C projects. "Creation of the Law of Ecocide will close the door to investment in high-risk ventures which give rise to ecocide" (Higgins 2012, p. 5). Stricter regulation of the financial sector in general will be an effective measure to influence corporate social investment strategies.

Structural changes

To protect the environment against irresponsible economic activity it is not sufficient to use traditional instruments such as injunctions or prohibitions and subsidies and fees. Higgins believes that stricter international environmental legislation is needed to change the structural framework.

The new laws must include clauses that stipulate that the Earth cannot be owned by private companies, those faceless entities that claim to have the right to destroy ecosystems. As it is today, companies can manage their own properties under short-term profitability considerations although the long-term damaging effects on ecosystems are disastrous.

Concluding remarks

To conserve viable ecosystems, Higgins states that global society needs laws that provide economic development based on creative collaboration and awareness of interdependence between human beings and the ecosystems. She claims that the implementation of the "Law of Ecocide" will be a powerful tool to expand our collective consciousness. Meanwhile, she warns against legislation which intends to reduce negative symptoms rather than ban environmentally harmful activities. She claims that symptom suppression measures often lead to situations where "the problem continues, often in time worsening" (Higgins 2010, p. xiv). Radical legislation is the most effective instrument for fundamental changes. Through her efforts, Higgins helped to give the term ecocide a practically relevant legal content.

MARGRIT KENNEDY

> Our monetary system currently allows us only the choice between two types of collapse: social or ecological.
>
> Margrit Kennedy

Introduction

Margrit Kennedy was for over thirty years an outspoken, engaged and influential critic of the prevailing globalized economic system. She argues that the current monetary system leads to serious social and ecological crises. The main problem is an interest system that stimulates exponential growth and inflation. To deal with the challenges it is necessary to decentralize financial institutions and introduce local currencies.

Biography

Margrit Kennedy (1939–2013) trained as an architect at the Technical University in Darmstadt. She continued with a master's in urban and regional planning (1972). In 1979 she was awarded her PhD in public and international affairs by the University of Pittsburgh in Pennsylvania.

Kennedy worked internationally in various research projects administered by OECD and UNESCO. She worked as urban planner and ecologist in Germany, Nigeria, Scotland and the USA. In the period 1984–1985, she was visiting professor in urban ecology at the University of Kassel. In 1991 she was appointed full professor of architecture (ecological building technology) at the Universität Hannover.

She is acknowledged as an active and influential commentator and critic of established interests and monetary policy. She believed it was necessary to reform the national and international monetary system by allowing for increased use of local currencies. Kennedy's most influential books in these topics are *Interest and Inflation-Free Money* (1987) and *Occupy Money* (2012).

The money system

Money has a prominent role in all forms of economic activities. The economy measures values in terms of money in the same way that physics uses kilograms and meters. According to Kennedy, economists rarely question the way the monetary system works. She points to a number of problems related to the fact that money, unlike kilograms and meters, does not represent a stable measure; monetary value varies more or less daily.

Kennedy shows that money is not only conducive to growth and development, it also leads to a number of serious problems, nationally and internationally. As examples she mentions that unemployment and environmental degradation are related to how the monetary system is designed and works. The principle of interest and compound interest is the direct cause of the world's poorest countries being in bottomless debt. Kennedy refers to the economist John L. King, who argues that the current monetary system is the free-market economy's invisible "wrecking machine." She worked to find ways to change this mechanism in a sustainable direction so that the effects are positive for the individual, society and the environment. She questions whether we are able to change the system before the next major breakdown occurs, or if the first change will happen after the current system has collapsed. The challenge is to develop a sustainable monetary system that helps us to find solutions instead of steering us in the wrong direction.

Four myths about the current monetary system

Money is one of the most ingenious inventions to facilitate the exchange of goods and services between people, regions and countries. Money creates the possibility for specialization and division of labor, which is important in order to increase efficiency and quality in the production of goods and services. The problem is that money also has the opposite effects: it prevents barter because it accumulates in people and businesses that have (too) much in advance. The explanation is that those who have (too) little need to pay a fee to those who own capital and thus increase the differences between rich and poor, nationally and internationally.

Kennedy points out that there are a whole lot of myths connected to money which are difficult to dispel. She mentions four myths (misunderstandings) which make it difficult to gain support for a paradigmatic shift of the monetary system.

1 There is only one type of growth

In today's economy, exponential growth, that is, something grows slowly in the beginning and then accelerates faster and finally grows in an almost vertical fashion, has been established as an indisputable truth within the current economic system. Kennedy points out that exponential growth necessarily leads

---

Box 10.2 Four myths about the economy

- There is only one type of growth.
- We pay interest only if we borrow money.
- In the present monetary system, we are all equally affected by interest.
- Inflation is an integral part of free-market economies.

---

to crisis in the economy. To avoid, or rather postpone, crises the economy must grow even faster, while the principle of interest and compound interest stimulates an almost unrestrained growth spiral.

According to Kennedy, a healthy economy must be rooted in natural growth. Natural growth represents the normal growth pattern found in nature (e.g. humans, animals and plants) in which everything stops growing at an optimal size. Kennedy points out that natural growth is not consistent with the current monetary system and therefore it is necessary to develop a monetary system that conforms to the natural growth curve.

2   We pay interest only if we borrow money

Most people think that they can avoid paying interest if they do not borrow money from the bank. "If we want to avoid paying interest, all we need to do is avoid borrowing money" (Kennedy 1995, p. 8). This is not correct, according to Kennedy, because interest is included in every price we pay. The higher the capital share in an industry, the higher the proportion of the price of products is interest and compound interest. On average, she claims that people in Germany pay approximately 45 percent interest on the prices at which they buy.

3   In the present monetary system, we are all equally affected by interest

This myth is based on the notion that since everyone must pay capital costs for the products we buy all are affected equally and thus it is fair. However, when we take a closer look there are huge differences. In practice, the system works in a way that transfers money from a large majority (the poorest portion of the population) to a small minority (the richest proportion of the population). As an example she mentions that workers transfer approximately 1 billion euros a day to those who can make their money work for them. This illustrates one of the least understood reasons why the gap between rich and poor keeps on increasing.

4   Inflation is an integral part of free-market economies

For many economists and politicians, inflation is perceived as a necessity, inherent in the market economy. According to Kennedy, inflation is caused by situations where the gap between income and debt increases. Inflation, a kind of tax, is a means to compensate for the increasing gap. The greater the debt burden is, the higher the inflation needed to avoid or at least postpone the crisis.

Creating interest and inflation-free money

If we do not succeed in changing the monetary system in a sustainable direction we will face a choice between two types of breakdown, social or ecological. To solve problems connected to an increase in debt within the current economic system, one solution is to stimulate growth. But growth leads into a vicious cycle that reinforces environmental problems dramatically. "Far too few of us are aware of how the structural defects in the monetary system undermine our lives" (Kennedy 2012, p. 5).

That the financial industry does everything it can to maintain "status quo" is, according to Kennedy, not surprising because it lives well within the current monetary system, where frequent changes in monetary value allow speculators to make quick money. Kennedy concludes that "those wealthy few are the ones keeping us from changing the system" (Kennedy 2012, p. 24)

To solve these problems, Kennedy outlines two strategies, one within the current system and one that requires fundamental changes on a systemic level. Without changing the system, banks can reduce interest rates to a minimum. To make profits they introduce new forms of fees and charges. As an example of fundamental change she suggests a system where money is differentiated and adapted for different purposes. By introducing complementary money, based on different principles, the resilience in the economic system will increase as a result of diversity. The new money concept should not aim to multiply profits. Instead it should focus on ecological, social and cultural benefits. The overarching objective is to stimulate qualitative growth, for example, growth in knowledge and skills. A living society depends on viable processes initiating qualitative development.

Regional currency

Kennedy claims that one of the most promising shifts is toward a decentralized money system. Regional currency helps to retain capital in local communities since money can only be used to purchase goods and services produced in the region. She also points out that most products we use on a daily basis, for example food, water, waste, energy, education and health care, will be cheaper and more sustainable if they are produced and traded locally. The explanation is partly due to reduced transport costs and more personal contact between the economic actors. Important repercussions are the establishment of dynamic networks of subcontractors. Regional currency not only helps to strengthen the region's economy, it also helps to develop people's identity and sense of belonging to their community. In this way, regional currency establishes a semipermeable protective "membrane" between the region and the world, which makes society less vulnerable to international fluctuations and crises.

To overcome the deep crises in the economy and the financial system it is necessary to establish collaborative integrated networks of local initiatives. Regional currency initiatives alone will not be enough. We need a transition process in which the creative power of money is transferred to decentralized networks of institutions that will "use this power to benefit society, thereby ending the domination of our compulsive, boundless expansion of money and debt" (Kennedy 2012, p. 88).

Concluding remarks

According to Kennedy, a sustainable monetary system presupposes that the prices of goods and services tell the ecological truth about products, so that we become aware of the impact our lifestyles have for future generations. Decentralization and the establishment of networks of smaller economic units contribute to making the economy more democratic and open. She mentions a number of advantages that are associated with the decentralization of monetary systems: focus on real value instead of "paper profit," money cannot be used for speculation, exponential growth is not stimulated because interest rates are removed and, of great importance, everyone understands how the system works.

Kennedy argues that the time is ripe to initiate processes that will ensure that the established monetary system is replaced with a new system that puts people before profits. We must realize that the function of money must be restricted to being a value standard for exchange of goods, not for financial speculation. In her book *Occupy Money* she points out that the creation of a stable monetary system that reflects real values will be for the benefit of all. "The time has come for the systematic adoption of sustainable money. Let's get moving" (Kennedy 2012, p. 93)

BERNARD LIETAER

Revising our monetary systems through the inclusion of cooperative currencies fosters the possibility of building a better world, one to enjoy now and one worthy of bequeathing to future generations.

Bernard Lietaer

Introduction

Bernard Lietaer questions why prolonged and vigorous efforts by national and international organizations, major business investment and agreements at a high political level have scarcely been able to handle the increasing problems associated with unemployment, environmental degradation and societal breakdown. Lietaer identifies that the explanation may be that we have not drawn attention to the real problems. He refers to Bateson, who summed up the current debacle by saying "The source of all our problems today comes from the gap between how we think and how nature works" (Lietaer and Dunne 2013, p. 32). Many of the challenges require changes in the monetary system: "It's time to rethink money" (Lietaer and Dunne 2013, p. 1).

Biography

Bernard Lietaer was born in 1942 in Belgium. He studied engineering at the Catholic University of Leuven, where he later became professor of international finance. He holds an MBA from MIT and he had a position at the Center for Sustainable Resources at the University of California, Berkeley. From 2003 to 2006 he was visiting scholar at Naropa University (USA).

Lietaer is the author (and co-author) of numerous books on economics, money and complementary currency. Lietaer has extensive experience of work with monetary systems in the EU and various developing countries. He has also been a consultant to several multinational companies.

The monetary system

Despite significant technological breakthroughs in several areas and serious efforts in public and private sectors, the challenges related to the economy, environment and society have grown both in scope and severity over the last decades. According to Lietaer many of the most pressing problems are connected to a monetary system which is not in accordance with the tasks in today's society. He maintains that there must be drastic changes to solve the problems: "It's not good enough to just simply think outside the box anymore. We need to throw the box away and think in an entirely different way" (Lietaer and Dunne 2013, p. 221). In other words, it is not possible to find sustainable solutions before the real causes are uncovered. Measures that reduce symptoms within the established monetary system are not sufficient; deeper change is required.

To understand the challenges, Lietaer claims that insight into how monetary systems and complementary currencies work help to develop the necessary new solutions. Lietaer defines money as an agreement between people within a social community to use "something" as a symbolic means of exchange. Hence, money is not a thing but a mutually binding agreement. The introduction of complementary currencies is necessary to create viable communities and regions. An important purpose of the introduction of complementary currency is to link the connection between unused (human) resources and unfulfilled needs. He uses the term complementary rather than alternative to stress that the goal is diversity, not a new, alternative system.

The potential of money

Lietaer interprets money from a systems perspective because "systems take into account a broader, more comprehensive arena than economics does; it integrates not only economic interactions but also their most important side effects" (Lietaer 2001). He describes how money exceeds the economy's domain and affects the interaction between people, nature and culture. One consequence of the flow of money through most parts of the community is that people have the potential not only to secure a viable economy, but also to create a lot of suffering and distress. In this context he refers to Francis Bacon's well-known statement: "Money is like manure; it's not worth a thing unless it's spread around."

Using this analogy, we can conclude that the existing monetary system that leads to an increasing gap between rich and poor must change. When manure (money) is concentrated in small areas and is absent elsewhere, the harvest will be far from optimal. Instead of stimulating unsustainable and unfairly distributed wealth through competition, the monetary system should contribute to sustainable and fair economic development through cooperation.

The function of money

To understand the strengths and weaknesses inherent in the dominant monetary system it is necessary to examine the functions of money. Money fulfills a number of different tasks, only two of which are essential.

In addition, money has become a commodity in itself, which increasingly encourages speculation and hoarding. Today, more than 95 percent of all foreign exchange transactions in the world are motivated by opportunities for big gains through speculation. Less than 5 percent is related to trade in goods and services. The established monetary system allows for the commercialization of increasingly larger portions of nature and culture. The result is that nature and culture have lost their intrinsic value and are divided up into pieces that are sold on the market as atomized commodities.

Lietaer also highlights the challenges posed by the established monetary system, which is extremely vulnerable because it is characterized by uniformity and monoculture. In most countries, there is only one accepted currency. Money, or lack of money, is a not-insignificant part of our lives. However, it

---

Box 10.3 The function of money

- A standard of measure. We compare the value of different commodities by expressing each of them on a monetary scale.
- A medium of exchange that is more efficient than older forms, barter for instance.

is not just the lack of money that prevents us from taking up and finding solutions to current challenges. The problems are caused largely because money has a one-dimensional functionality.

Monetary systems' efficiency and vitality

According to Lietaer, the objective is to develop an economy that is balanced between efficiency and resilience. Efficiency refers to the ability of the system to process volumes of whatever flows through it per unit of time, "in an organized, streamlined manner" (Lietaer and Dunne 2013, p. 32). Resilience refers to the extent to which the system is able to cope with changes in the environment while preserving its integrity. Efficiency and resilience depend on the structural characteristics of the system, diversity and interconnectivity. On the one hand, increasing diversity and interconnectivity leads to a strengthening of the system's resilience and thus the ability to adapt to change and various forms of external fluctuations. On the other hand, uniformity and simplicity strengthens the system's efficiency, that is, the ability to process ever more.

Unlike nature, where sustainable ecosystems are balanced between efficiency and resilience, the established economy has a one-dimensional focus on efficiency. Thus, the economy is extremely vulnerable to changes in external influences. Lietaer points out that "Too much efficiency leads to brittleness and fragility, and too much resilience leads to stagnation" (Lietaer and Dunne 2013, p. 62). The introduction of complementary monetary systems helps to develop resilient and effective communities that are able to deal with environmental and social challenges without collapsing.

Although most of the initiatives Lietaer describes are small scale, he argues that they will grow in scope and importance. The different initiatives are like seeds, which will flourish given good conditions. They have the potential to provide effective and resilient solutions with which conditions for human beings and ecosystems may improve radically. If allowed to grow, they will constitute a significant contribution to efforts to devise effective solutions to the challenges we have to deal with in the years ahead.

Box 10.4 Monetary ecosystem

- A global reference currency
- Three main multinational currencies
- Some private international scrip
- Scores of national currencies
- Dozens of regional currencies
- A multitude of local cooperative currencies
- A wide variety of functional currencies

Toward a multitiered monetary ecosystem

Lietaer argues that a monetary system based on diversity and interconnectivity fosters the possibility of building a better world. The most important characteristic of a monetary system based on ecological inspiration is a balance between competition and cooperation. Lietaer gives some idea of how such a multitiered monetary system would look (Lietaer and Dunne 2013, p. 199). Lietaer makes it clear that individuals and businesses do not take part on all levels, they participate in only a few of these systems.

Change is possible

By introducing complementary currency designed specially to encourage collaboration on long-term solutions that benefit the economy, nature and society, it is, according to Lietaer, possible to change the trend. Such an alteration can be completed because short-term thinking is not tied to human nature. It is imposed by a monetary system that focuses exclusively on growth and short-term profits.

Lietaer points out that the established monetary systems are inadequate because they are based on nationalism, competition and endless growth. Even if many attempts at money reform have proved difficult in the past, he believes there are several reasons why the current monetary initiatives have a better chance of success than ever before. Lietaer makes it clear that the change will not be initiated by politicians and business leaders (top-down), the process is catalyzed by bottom-up creativities: "ordinary people who are jumping outside the prescribed boundaries and simply rethinking and reengineering their money" (Lietaer and Dunne 2013, p. 204). He justifies his optimism in the following conditions (Lietaer 2001):

- A number of communities and regions have already introduced complementary currencies without attacking the official monetary system.
- Introduction of complementary currencies has already proven to be capable of addressing breakdowns of a new nature to which no solutions have been forthcoming within the conventional monetary system.
- The availability of information technologies has made it easier to implement new currencies. Increased use of information technology has also made it possible to democratize the established monetary systems.

According to Lietaer, more than 1,900 communities across the world use local currencies, independent of the national monetary system. While some communities, such as Ithaca, New York, use paper money; others in such places as Canada, Australia, Britain and France make use of electronic money. In Japan there are more than 300 private currencies used to pay for, among other commodities, social services. Time units are often used as a method of payment. In societies where money is scarce, time money has helped to create economic activity based on bottom-up initiative and creativity. Lietaer considers societies based on a multitude of complementary currencies to have great opportunities to develop a viable economy in harmonious interaction with nature and culture. Cooperative currencies allow ordinary people to make an amazing difference in their own local communities and in their own individual lives.

Complementary currencies

Time dollars (USA) and time banks (UK) are used in different states in the USA and in Britain to stimulate the local economy. The idea is that everybody, independent of their physical and psychical condition, has some service to contribute to the local community. It is a cooperative currency system that "allows transactions to occur that would likely not otherwise take place and provides a means by which to acknowledge and honour contributions and skills of people, matching their offerings with the needs of their community" (Lietaer and Dunne 2013, p. 79). Time-dollar transactions have proved to be an extraordinary tool for stimulating values such as reciprocity, trust, cooperation and co-production in a community. In addition, they are very democratic because everyone's time is valued the same. "A reflection of valuing everyone equally" (Lietaer and Dunne 2013, p. 79). Today, numerous time-dollar networks are active throughout the USA and the UK.

According to Lietaer, LETS (Local Economic Trading Systems) is the most widespread cooperative currency system in the world today. LETS were created in Canada as a debit and credit system, denominated in the national currency. The system was created to "facilitate much-needed trade within circuits in local neighbourhoods, villages and towns" (Lietaer and Dunne 2013, p. 76). Consumers wishing to purchase "cooking, driving, Web-designing, teaching English, or gardening" (Lietaer and Dunne 2013, p. 77) would simply phone in a transaction to a central coordinator and their LETS account would be debited and the seller's account credited. Currency is created by a simultaneous credit and debit in a transaction. Producers would then spend their credits with other members in the system. The system was essentially self-regulated, since members issue their own currency within the framework of their local community.

Concluding remarks

Lietaer states that even if we do not accept the (often unintended) consequences of our established monetary system, we must do something about it. Specifically, this means that we must create new arrangements for the change we want to take in local, national and international money systems. If we expect the challenges to find satisfactory solutions without our contribution, we will probably wait in vain. In his work Lietaer contributed to an expansion of consciousness that opens to see the opportunity to carry out changes in the monetary system that release creativity and human resources. According to Lietaer a cooperative local monetary system releases an important driving force behind social change. The introduction of new complementary currency systems will in the long term initiate self-reinforcing processes that promote balance between efficiency and resilience.

MALCOLM TORRY

The redistribution of income is always a redistribution of freedoms.

Malcolm Torry

Introduction

Malcolm Torry gives reasons for a general implementation of citizen's income (basic income). He argues, from different approaches, that citizen's income will make a substantial contribution to solving some of the main challenges in our societies, nationally and globally, such as the gap between rich and poor and unemployment. In addition, citizen's income will improve individual freedom. Torry concludes that a citizen's income for everyone will have a positive influence on the economy in general. Concerning practical implementation, he maintains that citizen's income is easy to manage and not very expensive to run.

Biography

Malcolm Torry has degrees in mathematics, theology, philosophy, social policy and economics and business management. He is senior visiting fellow in the Social Policy Department at the London School of Economics. In addition to being director of the Citizen's Income Trust, Torry is a Church of England priest. His publications include *Managing God's Business* (2005), *Bridgebuilders* (2010) and *Money for Everyone* (2013).

Citizen's income

Citizen's income means that the same amount of money is paid to everyone, independent of individual differences concerning social and economic status and personal conditions. This means that citizen's income is paid to each person, individually and unconditionally.

The growing attention to implementation of unconditional basic income as a right for everyone is first and foremost reasoned in ethical and social arguments. He claims that citizen's income is easy both to implement and to administer.

Torry elaborates on the potential social and economic advantages of introducing citizen's income. Citizen's income is defined as an unconditional income paid to every individual as a right connected to citizenship. He emphasizes that it is a right, not charity. Citizen's income "should be about strengthening compassion and rights, leaving pity and charity to individual consciences" (Torry 2013, p. xx).

The focal arguments refer to the ability to reduce inequality, increase individual freedom, expand social interrelations and improve the economic conditions for family life. In addition, citizen's income has positive influence on the economy in general and more specifically on the employment market. *Money for Everyone* represents an interesting and relevant contribution to the current debate concerning basic income and citizen's income in many countries all over the world. Basic income has influence on the local, national and global economy, the labor market and social trends.

Arguments for citizen's income

If citizen's income is discussed from scratch, without referring to the existing system, it is easy to agree on most of the principles Torry describes. The problem with our current system is that it is incoherent; the different parts are not harmoniously interconnected. The result is an unfair and inefficient system. In addition, it is confused, complex and expensive to administer. Torry argues that if we replace one system with another, some people would end up with more money and some with less.

He tries to avoid the common problem connected to our tendency to compare new ideas with what we do now, "as if somehow what we do now is normal and right, and what we might do [...] needs to pass the test that the current system passes, a test that might be irrational, irrelevant, or both" Torry 2013, p. 11). Instead of assuming that this is a problem with the new system, "it could equally mean that it is a problem with the present system and that the new system would offer a fairer distribution than the current one" (Torry 2013, p. 12).

A new system based on citizen's income would be easy to understand and it would be fair and resource-effective. Because of the secure income floor provided by the citizen's income, a much larger percentage of the population would be able to rise out of poverty. Society will be more cohesive and citizens are set free from bureaucratic intrusion. Some politicians and economists argue that if distribution of money were more equal and fair it would lead to a more efficient labor market and allow people more freedom to make choices about their employment patterns. At the individual level a secure income provides people with the chance to choose part-time work in addition to the basic income. Part-time work, often in combination with self-employment, is enough to top up their basic income. One consequence is work for more people, and reducing unemployment is important at a time when there is an increasing number of people and decreasing amounts of work due to, among other things, technological development.

Another consequence of less working time is more time for other activities. Individuals and families with enough money to provide a good standard of living will feel more secure and they can make choices to use more time for activities such as coaching a children's football team, going fishing or playing the guitar. By providing each one of us with a basic income, citizen's income would mean we were more productive, not lazier and "make more people more likely to be responsible citizens, with a greater sense of altruism and tolerance" (Torry 2013, p. xxii). Society as a whole would benefit, trust and solidarity would replace distrust and competition.

Arguments against citizen's income

The arguments against implementation of citizen's income vary depending on the choice of position from which the phenomenon is understood.

First, rich people don't need a basic income. Torry's comment is that there is no reason why the rich should not receive a citizen's income, because they are paying more than that in tax.

Second, we should not give people something for nothing. Torry's comment is that this is exactly what we are doing now in the existing system. We need, therefore, a change. Means-tested benefits often have a negative effect on employment.

Third, citizen's income is too expensive. How much citizen's income would cost depends on how the details in the system are arranged. If citizen's income is paid for by reducing tax allowances and means-tested and contributory benefits, then revenue neutrality would be possible.

Fourth, people would no longer work. According to, Torry people would be more likely to seek to increase their earned income if they were receiving citizen's income than they would be today if they were in receipt of in-work or out-of-work means-tested benefits.

Reflections on citizen's income

Torry refers to Wilkinson and Pickett's book *The Spirit Level*, in which they document that most social and health-related problems are worse in more unequal societies. Because citizen's income reduces the level of income inequality it will have positive influence on the level of welfare and quality of life.

Torry refers to Wittgenstein, who argued that no word has a univocal definition, and "poverty" is no exception. On the one hand, it is hard to draw a demarcation line, based on the level of income, between poor and rich. On the other hand, it is equally difficult to agree on basic human needs. The needs are related the concrete situation and individual and cultural differences. Torry concludes that it is hard to describe citizen's income in detail because it depends on the historical and geographical context.

Torry maintains that the question of injustice is closely connected to politics. The problem is that it seems as if a majority of the population do not want to reduce inequality. Since Rawls' theory of justice gives priority to the free market, it offers no real challenge to the current situation. According to Torry, citizen's income would be an efficient instrument to redistribute wealth and in so doing reduce injustice.

Concluding remarks

Torry's conclusion is that citizen's income is reasonable from different political positions. First, it represents a safety net, including everybody. Besides that, citizen's income will encourage individual freedom and social responsibility. Second, because more people would choose part-time jobs, citizen's income would be an effective tool to reduce unemployment. Third, citizen's income is both simple to understand and easy to implement in practice.

Torry is optimistic when he refers to Barbara Wootton, who pointed out that what seems an unrealistic utopia in one generation would be normal practice in the next. "The limits of the possible constantly shift, and those who ignore them are apt to win in the end. Again and again, I have had the satisfaction of seeing the laughable idealism of one generation evolve into the accepted common-place of the next" (Wootton 1967).

11 The beginning is near

The contributors in this last chapter in Part II describe the problems of our time as birth pains as we go through an era in which times are a-changing. Today, something new is about to be born. Evelin Lindner (Germany), Otto Scharmer (Germany) and Charles Eisenstein (USA) argue that the change is anchored in our consciousness. We are about to develop a planetary consciousness based on liberty, equality and fraternity. "I am because you are" is the slogan.

If "you" is extended to include all living beings we are moving from an ego-system toward an ecosystem approach. Through presencing (see the discussion of Scharmer, below) we can eliminate segregation and separation and develop our understanding toward wholeness and coherence. It is naïve to think that reputation building, green-washing and green growth can do more than reduce symptoms and hide the main challenges behind a veil of almost impenetrable fog.

EVELIN LINDNER

> In times of crisis, we need people of courage, people who step out of the beaten track of familiarity and look at the situation from a new perspective.
>
> Evelin Lindner

Introduction

Evelin Lindner points out that ecological sustainability and social cohesion require an increased focus on human dignity, and can only be implemented if we change our current mind-set, which is characterized by fragmentation, competition and humiliation, toward a mind-set of integration, cooperation and humility. Lindner argues for the necessity of a profound paradigm shift, not from one rigid paradigm to another, but in the direction of increased diversity. The concepts of dignity and humiliation are central to Lindner's work.

Biography

Evelin Lindner was born in 1954 in Hameln, Germany. She holds doctoral degrees in psychology (University of Oslo) and medicine (University of Hamburg). In addition, she studied philosophy at the University of Hamburg. In recent years, she has researched and practiced within problem areas associated with globalization, international relations and conflict resolution. Lindner has lived, studied and carried out research in Asia, Africa, the Middle East, USA and several European countries, including in areas affected by civil war and conflict.

She is co-founder of the research network Human Dignity and Humiliation Studies and the *Journal of Human Dignity and Humiliation Studies*. Lindner has united human dignity and environmental responsibility in the "Dignity Economy," which is her contribution to the efforts to create a better world.

Planetary consciousness

Lindner has developed fascinating thoughts and ideas about society and economy based on universal values such as dignity, mutual respect, care and compassion, combined with responsibility for all life in nature. To carry out the goals she has contributed to establishing and developing a global network of dedicated researchers and practitioners. The purpose is to raise awareness about the importance of social change that promotes peace, equality, welfare and quality of life.

Lindner uses the term "planetary consciousness" to emphasize the need for extending the individual consciousness. To see challenges from a holistic perspective it is necessary to establish arenas for dialogue between people who dare to break with established procedures and contexts of understanding. Based on interdisciplinary studies and extensive experience from various projects Lindner has developed methods that help to strengthen the public consciousness.

A key project in her program is the creation of the World Dignity University. This university is not tied to a particular physical location; it consists of a network of affiliated people, institutions and organizations. The university is thus a process rooted in dialogue and cooperation. The idea is that the whole can be recognized in parts while totality embraces all parts. The basic principle is "unity in diversity."

Box 11.1 Change of consciousness

- From fragmentation toward integration
- From competition toward cooperation
- From humiliation toward humility

Box 11.2 How to develop public consciousness

- Establish and develop global networks.
- Encourage multidisciplinary research.
- Communicate knowledge through the development of new educational programs.
- Intervene in processes at the micro, meso and macro levels.

Human Dignity and Humiliation Studies (HDHS)

HDHS is based on a multidisciplinary approach to social and environmental challenges, combined with close contact with practice. When academics and practitioners meet in open dialogue they establish the basis for development and awareness of dignity and respect for both people and nature. By calling for diversity in perspectives, scientific approaches and cultural context, Lindner stimulates creativity and cross-border solutions. She further argues that it is necessary to articulate new questions if we want to work out creative solutions that lead to a better world. She warns against applying old solutions to the new challenges we face.

In today's globalized reality, it is necessary to find solutions based on the principle of "unity in diversity." The coming society should be characterized by more cohesion, while allowing for increased diversity. Lindner points out that diversity based on a common understanding of goals helps to create exciting and stimulating communities. She warns strongly against extremes, global uniformity and divisive diversity. In this context, she refers to the French philosopher Chartier, who has argued that "Nothing is more dangerous than an idea, when you have only one idea."

Prevention versus therapy

Through her practice as a psychologist, Lindner experienced challenges that inspired her to initiate change on a systems level to tackle various forms of humiliating practices. Even if therapies focused on reducing negative symptoms are necessary, the long-term goal is to develop communities that prevent problems related to individual and collective humiliation. The most important task within HDHS has always been to encourage long-term change processes that contribute to eliminate all forms of humiliating practice. She claims that problems are caused by mechanical systems more than individual characteristics.

Local versus global solutions

Until a joint government throughout the "global village" is established, it is necessary to maintain a balance between local and global interests. The main thing is to emphasize that individual citizens in the global village maintain their individuality and dignity, and that they are not forced into limiting systems based on separation and specialization. Holism must be institutionalized in political and economic systems as a replacement for the divisive and undemocratic systems which apply today.

Lindner argues that local networks linked together globally provide the best basis for developing co-responsible human beings. The result is that local and national interests will not seem divisive in our shared responsibility as global citizens, while we avoid global uniformity. Diversity guarantees that relations remain dynamic and avoid settling down into a fixed pattern, which can, in the long run, lead to conflict and disunity. An important requirement for systems based on dignity is that they contribute to the development of respect and mutual care and that individuals are encouraged to live in accordance with ecological principles.

A new solidarity economy

Lindner is critical of the inhumane market economy that increasingly dominates the world. Commercialization means that workers and consumers become victims of a systematic market manipulation where they are objectified and deprived of their inherent dignity. In her book *A Dignity Economy* (2011) Lindner combines her rich experiences with extensive literature studies and concludes that the future economy should be arranged to encourage peaceful, fair and sustainable communities locally, regionally and globally. An important measure is the development of global democratic institutions which have the authority to regulate the world economy. She notes that local and global institutions should be rooted in the ideals of the French Revolution: liberty, equality and fraternity.

She points out the importance of establishing venues for constructive dialogues that give impetus to developing an economy based on equality and dignity. The goal is to create societies with high quality of life rooted in an economy that counteracts greed and ensures a sustainable future for all. Lindner points out that neo-liberal economics expects that we act like one-dimensional utility-maximizing machines. This is an abstraction that is inconsistent with our experience of being complex individuals with many different motives, feelings and values. In this context she cites Desmond Tutu: "I am because you are: I am human because I belong, I participate, I share."

Concluding remarks

Through the HDHS cooperation, Evelin Lindner focused on the negative impacts of increasing alienation and an accelerated overuse of planetary resources. She explains the negative trend by showing the irresistible temptation we have toward irrational behavior. We consume the Earth's resources at a pace that creates serious imbalance in the ecosystems, while the globalized market economy contributes to unequal distribution of wealth within and between nations and within and between generations. The tendency is reinforced by myths (such as "the market knows best") that promote herd mentality and irresponsibility.

OTTO SCHARMER

> The blind spot today is that we take mainstream economic thought for granted, as if it were a natural law.
>
> Otto Scharmer

Introduction

Otto Scharmer is well known as the developer of Theory U. Theory U says something about the changes necessary to create a better future and how they can be implemented. Scharmer argues that bridging the gap between ecosystem reality and ego-system awareness is the main challenge today. He also states that we organize our economic thinking around the really bad idea that we should work for money. Many problems would disappear if we decoupled work from income.

Biography

Otto Scharmer was born in Germany in 1961. He holds a doctorate in economics and management from the Witten/Herdecke private university in North Rhine-Westphalia. Scharmer is currently a senior lecturer at the Massachusetts Institute of Technology (MIT). He is founder of Emerging Leaders for Innovation Across Sectors (ELIAS). He was also a co-founder of the Presencing Institute and the Global Wellbeing and Gross National Happiness Lab. Scharmer has published numerous books and articles and has developed award-winning leadership development programs for, among others, Daimler, PricewaterhouseCoopers and Fujitsu.

Presencing

Scharmer argues that such global challenges as climate change, poverty and health problems cannot be solved within the framework of current economic theory and practice. A solution requires fundamental changes at both the individual and systems level.

According to Scharmer, the tendency among current managers and leaders is to seek solutions using methods and experiences from the past to tackle the problems of today. Through the development of Theory U Scharmer claims to have found the key to a better future. "Presencing" is the core concept in Theory U; it is what makes it possible to break with established patterns of behavior. Presencing is composed of the words "presence" and "sensing" and describes a process leading to expanded awareness on a deeper level. By releasing policymakers from learned forms of understanding and established solutions, it enables access to a virtually unlimited source of creativity.

Theory U

Theory U describes how we move from perception of the current reality (mind) down to presencing of opportunity (heart), then move up through increasing concretization into practical action (will). If we succeed in developing a balanced interaction between an open mind, an open heart and an open willingness, we are also able to "move" our attention to a new position so that alternative ways of thinking and acting become possible.

Scharmer describes how Theory U moves through the following phases:

1   Observation (mind)

In the first phase, the focus is on observing in as unprejudiced a manner as possible to avoid the old mind-set blocking new questions and new answers. To liberate ourselves from established patterns of thinking and open up to creativity and innovation, it is necessary to become aware of our "prejudices." The ability to listen to others and to ourselves is important to aid this process. In addition to physical perception, Scharmer states that intuition makes it possible to search impressions from new sources. The seeds of change lie in varied observation that are as free as possible from past experiences and assessments.

2   Reflection (heart)

In the second phase, the focus is on reflection on impressions in order to give new ideas and new opportunities the opportunity to become conscious. It is about creating a space where the future may materialize freed from the straitjacket of the past. Through presencing, a deeper awareness is developed and this is a prerequisite for the creative moments where we sense (intuition) which way we should go.

3   Specification (will)

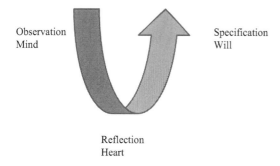

Observation
Mind

Specification
Will

Reflection
Heart

Figure 11.1 Phases in Theory U

In the third phase, the new ideas are set out clearly and practiced. In this process the ability to improvise is of great importance. Improvisation presupposes, among other things, courage to put measures into practice which involve a degree of uncertainty. Uncertainty is reduced through the learning process based on reflections on new experiences. Knowledge generated through this process is used to adjust behavior in different situations. The learning process could be delayed because it is difficult to let go of established safe systems and models which are based on well-documented knowledge.

Changes

Scharmer points out that many serious crises in the economy, society and nature are deeply rooted in the dualistic worldview characterizing Western culture. To solve these problems we need to change our understanding of wholeness and coherence instead of focusing on atomized parts.

At the personal level, we must move away from "I" to "we" consciousness, while at the systems level we must move away from an ego-centered to an eco-centered economy. One consequence is that we develop relationships not only with others but also the whole system and with ourselves.

We have to establish arenas for "premarket cooperation" if we are to achieve this. Basically, this means that we must initiate relationships that create a dynamic balance between different positions.

Scharmer provides no simple recipe for how these changes can be implemented, but he does point out that by opening our minds to a diversity of perspectives we will be able to see how we can transcend our learned pre-understanding. There are in principle two different forces which help to create the required shift of direction. External challenges (the push factor) and expanding individual consciousness (the pull factor). Scharmer believes that the time is ready to implement fundamental changes because both forces are present today. The external challenges are so severe that they cannot be ignored, and in our time there is increased focus on the

---

Box 11.3 Bridge the gap between different positions

- Finance economy and the real economy
- Economic growth and ecosystems limits
- Those who have and those who have not (poverty)
- Institutionalized management and people (commitment)
- GDP (gross domestic product) and quality of life
- Governments and the people (democracy)
- Private ownership and what serves the community
- Technology and society

extended self which is inspired by the influence of Eastern religion and philosophy.

Obstacles

Scharmer states that the main obstacles for creating fundamental changes are:

1 Ignorance
   People are too busy with daily tasks to bother with the serious global challenges. When we encounter a new situation, we employ established thought patterns that overshadow the new. Experiences from the past are blocking fundamental change.

2 Cynicism
   Cynicism creates a distance between our actions and the negative effects they have on environment and society. We are experiencing challenges so threatening that we protect ourselves against them by distancing ourselves from them. The result is that we block any commitment to active problem solving.

3 Depression
   The challenges perceived as so overwhelming that we lose all energy to do anything. Fear of failure is so great that we dare not let go of the old solutions to create a new future.

Concluding remarks

Scharmer points out that the future is not waiting for us, the future is the result of our actions today, and we create it continuously. The future is connected to our deepest purpose and wants and it can only occur to the extent that we are willing and able to let go of the desire to have full control and develop the ability to live with uncertainty associated with moving into uncharted waters.

Scharmer argues that the economy has changed at the same pace as the evolution of human consciousness and today we face a historic turning point where "the essence of the new economy is to transform economic thought from ego-system awareness to eco-system awareness." Such a change presupposes that, first, production is linked to consumer needs, and second, that consumers develop empathy for others (consumers), and third, that the individual consumer becomes aware of his or her own needs.

CHARLES EISENSTEIN

The path to achieve the impossible consists of many practical steps, each of them possible.

Charles Eisenstein

Introduction

Charles Eisenstein provides an exciting contribution to holistic understanding of the social and environmental challenges we face. He explains the problems by referring to an ingrained understanding of reality that is characterized by segregation and separation between humans and between humans and nature. Raising awareness of the interconnectedness in nature is a prerequisite for the solution Eisenstein discusses. We must be aware that everything in reality is integrated and that we are part of the whole and that we all have the totality within us.

Biography

Charles Eisenstein (1967) studied mathematics and philosophy at Yale University. During a stay in Taiwan he learned Chinese, and worked for several years as a translator. Eisenstein has studied Eastern philosophy and religion for many years. In addition to writing books and essays, Eisenstein has lectured at Goddard College, and Penn State University of Science, Technology and Society. He has also practiced as yoga teacher.

In recent years, Eisenstein has been very active as a speaker at conferences, seminars and events organized by various organizations, businesses and government agencies. According to him this contact and interaction with different people has given life to his extensive thinking and writing.

Agents of change

In a time characterized by social and ecological crisis, Eisenstein has examined what we as individuals can and should do to make the world a better place. He has been particularly focused on finding effective antidotes to cynicism, frustration and paralysis. We all have possibilities to become effective agents of change with a positive influence on the global development. In *The Ascent of Humanity* (2007), Eisenstein elaborates on what he means by the term separation (or segregation). He explains its origin, development, ideology and effects, and how separation can be countered through awareness of interbeing (being one with everything). Eisenstein approaches the challenges by reflecting on our own identity.

Separation

According to Eisenstein, many of the most serious challenges we face are caused by a mythical understanding of reality which implies, on the one hand, that the individual is separated from other people, and on the other hand, that people are separated from nature. Our identity and our way of being are largely linked to the experience of the "separate self." This separateness is characteristic of our culture and it explains, on the negative side, the development of technology which is effective in the exploitation of both eco- and social systems. On the positive side, the separated self is the explanation behind the development of goodness and beauty. Overall the negative side dominates and we stand today at the brink of total collapse. The main focus of Eisenstein's books is how we can move forward to create a better world.

Sacred economy

In his book *Sacred Economics* (2011), Eisenstein describes the history of money from the ancient gift economy to modern capitalism. He discusses how the monetary system has contributed to alienation, competition, scarcity of resources and a malicious growth ideology. But, as he says, crises always carry the seeds of new solutions that allow for a more integrated, ecological and sustainable approach.

To create a new economy requires fundamental systemic changes: negative interest, local currencies, the resource-based economy, the gift economy and a focus on the common people. But changes in individual behavior are also required. The challenge is related to how it is possible to live according to these ideals in a world where a monetary-based system draws us in the wrong direction. In *Sacred Economics*, Eisenstein states that what economists often refer to as growth in reality means that scarce resources are extended to apply to areas of life that previously were characterized by abundance. As an example he mentions that fresh water, once more than enough for everybody, has become scarce after it became a commodity that we have to pay for.

One important explanation behind the economic growth spiral is found in the fact that increases in debt and higher requirements from returns on investment have created a demand for growth in production and sales to repay the debt. So the debt spiral contributes to an increased focus on activities in industries that generate money. Since the debt is always greater than

---

Box 11.4 Consequences of the dominant money system

- Alienation
- Competition
- Scarcity of resources
- Malicious growth ideology

Box 11.5 Dimensions in the required systemic change

- Negative interest
- Local currencies
- Resource-based economy
- Gift economy
- Focus on the commons

the money supply, the result will be, according to Eisenstein, constant pressure to produce more goods and services with higher profits from the production of commodities that satisfy the fundamental need for healthy food, for instance.

Just as all forms of natural resources, such as fossil fuels, minerals, forests, fish and water, are converted into products sold on the market, the same is about to happen in the social, cultural and spiritual worlds. Things that have been free throughout human history, such as stories, songs, pictures, knowledge and ideas, have been copyrighted and patented to ensure that they are being traded through market transactions.

Motivation for economic activity

If we want to develop an economy that is sustainable in the long term we must look closely at the real motives behind economic activity. Eisenstein asks how it would be if business decisions were taken on the basis of ecological and social considerations. An increasing number of companies already base their decisions on values described as the triple-bottom-line. The rationale is often that environmentally and socially responsible practices give the company a stronger position in the market because it creates positive attitudes among consumers, politicians and governments. Environmental responsibility also leads to lower costs, because resources are utilized more efficiently. An environmentally responsible attitude stimulates, in addition to developing, creativity both in production and organization. In addition, employees in companies who practice environmental and social responsibility have higher morale because they can easily identify with business practice.

Although many of these propositions seem reasonable, Eisenstein argues that by appealing to economic arguments for sustainability the results will be marginal and will just help to maintain "business as usual." Greening the business because it pays, gives support to the idea that profitability is the most important goal in economics. In contrast to the greening practice, Eisenstein asks the following question: "What if I said to you 'live your life in service to the planet, based on values such as love, care and the desire to serve all life'?"

What can be done?

Eisenstein does not think it is naïve to believe that reputation building, greenwashing and A green economy will eventually give way to an economy based on more fundamental values. We must not let ourselves be fooled into thinking that a greener economy within the established system gives significant results. He points out that there has been no fundamental improvement in the last ten years, despite increased focus on environmental and social responsibility in business sectors. The environment continues to deteriorate, the ocean becomes more acidic, sea life is threatened, drought is spreading across the globe, military spending increases worldwide and the concentration of wealth has been intensified.

One day, hopefully soon, we will begin to ask deeper questions: such as "who am I?"; "what is important?"; and "what values will you prioritize?" By asking such questions we can get the ball rolling for real change. Changes occur when a sufficient number of people have developed a holistic world-view experience and, as Eisenstein says, "perhaps it needs just the weight of one more person taking one more step into interbeing to swing the balance. Perhaps that person is you."

Concluding remarks

Eisenstein has given inspiring and multidisciplinary contributions which indicate that the solution to the most pressing social and ecological crises requires change at several levels. Extended consciousness on an individual level is important, but changes at the system level are a necessary precondition for real changes. The profit-motivated competitive market economy is so strongly rooted in business and politics and among people that it will require a profound structural change to provide the basis for developing a gift-based collaborative economy. Eisenstein argues in all his books that the main change is elimination of the ingrown idea of separation between human beings and between man and nature. Today, we are approaching a common understanding that everything is interconnected in one living entity, Gaia. Such holistic experience will make each of us a significant agent of change with substantial positive impact on developments, locally and globally.

Summing up Part II

Part II consists of multifaceted ideas presented by numerous contributors from different part of the world, from different time epochs and representing different scientific and philosophical positions. Despite huge differences in sources of inspiration, perspectives and topics focused on, it is surprising how they agree when it comes to understanding problems and suggested solutions. The different chapters present a mixture of creative and adventurous ideas dedicated to understanding the problems and how to find a path toward a brighter future. The exciting differences in description of the actual situation and the content of the change processes are colored by the contributors' interpretative context and perspective.

The new economy

The variety could be illustrated by the different concepts used to characterize the new economy: socio-economics; dignity economics; living economy; sacred economics; Buddhist economics; bio-economics; evolutionary economics; peace economics and many more. The different articulations of ecological economics are all in to varying degrees inspired by the four sources of inspiration: thermodynamics, Darwinism, anthroposophy and Buddhism. All of these versions of a new economy represent interesting and relevant contributions to the ongoing work to develop ecological economics as a realistic and relevant alternative to the current dominating position of neo-classical economics.

Challenges

The challenges we are facing, locally, nationally and globally, that are described in Part II span a wide range of issues: depletion of the soil, desertification, extinction of plant and animal species, overconsumption of natural resources, increasing amounts of waste, climate change, poverty, aggression, war, financial crises, overpopulation, increasing flows of refugees, terrorism, clean water, debt crises, unemployment, health problems and many more. The variance could be explained by referring to the main source of inspiration.

First, contributors inspired by thermodynamics are focused on problems connected to exponential growth. Second, economists referring to evolutionary theory describe the market as an integrated network. Third, thinking about the alternative economy that makes reference to anthroposophy replaces competition with cooperation as the fundamental principle in economic activity. Fourth, from a Buddhist perspective, personal development of consciousness and simplicity become the focus.

Science

Since most of these problems refer to the serious conflict between the economy, nature and culture, most of the contributors comment on epistemological questions. They argue that it is necessary to integrate knowledge from many different sciences to catch the problems and to come up with good solutions. A variety of concepts are used to describe the border-crossing approaches in ecological economics: multi-disciplinarity; scientific pluralism; multi-paradigmatic; paradigmatic pluralism; interdisciplinarity; transdisciplinarity and more. The point is that ecological economics does not represent a new paradigm, rather ecological economics opens up a variety of perspectives and interpretations. Here we find the explanation for the capacity of the four sources of inspiration to exist side by side, or more strongly integrated, even if they represent contradictory perspectives.

Problems on the individual and the structural level

These complex problems can be described on the individual and on the structural level. On the individual level, the thinkers surveyed often mention greed, envy, lack of belonging, egocentrism and a one-dimensional focus on materialistic consumption. On a structural level, they refer to economic models looking at nature as a lifeless resource, the separation between humans and separation between humans and nature, competition, globalization, one-dimensional focus on economic growth, unfair distribution of wealth and international institutions that promote destructive and unjust economic order. Buddhism gives priority to individual change, while sociological perspectives give priority to structural change.

Change

On a general level, most of the contributors agree that the current problems are connected to our mistaken worldview. The dominant competitive market economy presupposes an abstract mechanistic ontology where everything is connected as in the parts of a big machine. The economy is ruled by market and prize mechanisms. On the epistemological level, everything can be explained as cause–effect relationships. On a methodological level, knowledge is developed through empirical experiments. In the mechanistic worldview, the deeper meaning is replaced by concepts like efficiency, profits and growth.

One the one hand, it is possible to argue that the system depends on human beings. To change the system, we, as individuals, must change first. On the other hand, if the systems are bad, people will behave badly. So we have to change the systems first. Even if some of the contributors focus on one or the other solution, there is a general agreement that we have to start from both ends simultaneously (cf. push and pull). The two levels are mutually dependent: structural change presupposes individual change and individual change presupposes structural change. The objective is to implement a process which leads toward a society characterized by a high quality of life, resilient societies and a viable economy within sustainable ecosystems.

The contributors use a variety of concepts to describe some of the most crucial elements in this process, such as happiness, meaning, equity, cooperation, eco-centrism, simplicity, well-being, equitable distribution of resources, democracy, dignity, serenity, peace, resilience, integration, humility, responsibility for all life in nature, mutual respect, compassion, establishing collaborative networks of smaller self-organizing societies, international laws and regulations that protect social and natural environment.

A utopian story

If we accept that our actual mechanical worldview (categorial scheme, paradigm or myth) is not in accordance with real-world conditions and we decide to use this map anyway, we cannot be surprised when a whole lot of unintended negative consequences are the result.

All the chapters in Part II provide valuable contributions to developing a utopian narrative, telling a story that we live in an organic world where we are integrated parts in the web of life. The mechanical parts are interpreted in an organic context. The implications for economics are systemic change toward a partnership approach, decentralized networks, cooperation, mutual responsibility and circular value chains. In addition, to prohibit ecocide a juridical framework has to be established.

On a business level, administration and leadership theories emphasize the triple bottom line, indicating that all decisions should take into account economic, social and ecological factors. Spiritual leadership argues that all stakeholders should be included in the extended self. To handle discrepancies in the prioritization between bottom-up and top-down initiatives, most of the contributors propose change in both directions.

In Part III, I cultivate different utopian narratives based on the context of interpretation and content presented in Parts I and II. The point is not to come up with correct answers but to describe utopian perspectives that make it possible to move outside the established ideology to get a better understanding of the current situation and inspiration to develop realistic processes based on knowledge and insight. The description of utopia is a never-ending process where all members of society take part. In other words, working with utopian narratives is a procedure, not an objective method for finding the correct solutions to concrete problems. To ensure life-enhancing processes, the following criteria are absolute: scale (consumption within the ecosystem's source and sink capacity), equity (fair distribution of resources) and cooperation (decentralized cooperative networks).

Part III

Ecological economics

A utopian narrative

Thomas Aquinas, the thirteenth-century philosopher, theologian and jurist, claimed that even the most slender knowledge obtained of higher things is more desirable than certain knowledge of lesser things. These days we draw a distinction between exact and relevant knowledge. Even knowledge that is correct in all its details may well be unhelpful or misleading to the under-standing of the actual situation. In the following chapters I will reconstruct a meta-story that is both precise and relevant for the understanding and the resolution of some of the most serious challenges facing modern society and try to integrate them with the main ideas presented in Part II. My aim is to present a narrative based in part on descriptions of reality as it exists and partly on the interpretations that influence our understanding of reality.

This approach is inspired by a critical realism which argues that even if science is a mere human construction it still contributes a picture of reality that is relevant and provides us with a deeper understanding of the world we live in. Even if utopia could never be given an exact positivistic interpretation, utopian stories have, nevertheless, great importance as a context for under-standing how specific phenomena are interconnected and how everything is in continual state of change. It is through language that we express our struc-tures and influence each other. Utopia is imagined as "the crossing, the place-less meeting point, or the conjunction of philosophy and art, where concepts are enacted and dramatic action puts thought in motion" (Vieira and Marder 2012, p. xiv).

Utopia is driven by dialectical processes inspired by different sources of inspiration and interpretations are advanced within the framework of a pro-cess of philosophical tradition. My version of utopia is far from being the only one possible; descriptions focusing on other aspects and other contexts of interpretation are also relevant. Instead of claiming the one true and final interpretation I am open to a diversity of prospects. The portrayals of how the economy would function in a utopian society diverge in relation to the review-er's position in history (time) and cultures (space). According to Sargent:

204 *A utopian narrative*

> We must choose the belief that the world can be radically improved; we must dream socially; and we must allow our dreams to affect our lives. The choice of Utopia is a choice that the world can be radically improved.
>
> (Sargent 2011, p. 306)

In Part II it was argued, from a variety of points of view, all convincing in their own way, that it is not enough to make mere adjustments within the existing system. We need radical systemic change. We need an approach so radical that old problems may be simply forgotten or dismissed as irrelevant, rather than taking trouble to solve them. Instead of reducing the negative symptoms of the current dominant ideology it is infinitely more relevant to spend our energy developing a utopian story which points out a possible path to a future economy which is based on the creation of harmony between humans, nature and society.

The concepts, models and theories presented in Part II are taken apart, reconstructed and rewritten, as a holographic narrative, which is to say that Part III will tell the same story from diverse perspectives and focal points. One central question is how the new economy interconnects with changes on different levels in society as a whole. Individuals, society, nature and the economy are interwoven and impact on each other. Anchored in the acceptance of the idea that "becoming" is more real than "being" I will offer some insights to help us to understand more about fundamental ideas, patterns, processes, rhythms and the principles involved in the developmental processes.

Even if the basic understanding is similar, in practical terms it could take many forms because of the almost infinite variety of individual, cultural and ecological contexts. Diversity is a precondition for resilience. The utopian narratives which characterize ecological economics in Part III are not meant to be taken literally but more as visions and descriptions to be further developed and adapted to local and regional conditions through a process of practice and assessment.

12 A narrative approach

It is usually assumed that social life consists of a combination of our intended actions, the decisions we make and events that just happen to us. We are responsible for our actions but not for events. Actions are given meaning in terms of their context. A meaningful action, if you like, may be seen as a text while living is more like writing a book. Experimenting with innovative narratives helps to connect utopia to the reality from which it stems. It is of vital importance that utopia is connected to reality because "we can evade reality, but we cannot evade the consequences of evading reality" (Lindner 2011, p. xxix).

Since individual narratives are connected to a social context it is obvious that we write our book together with other people and other living and non-living entities with whom we share planet Earth. To understand our own life, we have to materialize it in a narrative, that is, a text. When we shape other people's narratives we demonstrate power; when the narratives are written through a dialogue we become co-authors in each other's lives. Social theory and practice can be treated as narratives within narratives. An interesting task is to find out how they are constructed, used and misused. According to, among others, Nietzsche and Mannheim, theories are often connected to ideology, interest and power.

Economists tell stories and use abstract concepts and models to describe and explain economics and economic practice. In order to make social sciences and economics more "down to earth" Whitehead suggested principles which have applications outside their original context. It is important to make clear that the success of this procedure is linked to the necessary condition that ideas derived are generalized and expressed in a way relevant to the context and logically consistent.

More precisely, Whitehead described a philosophical method which includes both empirical and rational criteria in order to decide which scheme of interpretation is the most relevant. First, empirical criteria indicate that the categorial scheme must be both applicable and adequate. Applicability indicates that the categorial scheme illuminates knowledge that is useful in different situations. Adequate means that the categorial scheme expresses knowledge that is valid in concrete practical situations. Second, the rationalistic criteria indicate that contents of the categorial scheme must be coherent and logic. Coherence means that the basic ideas employed in constructing the understanding require each other. It follows that they cannot be isolated from each other without losing their meaning. Logic indicates that the stories must not contradict each other.

From the narrative approach it must be possible to give convincing arguments validating the utopian description of the economy, nature and culture, and present them as integrated parts of an indefinite whole which must be satisfied. In addition, the analysis of ecological economics must satisfy the claims of logic, such as truth (correspondence with reality) or coherence (with other texts). The content of scientific texts is given validity and reliability by referring to the stringent use of scientific methods, but we should note it could also be a consequence of institutionalized research practice (categorial schemes or paradigms), that is, it could often be more accurate to speak in terms of "conformity" rather than "reliability." According to Czarniawska, "It is not the results that are reliable but the researchers – who are conforming to dominant rules" (Czarniawska 2004, p. 133).

Dissatisfaction with existing institutionalized criteria for good scientific texts led to a demand for alternative guidelines. Utopian narratives could be a way of both knowing and a way of communicating. Rationality in narratives is defined as coherence and integrity; in other words, the credibility of a narrative is established through the presence of sound reasons and consistency based on facts, logic, metaphors and stories.

Czarniawska states that the narrative approach does not offer a method or a clear-cut paradigm, or even a set of procedures to check the accuracy of results. Instead "it gives an ample bag of tricks – from traditional criticism through formalists to deconstruction – but it steers away from the idea that a rigorously applied procedure would render treatable results" (Czarniawska 2004, p. 136). Use of narrative methods should lead to far more inspired reading – and writing.

In the following chapter I interpret, deconstruct and put together the texts described in Parts I and II, and rewrite an integrated story (narrative) of ecological economics. In the deconstruction of the texts I focus on disruptions and contradictions, goals and values, the most distinctive concepts and elements in the different texts and metaphors used by the different authors, and separate the general and specific contents of the texts. "A metaphor can bring a point to a story while a story can exemplify a metaphor" (Czarniawska 2004, p. 108).

The story must include several thematic areas:

1   It must give meaning and purpose to life.
2   It must give us reason to believe that despite powerful opposition the necessary changes are possible.
3   It must address the claim that we are, by nature, individualistic, greedy and competitive.
4   It must signpost the way to a viable human future.

As a starting point, I accept that the only valid purpose of an economy is to serve the flourishing of life in all kinds of social and ecosystems. An economy has to be viewed as an integral part of society and nature if economic activity is to be filled with meaning. Every activity and every process within the economy should be a servant of life.

13 Utopian narratives of ecological economics

Georgescu-Roegen argued that instead of asking what the future *will be* we should reflect on what *we want* the future to be. The idea behind this reasoning is interesting when we see it in the light of Merton's reflections on self-fulfilling prophecies. Owing to the positive feedback between belief and behavior, any prediction (or prophecy) about the future causes itself to become true. He formalized and structured the consequences of "self-fulfilling prophecy" in this way: "If men define situations as real, they are real in their consequences" (Merton, 1948, p. 193). If we apply Georgescu-Roegen's advice to redirecting the focus of science, we can conclude that utopia could be a means for change.

The first part of Merton's theorem provides a reminder that we do not only respond to the objective features of a situation but also to the meaning this situation has for us. In harmony with this reasoning, Giddens emphasized that our behavior is affected by how we interpret the world surrounding us. Human behavior cannot be separated from the individual's conscious (or unconscious) worldview. Furthermore, the interaction between worldview, social structures and human agency is cyclical (Figure 13.1). "Social structures are both the precondition and the unintended outcomes of people's agency" (Capra and Luisi 2014, p. 326). Merton goes deeper into this connection and argues that once people "have assigned some meaning to the situation, their consequent behaviour and some of the consequences of that behaviour are determined by the ascribed meaning" (Merton 1948, p. 194). It is of great importance to note that this connection does not exist in the world of nature. For example, Merton mentions that all or any predictions of the return of Halley's comet in no way influence its orbit. In other words, a definition of a future situation based on a utopian narrative evokes behavior that makes the described situation come true. Statistical forecasts of "how the future will be" are part of the established ideology, while descriptions of "how we want the future to be" could be utopian. The validity of self-fulfilling prophecies depends on how we react to them.

To make any substantial changes we have to look at utopian narratives. Any definition of a future situation affects our behavior today because it becomes an integral part of the present. As long as the definitions stay rooted within the existing ideology only marginal changes are possible (e.g. greening the economy). Utopian stories will evoke radical behavior because the descriptions are outside the existing ideology. It is important that utopias challenge established conceptions and question assumptions in former theories. From this we can draw the conclusion that utopias are of great importance if we are to stimulate fundamental change. However, it is necessary to be aware that not all change is good even if betterment does presuppose change.

On the other side of the coin from self-fulfilling prophecies, self-defeating prophecies prevent what is predicted from happening – something often known as the "prophet's dilemma." It is important to distinguish self-fulfilling prophecies that predict a negative outcome from self-defeating prophecies. If a prophecy of a negative outcome is made, for example, a group of people, due to ignorance, cynicism or depression, think they will not succeed in solving the problems they face, they will give up and stop working toward this end. On the other hand, if a prophecy with a negative outcome is made, and a group of people want to falsify the prediction by behaving in opposition to it, then the prophecy could be self-defeating. With exactly that same line of reasoning, Whitehead argued that the future depends on the choices we make today. We can say that the present exists at that very point where experiences from the past meet the visions of the future.

The prospect of a utopian future could be an incitement to self-fulfilling or self-defeating prophesies. Our challenge is to offer a description of a utopian society that is dynamic, based on plurality, individual freedoms, equity and harmony with nature. To be utopian in any real sense, utopia must initiate changes that are much more than mere descriptions of measures to reduce negative symptoms within the existing narrative of the neo-liberal ideology.

From a philosophy of science perspective this model includes reflections on ontological and methodological individualism and holism (collectivism). Depending on the ontological preconditions on the level of worldview, methodological explanations are defined. On the one hand, ontological individualism presupposes methodological individualism. On the other hand, ontological collectivism gives relevance to both methodological individualism and collectivism. To illuminate these concepts I refer to the definitions given by Capra (1996) and Samuels (1972) respectively. According to Capra holistic ontology emphasizes the whole as "holistic, organismic, or ecological" (Capra 1996, p. 17) and implies a system of thinking which looks at the web of life as networks within networks. Individualistic ontology means that the material universe can be understood completely by "analyzing it in terms of its smallest parts" (Capra 1996, p. 19).

Samuels refers to methodological individualism as "the view which holds that the meaningful social science knowledge is best or more appropriately derived through the study of individuals" and methodological collectivism (or holism) as the view which holds that meaningful social science knowledge is best or more appropriately derived through the study of group organizations, forces, processes and/or problems (Samuels 1972, p. 249).

Box 13.1 Ontology and methodology

	Methodological individualism	*Methodological collectivism*
Ontological individualism	green economy	impossible
Ontological collectivism	ecological economics	ecological economics

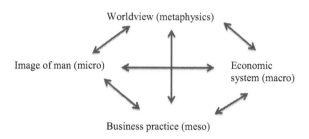

Figure 13.1 The fourfold mapping of the economy

In Box 13.1. I have illustrated the connection between ontology and methodology in a dual table indicating the connection between ontological preconditions and methodological explanations in economics. Green economy is categorized as a part of the dominating ideology based on ontological and methodological individualism. Ecological economics, as the utopian alternative, is based on ontological collectivism which opens for both individualism and collectivism concerning methodology. The consequence of this is that a shift in business practice (meso) could be explained by referring to development on either individual (micro) or systemic (macro) levels. Green economy focuses on changes on the individual level through, for example, nudging and use of market economic tools.

In the following sections I look in detail at the utopian vision of what ecological economic practice would look like within a future society based on interplay between the four different levels: worldview (metaphysics), economic system (macro), business practice (meso) and image of man (micro).

Even if the narrative "Utopia VSO" (viable organic society) is very different from what we see today, it is not breaking any fundamental natural and social laws. Because of the theorem of self-fulfilling prophecies, the Utopia VSO is in a position to have massive influence on the processes of change. The four different dimensions are defined in the following ways.

Worldview (metaphysics)

To outline the worldview, we divide it into two main classifications – mechanistic and organic. One the one hand, a mechanistic (or atomistic) worldview states that the nature of everything that exists is like machines composed of parts lacking any intrinsic relationship to each other. Being is more real than becoming and objects are more important than relations. The source of any kind of activity is influenced from outside and not from the entity itself. "A machine must be controlled by its operators to function according to their instructions, so the main thrust of management theory has been to achieve efficient operations through top-down control" (Capra and Luisi, 2014, p. 59). Scientific management and new public management are illustrative examples.

On the other hand, an organic (or holistic) worldview states that the nature of everything that exists is like a living organic whole. Everything is interconnected through a variety of relations. When we shift to an organic understanding we realize that becoming is more real than being and that relations are more essential than objects. Activity is initiated by the organism itself, from within. "According to the theory of autopoiesis, a living system relates to its environment structurally – that is, through recurrent interactions, each of which triggers structural changes in the system" (Capra and Luisi, 2014, p. 135). Social connections are progressively being constructed and reconstructed through flexible networks rather than formal organization.

Economic system (macro)

The economic system is divided into the following two categories: market economy and circulation economics (Ingebrigtsen and Jakobsen 2007). Market economy is based on competition between autonomous actors. According to Blaug, the market economy can be characterized by a concept of "atomistic economic agents, interacting in self-adjusting and self-regulating competitive markets […] a paradigm which still retains its grip on current thinking" (Blaug 1978, p. 720). The motivating force is made up of profit by firms and maximization of satisfaction by consumers. Originally it was an essential requirement that "the invisible hand leads private interest to serve the public welfare" (Daly and Cobb Jr. 1994, p. 13), while today the authorities define laws and regulations for market behavior.

Circulation economics is a transdisciplinary field of research that defines economy as a subsystem of the ecological and social systems. Circulation economics refers to the interplay between the economy, nature and society as decentralized networks based on cooperation. Systems thinking and co-evolution are core concepts in circulation economics. "There is a common focus on dynamic and evolutionary processes and concepts such as path dependence, lock in, emergent properties and multi-level perspectives" (Martinez-Alier and Røpke 2008, p. xxxi).

Business practice (meso)

Business practice is divided into strategic management and partnership approach. Within the strategic management model firms operate in competitive markets focused on shareholder perspectives. Maximization of net revenue for the owners is the overriding objective in the face of given prices and a technologically determined production function. Cyert and March claim that rationality in the business model can be reduced to two propositions: "(1) firms seek to maximize profits; (2) firms operate with perfect knowledge" (Cyert and March 1963, p. 8). More generally, Kourdi defines business strategy as "the plans, choices and decisions used to guide a company to greater profitability and success" (Kourdi 2015, p. 3). The focus is on describing strategic action plans that increase the firm's competitive power compared to others in the market.

A partnership approach is defined by the following characteristics: cooperation, stakeholder engagement, responsibility and long-term perspectives. This means that all actors in the market are interrelated and interdependent. In addition, the firm is integrated into both the social and natural systems. A partnership approach is based on establishing a compatibility between "economic needs and ecology, because what destroys the environment also destroys economy" (Barash and Webel 2014, p. 442). Through partnership agreements the actors take the initiative to find solutions based on a holistic frame of reference and the focus is on how to develop action plans that clearly demonstrate that the firm's activities are for the benefit of all the actors in the (local) society.

Image of man (micro)

On micro level I draw a distinction between "economic man" and "ecological man." Economic man (*homo economicus*) is an egocentric actor behaving in accordance with instrumental rationality. It is possible to explain and predict the behavior of economic man because he is always trying to maximize his own self-interest. Since the quest for private gain is recognized as "intelligent" all other modes of behavior are looked on as less rational or even irrational. "The assumption that rationality largely excludes other-regarding behavior has deep, although conflicting, roots in the Western theological understanding of human nature" (Daly and Cobb Jr. 1994, p. 5). Economic man's egocentrism was acceptable because it was a precondition for competition and the efficient use of scarce resources.

Ecological man (*homo ecologicus*) is integrated in ecosystems and social systems as an inherent principle of human existence. According to Becker, the relationship between ecological man and nature is "beyond economic self-interest and biological survival" (Becker 2006, p. 20). Ecosystem awareness is developed by moving into today's complex, unstable and disturbing challenges to try to understand how everything is interconnected, that is, "the mutual dependence of all life processes on one another" (Capra and Luisi 2014, p. 353). By linking the four different dimensions we can outline some of the main differences between two paradigmatically different maps or categorial schemes, ideology and utopia.

A sketch of two divergent economic maps

We live in a world of uncertainty, a world rich in potential for disaster but at the same time open to positive changes. We have to realize that old maps, no matter how familiar and comforting, will never offer solutions to our current challenges and if we are to do more than merely reducing negative symptoms we have to initiate change on four levels. Metaphysical questions have been absent from mainstream economics and this has let us dodge fundamental conflicts. "These conflicts have led to a whole range of negative symptoms such as climate change and financial crises" (Ims and Jakobsen 2010, p. 17).

The dominant ideology

In the current and dominant ideology economics is based on a mechanistic worldview (metaphysics). A mechanistic worldview is in harmony with a market economics (systems level) anchored in atomistic competition. The main challenge for business (practice) is how to develop strategic plans based on competitive advantage and instrumentality. In brief, the whole system is based on the idea of an instrumental rational economic actor giving priority to egocentric maximization of utility. Because economic activity is explained by referring to individual choices and actions in an atomized market, the model is based on both methodological and ontological individualism.

With reference to social and environmental responsibilities the economy within the dominating ideology concerns itself more, if not exclusively, with short-term solutions aimed at reducing the most pressing negative symptoms rather than discussing economic metaphysical presuppositions. "By using increasing doses of the prescribed old medicine, negative symptoms are muted so that the pathological causes remain indistinct" (Ims and Jakobsen 2010, p. 17). Symptoms suppression measures often lead to situations where the problem worsens in time.

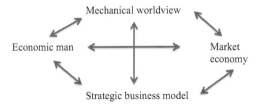

Figure 13.2 The dominant ideology

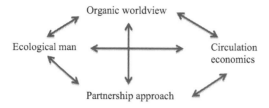

Figure 13.3 Utopia VSO

Utopia VSO

How will a shift toward an organic worldview influence all the other dimensions? In my interpretation of Utopia VSO it is possible to create other utopian stories from the same ontology. Acceptance of an organic worldview leads in the direction of circulation economics anchored in cooperative networks, a partnership approach and the image of ecological man. An organic worldview refers to ecological knowledge which throws light on the interplay between nature's different living and non-living entities by maintaining that nature is much more like a series of synergic networks than a system of mere destructive competition.

The application of this picture to economics actualizes a shift from competition to cooperation in addition to a shift from linear value chains to circular value chains and from atomized markets to nested networks. On a business level this shift is concretized by an increasing number of integrated, locally based, small-scale businesses rather than monster organizations. An influential element in this process is the transformation from egocentric one-dimensional consumers to integrated human beings characterized by deep authenticity. Deep authenticity depends on our ability to "flip to an organic worldview where awareness of an 'eco-centric self' becomes possible" (Ims and Jakobsen 2011, p. 221). Since economy in Utopia VSO is grounded in ontological collectivism, it follows that both methodological individualism and collectivism are relevant to our understanding of (ecological) economic activity.

Change processes

Chief among the thoughts behind the fourfold model is the idea of change based on dynamic imbalance. A shift on any of the four levels will cause disturbances that could lead to changes in the other dimensions. If we accept that the future may "contain multiple possibilities far in excess of seemingly fixed actualities" (Davis 2012, p. 136), and combine this with a growing recognition among politicians and business leaders (Chouinard, Ellison and Ridgeway 2011) that we must accept "responsibility for our relationship with Earth's biosphere, and restructure the institutions of the economy accordingly" (Korten 2010, p. 138), then we can quite clearly see that change is possible.

A major question we face is how to initiate a shift from the ideological toward the utopian model. On the one hand a change toward circulation economics on the systems level will inspire a change toward an organic business model on the meso level and toward ecological man on the micro level. On the other hand, an organic worldview, in combination with a change in consciousness, will inspire a change in the economic system and in business practice. In isolation, a change in business practice toward increased environmental and social responsibility will only have minimal effect as long as the rationality of economic man is ruling within a competitive market economy.

Today we recognize disturbance on all levels: at the individual level an increasing number of people no longer feel like one-dimensional consumers; at the business level networking is developing to bring local resources and markets together; more and more people are beginning to question far more critically than ever the claims made by the competitive market economy not only to understand but also to solve the many interlinked crises we face today. It is fair to say that among the questioners we can, finally, include many economists. Capra and Luisi refer to this change in awareness by referring to changes in the immediate surroundings in combination with individual reflection. Our awareness is a "subtle blending of cognition (including perception, emotions, and behavior) and consciousness in the sense of self-awareness" (Capra and Luisi 2014, p. 258).

At perhaps the deepest of all levels our worldview has changed and is changed forever. Man's landing on the moon in 1969 "with its view from space over this blue planet of ours, was probably the moment at which modern global consciousness was born" (Safranski 2003, p. 5). In addition to the birth of the Gaia hypothesis, human consciousness has made a massive and dramatic shift toward holism and organic understanding.

Concluding remarks

The next sections, based on the fourfold mapping of the economy (Figure 13.1), are structured in the following way: by way of introduction, I give a brief description, at the specific level, of some of the most challenging problems faced by the ideology which is currently dominant. Later, the utopian narrative will be described in more detail. Each section ends with a brief reflection on how the four specific dimensions are connected to the other dimensions. My intention is to include the "whole" in every story, rather like a hologram. Each of the four stories, for sure, has its own focus but, on a deeper level, they all point to the same reality. By interpreting one level in terms of the others and by switching between the different levels it is possible to achieve a far deeper understanding of how everything is interconnected and how the different stories fit together in, and contribute to, the greater whole. An ability to shuttle back and forth between the levels, finding relations and patterns, is essential to the process. Systems and practices are created by individuals (methodological individualism), and this created reality makes the individuals (methodological collectivism). In other words, society is produced and reproduced in an always changing and never-ending process and the utopian story emerges and changes, and is driven by, the existence of complex contextual networks integrated on the micro, meso, macro and metaphysical levels.

Utopia VSO is an enduring process that detaches itself from the dichotomy of methodological individualism and collectivism by emphasizing the existence of dynamic integrated networks. If we are to understand this fundamental interconnectedness a transdisciplinary science is called for, one that can capture all the relationships, both physical and spiritual, in a new and complex reality. Solutions that seem unrealistic from a fragmented scientific perspective may very well be realistic from a transdisciplinary perspective.

WORLDVIEW

Introduction

Ray and Anderson define "worldview" as the content of everything you believe is real: "God, the economy, technology, the planet, how things work, how you should work and play, your relationship with your beloved – and everything of value" (Ray and Anderson 2000, p. 17). But this worldview only becomes visible at the point it is threatened by something, or, referring to Kuhn, when the growing level of anomalies challenge the existing paradigm. From this point of view the worldview is closely associated with ontology as the metaphysical study of the nature of existence itself, with a special focus on its two basic categories – being and becoming.

Even the briefest look at the state of the world today makes it clear that the major problems stem from the dominating mechanistic worldview and it becomes increasingly evident that the Earth is an interconnected "living" organism. Pope Francis states that interdependent systemic solutions are required because

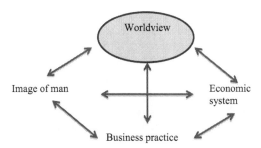

Figure 13.4 Focus on worldview

> Our common home is falling into serious disrepair [...]. [This is] evident
> in large-scale natural disasters as well as social and even financial crises,
> for the world's problems cannot be analyzed or explained in isolation [...].
> It cannot be emphasized enough how everything is interconnected.
>
> (Francis 2015, paragraphs 61, 138)

Instead of seeing the connections between our major problems, most political and business leaders tend to focus on separate single issues and simply shift the problem from one part of the system to another, and such piecemeal solutions, on which future generations depend, end up hidden in a veil of fog. For example, in their fixation on stimulating economic growth, they pile up environmental problems for the future – such as loss of biodiversity and climate change.

Many of the most challenging problems we face today come from our inability to make the dominant mechanical worldview and reality match up. In other words, our roadmap is not in accordance with the real world. Stories based on mechanical thinking become confused with reality and almost nobody ever asks critical questions about them; instead we behave in a way that turns them into self-fulfilling prophecies which become even more resistant to pressure and challenges.

Examples which illustrate this point very clearly are economists and politicians who try to operate within the globalized growth economy by referring to price mechanisms, market forces and atomized competition between autonomous actors. Such mechanical stories are so heavily incorporated in Western culture and science that we have become immune to them and don't even try to fight or falsify them because we no longer realize they are there. Even if an increasing number of economists and politicians accept quite openly that both nature and society are endangered by the modern economy and our lifestyle they are still not willing, or even point blank refuse, to revise their worldview. This view is deeply rooted in history and one of the origins of the modern mechanical myth is René Descartes and his claim: "I have described the earth and the whole visible universe in the manner of a machine." We are still struggling to recover from the effects of Cartesianism.

In mainstream economics, this clanking, tired, mechanical view of the world is transferred into concepts, models and theories which eliminate life, emotions and spirituality as real phenomena and in their place put a one-dimensional focus on egocentric maximizing of utility. This limited, linear way of thinking and behaving in the real world brings about a whole lot of negative unintended (and often) irreversible consequences. Today these negative consequences represent anomalies that threaten the economy, societies and ecosystems throughout the world.

To reduce some of the most serious negative side-effects of the mismatch between the mechanical myth and the real world, economists prescribe for us increasingly stronger doses of the same old medicines with which we are all now more than familiar; procedures that stimulate growth, increasing bureaucratic control, privatization, commodification of both nature and culture, and competition. By these means the Earth is about to be transformed into a giant supermarket, where everything is for sale and the only goal is egocentric maximization of profits or utility. When an organism is split up into pieces it loses all vitality and ends up being a lifeless machine. It's the same with natural resources: fossil fuels, minerals, plants, animals and water are converted into products to be sold on the market, and the same is about to happen in the human sphere. Social, cultural and spiritual phenomena are transformed into commodities. Things such as stories, songs, pictures, knowledge and ideas that have been free throughout human history become increasingly copyrighted and patented to ensure that they are being traded through market transactions.

It can be no surprise to anyone that economists and politicians struggle to come up with any new solutions when they are so trapped in the quicksand of the dominant mechanical ontology. To be aware of the true nature of this tired ontology we must take a brave step into utopia. Success in our search for appropriate solutions presupposes that we have the stories right. There has always been a holistic organic component in the Western culture, "espousing an animistic understanding, that ran alongside the reductionist scientific mainstream" (Harding 2009, p. 35), and this holistic tradition is outlined in the following paragraphs. Culture is the sum-total of all tangible and intangible elements that build our identity.

Utopia VSO

The world of Utopia VSO implies a remarkable change in ontology, a move away from a view of the universe as a big machine, toward an understanding of the universe as something alive, self-organizing and flourishing. Contemporary scientific understanding suggests that the cosmos is an interrelated whole where the various parts are all linked in a network of mutual dependence. Human beings are tied together by social relations, as well as being integral parts of nature's ecosystems. Instead of being a pyramid of life forms we see the living Earth "Gaia" as a series of ever-widening circles encompassing humankind, the sentient world, the material world and all-holding, omnipresent nature. Moreover, within this holistic ontology every life form, on every level, has intrinsic value.

Just as the human body consists of different mechanical parts, for example, knees and elbows, a living community integrates mechanical parts like buildings and transport systems. Mechanical parts are embedded in the web of life. This holistic approach involves a shift away from objects and toward processes and relationships, away from hierarchies toward networks and away from objective knowledge to contextual knowledge.

Basically, we cannot understand either physical nature or life unless we fuse them together as essential factors in the composition of the whole universe. This interconnectedness is non-linear in the sense that freedom is considered to be the claim for self-assertion. One important consequence of the organic worldview is that organizations are no longer reduced to parts in a big machine governed by external laws and explained by referring to scientific rationality. Instead, we understand the market as interconnected partners unified in dynamic networks. In this kind of complex framework we come to see that economic behavior is both multifaceted and context-dependent.

As human beings we accept that we are responsible for treating Gaia's ecosystems with respect and dignity. Instead of dominating nature we learn from nature and we are committed to adapting and stimulating the ecosystem's capacity for self-regulation and self-organization. As soon as we acknowledge this holistic consciousness we behave in a more flexible manner and become aware of our mutual responsibility for the interplay between all ecological and social networks.

Human communities are like living organisms which are constantly changing. The social context is an integral part of our existence as individuals and, in a real sense, we are all members of each other. Diversity is a guarantee for keeping the relations dynamic and avoid settling into hardened and fixed patterns. In accordance with the communitarian outlook we feel society is not reduced to a mere collection of isolated atoms, but rather we accept that societies are integrated communities, a "vibrant societatis organiscimus" (VSO).

On a more general level every organism is understood in terms of its physical and spiritual environment. This means that even in an organic worldview we must pay attention to mechanical phenomena as well. Wholeness indicates that everything is integrated and interconnected through a myriad of relations. Wholeness is what we experience within time and space. However, on a deeper level, behind time and space, there is a oneness. There are different paths to experience oneness, from presencing to meditation and art. To understand wholeness it is of great help to have experienced oneness in one way or the other.

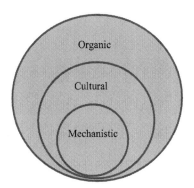

Figure 13.5 Ontological development
Source: Storsletten and Jakobsen 2015, p. 343

One characteristic of the organic worldview is the existence of an inherent cosmic spirit, or in everyday language, "life." Life is characterized by dynamic change and evolutionary processes. Life develops from inside, life is process, life is integration and life is creativity. This point of departure leads in the direction of being conscious of the fundamental meaning of relations as more important than objects and even further that becoming is more important than being. But it is important to remember Whitehead's statement that "the art of progress is to preserve order amid change and to preserve change amid order."

The organic story tells us that all problem solving is dynamic. In other words, it is far from enough to search for new answers to traditional questions; instead, we have to ask deeper questions. An obvious consequence of organic thinking is that our consciousness allows us to be aware of questions concerning life and meaning. It is almost impossible to come up with such questions when we see the world from a mechanical worldview. When we exchange our stories and take a look at reality from an organic point of view we discover things that were hidden in the mechanical story. One of the first things we become aware of is the necessity to develop a holistic research model that takes into account the complexity in understanding the key interactions, processes and features at local, national and global level.

Transdisciplinarity has been introduced in modern universities and represents a dramatic change in scientific theory and practice. Both weak and strong versions of transdisciplinarity are relevant. The weaker form is practiced as a dialogue between researchers from different fields of science or different scientific disciplines and is in accordance with the definition of wholeness as interconnectedness between different parts. Strong transdiciplinarity is about oneness, or a more concrete focus on a reality where the demarcation lines between the different sciences vanish. There are centers practicing strong transdisciplinarity at universities. Different topics are studied by integrating inspiration, intuition, imagination and creativity in scientific theory and practice. Negative and positive prehensions inspire creative development by connecting entities that naturally belong together and avoiding entities that initiate disharmony and conflict. In this intuitive process we can develop our presencing abilities.

This position in the philosophy of science makes it possible to grasp the essence of communities as living entities where life forces and creativity develop from within. The economy is understood as an organ integrated in other organs such as culture, politics and nature. A healthy evolutionary process depends on a harmonious balance between the different organs; no one dominates the others. Ecological economics develops in a way that lights up the path to harmony between economic activities and the dynamic patterns and rhythms of nature.

Reflections

Living in an organic world has implications for systems, practice and the image of man. Positive thinking, constructive dialogues and meaningful action

Box 13.2 Characteristics of an organic worldview

- Organic
- Holistic
- Process

- Integrated
- Relations
- Non-linear

- Diversity
- Resilience
- Creativity

- Self-organizing
- Becoming
- Meaning

are all fundamental characteristics of the organic worldview. Translated to economics, the organic worldview leads to a cooperative economy where all kinds of activity are interrelated and mutually supportive. Business practice is coordinated through communicative processes where every economic actor is invited to participate. To succeed in such a dialogue-based network economy the actor can rightly be described as an "ecological man." It follows then that a change in worldview cannot be separated from changes in the economic system, business practice and the image of man. Even if the change in world-view represents a fundamental precondition for the whole process, its success depends on how the different levels have become integrated parts of the transition. Ecosystems and economic systems are characterized by the relations connecting the entities together in dynamic networks.

Ecosystems, social systems and economic systems totally depend on functioning together and cannot survive when split up and atomized, any more than any organism can survive in fragments. Man's well-being depends on coexistence in resilient ecosystems and economic systems. To help us understand the dynamic interconnectedness in a real way, holistic research models, based on transdisciplinarity, are vital.

ECONOMIC SYSTEM

Introduction

An economic system is defined by referring to the principles governing the allocation of resources in any society. Mansfield argues that the economic

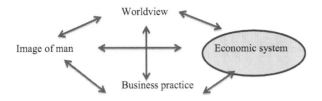

Figure 13.6 Focus on economic system

system is characterized by functional rationality. "By this he means that the economic system's rationality is independent of the intentions of the instrumentally acting agents" (Ingebrigtsen and Jakobsen 2006, p. 61). According to the *Stanford Encyclopedia of Philosophy*, "Economists are concerned with phenomena deriving not just from rationality, but from rationality coupled with the desire for wealth and larger consumption bundles" (Hausman 2013).

Hopkins argues that the stories underpinning our existing economic system tell us that "the future will be wealthier than the present, that economic growth can continue indefinitely, that we have become such an individualistic society that any common goals are unthinkable, that possessions can make you happy and that economic globalization is an inevitable process to which we have all given our consent" (Hopkins 2009, p. 14). These stories are as false as they are dangerous for the economy (financial crises), ecology (climate change) and society as a whole (stress, poverty and unfairness) and have to be changed straightaway. Our existing economic system glorifies free trade and has a strong affinity for simplistic explanations to complex problems and clashes with and rejects any alternative solutions based on a long-term responsibility for nature and society.

Even if it is obvious that we need a new economic system, there is strong resistance to such a change. It is believed that if we were to replace one system with another there would be winners and losers and those who come out badly will naturally oppose the amendments and argue that there are problems with the new system. If we change the perspective it could equally be argued that there are massive problems with the existing system and that the new system would offer a fairer means of distribution. Today we know that many serious negative consequences come about more through the dominant economic paradigm and not from individuals with bad intentions. Individual behavior and business practice are to a large extent encouraged, if not dictated, by the economic system. According to Galtung a shift from a "killing," life-destroying economy to a "living," life-enhancing economy depends on our success in rejecting the mechanical worldview.

Emancipation from the market economic system depends on our ability to overcome our current way of thinking. The context of understanding used in economic theory and practice is culturally determined and consists of assumptions about how reality is constructed and functions along with values and norms for social interaction. Habermas uses the concepts of system and lifeworld to make a distinction between the two aspects of the cultural context. "Lifeworld and system are the respective homes of communicative and instrumental action" (Finlayson 2005, p. 51). Because a well-functioning system depends on the lifeworld, we are in big trouble in any situation where the system, to a large extent, has conquered ever-larger parts of the lifeworld. This means, among other things, that instrumental economic values have replaced natural and inherent cultural values in an expanding number of arenas. Environmental and social responsibility have been reduced to what is economically profitable and we must not be seduced by the idea that a greener economy operating within the established system will solve all our problems.

Man's ecological footprint depends on several factors, among them population size, material standard of living, ecosystem productivity and efficiency in the exploitation of natural resources. Competitive market economies promote growth through constant changes of model, combined with low prices and massive advertising. Capra and Luisi argue that the myth of perpetual growth – promoting the impossible idea that indiscriminate economic growth is the cure for all the world's problems – is, in fact, "the disease that is at the root of our unsustainable global practices" (Capra and Luisi 2014, p. 368).

Underlying the idea of an ever-growing economy is a strong belief that growing consumption leads to increasing human happiness, when in fact it brings the accelerating overexploitation of natural resources. Unhealthy progression is characterized by slow growth in the beginning and then an exponential growth pattern. A healthy economy must be rooted in natural growth. Natural growth is fast in the beginning and then it flattens. This kind of growth pattern is found in nature, where everything stops growing at an optimal size. The conventional, linear, one-dimensional monetary measure of progress called gross domestic product (GDP) is far too limited and reductionist. It has to be replaced by a holistic, qualitative, integrated and balanced approach to development. In other words, qualitative development should replace exponential growth.

Utopia VSO

Revolutionary consequences follow when we accept a shift to an organic worldview: nature overpowers economy and nature itself changes from being a mere economic resource base to being the very frame of reference for all kinds of economic activity. Our challenge is to develop an economic system that contributes to life-processes in nature instead of extracting resources from nature. Put simply, the economy changes from being nature's master to being its humble servant.

This new economic system is oriented toward qualitative development (prosperity) rather than quantitative growth. Instead of maximizing production and consumption measured as GDP, the goal has to be changed toward maximizing enjoyment of life measured in GNH (gross national happiness). It is not only a question of happiness for human beings; non-humans and the whole ecosystem are included. Well-being of the ecology of our planet is tied to human quality of life. Within an organic worldview there is more focus on communicative rationality, intentionality, integrated cooperation, cultivation and value plurality. Circulation economics is based on the idea that the ultimate desire of all human beings, regardless of time and space, is to live a good life. The profound needs of human beings are not necessarily material or physical; there are other dimensions of life, "natural, social, cultural, intellectual, spiritual, psychological, aesthetic, moral, that make life worthwhile and meaningful, and that they need to be nurtured" (Powdyel 2014, p. 2).

Strong transdisciplinarity includes the spiritual dimension, integrating emotion, imagination and intuition. Its purpose is to raise awareness about the importance of change that promotes peace, equality, welfare and quality of life. The principles of circulation economics, based on universal values such as dignity, mutual respect, care and compassion, combined with responsibility for all life, can be introduced both in theory and practice. As a practical example, fair trade means a trading partnership based on dialogue, transparency and respect which promotes greater equity in trade. Organic understanding of reality is accepted and economics has moved in a direction where each economic activity contributes to the development of viable societies within a resilient and dynamic nature. Cooperation within networks gives priority to communicative action which is practiced in lifeworld arenas for dialogue. To initiate the change processes we need dialogue between scholars representing different scientific perspectives. Transdisciplinarity presupposes well-functioning arenas for dialogue in order to develop a context for meaningful economic activity.

When we accept that social systems and ecosystems are integrated networks, we have to establish the necessary technical requirements for building dynamic interrelations between the actors. Decentralized networks are materialized through interconnected villages and transition initiatives in local societies. The economic system, anchored in decentralized networks, is strengthened by the use of a local currency.

On the global level society is composed of small, self-sufficient, self-governing communities, grouped into regions and nations, each governed by representatives elected by its constituent units. On the national level there is an institutionalized cooperative network of communities. Economic actors are integrated in cooperative networks searching for solutions leading to enjoyment of life within resilient ecosystems and viable social systems. The aim is to change the economy in a direction where it is possible to create a high quality of life without over-using natural resources. Overarching goals are to satisfy the need for water, food, clothing, housing and other necessary goods for all humans. Qualitative values such as public health, cultural development and access to nutritious and environmentally responsible food are vital elements in ecological economics.

Creative solutions are initiated through bottom-up processes and engaged participation. This process starts when groups of motivated people within local communities come together to exchange ideas about how to develop existing local societies in an environmentally friendly and socially integrative way. Equity is developed through cooperation and development of fair structures. Arenas for open dialogue are established as necessary preconditions to strengthen mutual responsibility and to give each person a voice in decisions on which their individual well-being, the well-being of the whole society and that of the ecosystem depend. A network of integrated actors develops a market where customers, suppliers, competitors, communities and other stakeholder groups meet to decide practical questions concerning production and distribution. By observing the market from a holistic perspective we start to develop values such as trust and responsibility.

Change and development depend on building and rebuilding relations between all available entities (human and natural). Creativity is stimulated by measures that strengthen all kinds of bottom-up initiatives. Arenas for communicative processes are of vital significance in the development of resource-effective solutions that reduce as far as possible the ecological footprint of economic activity. Redistribution is introduced and consists of several sub-functions, collecting, sorting and recycling of various materials. By establishing circular value chains, it will be possible to reduce both the consumption of virgin natural resources and the amount of waste that goes back to nature. Business strategy based on the idea of circularity will expand the linear perspective of "from cradle to grave" to a circular reincarnation perspective of "from cradle to cradle" (Figure 3.3).

In addition, circularity is the basis of the connection between economy and nature. Finally, economy and culture also have a circular connection. Knowledge and values are essential if we are to develop a life-enhancing economy and gain experience from the processes which lead to new knowledge.

It is accepted that sustainable development demands more than merely reducing the negative impact on nature; other equally important measures are fairness and striving to reduce the gap between rich and poor. Justice is a necessary precondition for peaceful development. Problems connected to environment and poverty are linked to earlier systems which were based on ego-centered utility maximization of the goals of growth in production and consumption. To deal with the environmental challenges, changes at the systems level have to be implemented.

Greed, competition and growth are now replaced by solidarity, cooperation and compassion. It becomes inappropriate to talk about a single business as being in anyway sustainable, because all businesses are integrated into social and ecological networks. Likewise, green cities are impossible as long as the population remains dependent on capital goods and services from outside, something in clear conflict with ecological and humanistic values. Our challenge is to find new forms of interaction that allow solutions within a larger ecological and social context. Ecological economics is dynamic and assumes continuous development without any increase in the consumption of natural resources.

The main thing is the general acceptance of a level for total production and consumption that does not exceed the threshold point. Production and consumption above this level have negative consequences for individuals, society and nature. Dialogic processes including representatives from different stakeholder groups are important to maintain a co-productive balance between the economy, society and nature. In addition, dialogues should be more than rationalist exchanges of arguments; they should integrate a genuine fusion of minds, hearts and hands.

Values incorporated in the concepts of the threefold principle and triple bottom line are inherent in all economic decision processes. The threefold principle states that the ideals in the French Revolution – freedom, equity and brotherhood – are of vital importance. Culture is based on freedom, politics and law are based on equity, and the economy is founded on a principle of brotherhood or cooperation.

A healthy society is characterized by a balanced interplay between the three sectors. Negative consequences come about if one of them dominates the others. If the economic sector has a dominant position the result is the commercialization of culture and nature. If nature dominates the other sectors we could end up in a system where economic and societal values are depressed. If the cultural sector dominates in a society theocracy could undermine all humanistic and nature-based values.

In accordance with process philosophical principles it is accepted that everything is changing all the time, some things quickly, others more slowly. Diversity based on a common understanding of goals has inspired the creation of colorful and exciting communities. The juridical frame for economic action has changed in a direction where laws prevent ecocide. In combination with ethical and economic responsibility, juridical regulations provide a healthy, meaningful livelihood for all based on a just and equitable sharing of real wealth. The new laws include clauses stipulating that private companies, faceless entities that have the right to destroy ecosystems, cannot own the Earth.

The established monetary system contributed to alienation, competition, scarcity of resources and a malicious growth ideology. When economists attempt to impose monetary price tags on the whole of nature, plants, animals, human beings – life and ecosystems – are reduced to substitutable and exchangeable units. Fundamental systemic changes are required to create a new economy – negative interest, local currencies, a resource-based economy, a basic income for all and a focus on the common people. Management of money, the blood flowing through the economy, will have to change and banks will need to give credit in response to local needs and opportunities through a process that is transparent and democratically accountable. Money has to be oriented toward initiating the development of the local communities that the banks serve and, in accordance with the principle of cooperation, the banks will be owned cooperatively and rooted in the community.

Money – including profits and interest – should circulate locally on a fair basis but with a long-term view of eventually having a decentralized money system. Regional currency will help to retain capital in local societies, as money, in the new order, can only be used to purchase goods and services produced in the region. By introducing complementary money, based on new and different principles, the resilience in the economic system will increase as a result of diversity. Multiplying profits is not the aim of the new money system, whose defining characteristics are to stimulate qualitative development, that is, among other things, growth in knowledge and skills.

Regional currency will help to strengthen the region's economy and give people a far deeper sense of identity, of belonging to their community. Regional currency will, if you like, establish a protective membrane between the region and the world to make the society less vulnerable to international fluctuations and crises. Regional currency is important to promote local self-sufficiency through local production and local consumption but to produce larger commodities, such as cars, TV sets and airplanes, large-scale industries will be necessary. This branch of the economy will use national or international currencies. Large-scale industry will be kept to a minimum and will always be based on intermediate technology. Individuals will alternate between roles as owners and workers, borrowers and lenders. Some may have a bit more, some a bit less – but without any formal or clear class divisions.

The introduction of complementary currency is designed specifically to encourage collaboration on long-term solutions that benefit the economy, nature and society, as a means to initiate an expansion of consciousness to release creativity and human energy. A cooperative local monetary system will release an important driving force behind social change. Such a revolution in the money system will succeed because short-term thinking is not a part of human nature but imposed by a system capable of focusing exclusively on growth and short-term profits. We have created new dialogue-based arenas for the ongoing change processes in local, national and international money systems. We are confident that the challenges will have satisfactory outcomes as a result of these processes. The introduction of new complementary currency systems has initiated self-reinforcing processes that promote a healthy balance between efficiency and resilience. In a system anchored in the principles of ecological economics, income is decoupled from work. Citizen's income will be introduced to give people the opportunity to live a better, freer life.

The new system based on citizen's income is easy to understand and it is accepted as fair and resource-effective. Because of the secure minimum income provided by the citizen's income, a much larger percentage of the population will be taken out of poverty, giving greater social cohesion as citizens are set free from the weight of bureaucratic intrusions. Politicians and economists change their tune to argue that the distribution of money should be more equal and fair, while labor markets allow workers more freedom to make choices about their employment patterns. On the individual level a secure income provides people with the possibility to choose part-time work in addition to the basic income. Part-time work, often in combination with self-employment, is enough to top up their basic income. One positive consequence of part-time jobs is work for more people. This is an important consideration at a time of rising populations and decreasing amounts of work due to, among other things, technological development.

Freedom is of great importance if we are to vitalize the cultural sector. Cultural institutions, such as education and health care, are governed by freedom. Universities and hospitals will give priority to knowledge and health rather than focusing, as they do now increasingly, on economic growth and profits. A living economy's fundamental purpose is to create the best possible basis for a good life for many people. Viable communities are best established within the framework of sustainable nature with change initiated in the direction of decentralized networks of eco-villages. The economy is adapted to the new and decentralized social structure of small, relaxed and interdependent eco-village communities. Since small eco-villages are to form the basic units of the economy, the scale of industrialization is developed accordingly. Decentralization and the establishment of networks of smaller economic units have contributed to making the economy more democratic and open. Local networks linked together globally provide the best basis for developing co-responsible human beings. An important measure is the development of global democratic institutions which have the authority to regulate the world economy. A key point to emphasize is that individual citizens, even though they are in the global village, maintain and enhance their individuality and dignity.

Production is decentralized and each community is relatively self-sufficient as far as its basic needs are concerned. Eco-village-style neighbourhoods and districts are organized as locally owned, self-sustaining economic units; they offer a variety of locally owned commercial and recreational facilities as well as investment and employment opportunities which reflect the distinctive tastes, interests, skills and personal preferences of their residents. Each of the region's distinctive eco-villages makes its unique contribution to the diverse, resilient, self-reliant life of the whole.

Work is not only focused, as it mostly is now, on effective production processes; through work in the new system people develop their self-respect, and, by increasing their capacity to cooperate with others, they reduce the tendencies to egocentrism. A living economy is characterized by the quality of its actors and the societies it creates and not the quantity of its material objects. A living economy has moral and cultural implications for the humanity of the process of production; it strives to achieve sustainable development, a more balanced relationship with nature, the right to gainful employment within a decentralized production system. The role of the state will be redrawn to strengthen the possibilities for everyone to have a good life in a good society.

Box 13.3 Characteristics of circulation economics

• Economy as a nested system
• Bottom-up

• Economy as networks
• Associative economics
• Communitarian approach

• Economy as an open system
• Local self-sufficiency
• Prosperity

• Economy as cognitive interactions: a sense of ethics

Reflection

To understand the social organism, every sector must work in harmony with all the rest, and none can see themselves as working in a vacuum, as it were. For example, schools are aware of juridical regulations and economic conditions. Politics depends on culture and economy, and all kinds of economic activity depend on juridical regulations and cultural creativity. Legal regulations have great influence on human behavior and introducing strict environmental laws lays the foundation for new practice as it influences our mind-set and governs our behavior. This clear systemic understanding underlines that a change toward an organic worldview is an imperative not only for human well-being but also for the sustainability of Gaia as a whole.

Circulation economics is based on the fundamental idea that economic activity is anchored in cooperative, decentralized, nested networks. This means that people living in a local society are free to develop and are responsible for the development of economic activity within accepted frameworks especially in relation to natural conditions and juridical regulations. Change on a systems level is a prerequisite for changes in business practice. Within the existing system "greening" is seen as the only possible strategy, but far more fundamental developments depend on changes which affect ecological economics on systems level.

BUSINESS PRACTICE

Introduction

If we are to evaluate the result of mainstream business practice then three main criteria are of vital importance – effectiveness, efficiency and equity. Effectiveness refers to the ability to reach defined goals. Efficiency refers to the degree economic goals are reached with a minimum of negative impact on

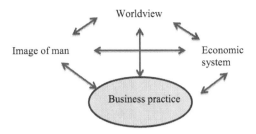

Figure 13.7 Focus on business practice

nature and society. Equity refers to how wealth is distributed. Equity can be defined as unity of interests and responsibilities, in other words solidarity put into system. On the one hand, within integrated communicative networks, it is possible to take care of individual freedom and creativity without disturbing the ends of the whole society.

On the other hand, it is naïve to think that reputation building, greenwashing and green growth will give way to an economy which is in harmony with ecological limits and humanistic values. We must appeal to the systems level and/or the individual level to find real motives to implement a real change in economic practice. A growing number of people within the business community are coming to realize that our economic system is "the driving force" behind the clear and obvious global environmental destruction. They are also beginning to accept the need for a fundamental reorganization and reorientation of business practice. An environmentally responsible attitude stimulates the development of creativity both in production and organization. A partnership approach at the business level deals with challenges concerning how to integrate all stakeholders in cooperative networks. A partnership approach includes ecological, social and economic dimensions. Employees in companies who practice environmental and social responsibility have a higher morale because they can easily identify with the business practice. To achieve common goals it is necessary to develop organic structures that initiate collaborative networks (associations). In order to maximize creative potential it is crucial to understand the interplay between the different actors who make up the self-generating networks.

Figure 13.8 illustrates the current situation where nature is interpreted as a resource base for economic activity. Nature is divided into small pieces – metal, sources of energy, trees, animals – in short everything and anything that can be sold for a profit on the market. In a mechanical world this seems to be non-problematic. In an organic world everything that is separated will die. In other words, as long as the market economy represents the frame of reference for strategic management it is impossible to come up with anything more than short-sighted solutions which focus on reducing negative symptoms of the existing system.

In order to handle the environmental and social problems of today it is necessary to accept a fundamental shift in economics, business administration

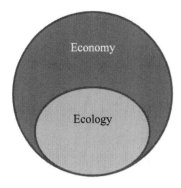

Figure 13.8 Economy as context

and leadership, away from the idea that the market functions as a machine driven by physical laws. An acceptance of this shift from an instrumental approach to an approach based on the inherent value of Gaia is found in the *Harvard Business Review* for October 2011:

> No one these days denies the need for sustainable business practices. Even those concerned about only business and not the fate of the planet recognize that the viability of business itself depends on the resources of healthy ecosystems – fresh water, clean air, robust diversity, productive land – and on the stability of just societies. Happily, most of us also care about these things directly.
>
> (Chouinard, Ellison and Ridgeway 2011)

The question is: what would business practice respecting the inherent value of Gaia look like in practice?

Utopia VSO

Organic business practices give priority to production processes, distributing systems and reprocessing of waste which satisfies human needs, individually and collectively, to stimulate life processes in both nature and society. All kinds of businesses will be organized in order to allow individual abilities to flourish. The interplay between the businesses is structured into nested networks specially designed to better coordinate needs and production, secure more appropriate utilization of labor and the optimal use of natural resources and technology. Through dialogue and value-based reflection the actors are able to decide whether the decisions taken are in accordance with the interests of the business firm and the social and natural environment. Collaborative networks also help to establish a broad understanding between producers, distributors and consumers to ensure that commodities and money circulate in the (local) societies. Mutual trust between the actors is a necessary condition for the partnership approach to function in the best possible way.

Economic, ecological, and social challenges are solved through integrated interaction between the actors in the market (the triple bottom line). The actors in the market regard each other as interdependent partners. Cooperative interactions between the businesses stimulate creativity to make substantial contributions to community life. In this perspective business and society require each other; the market consists of partners integrated in living, natural and social systems.

Figure 13.9. gives an impression of business practice within an organic context. The question now becomes how to pay attention to the development of business practices that stimulate resilience in nature and society. To reach such a goal, co-operation rather than competition is introduced in combination with networks in place of atomized markets. The partnership approach is based on voluntary agreements and binding cooperation between all actors in the market. "A more complex and dynamic framework takes into consideration that economic behavior is both multi-faceted and context dependent" (Storsletten and Jakobsen 2015, p. 343).

It is inappropriate to talk about a single business as being in any way sustainable. The reason is that all businesses are integrated into social and ecological networks and so the challenge consists of finding new forms of interaction that allow solutions within the larger ecological and social context. When the market is understood as a network of interdependent actors then responsibility of business is extended from shareholders to all stakeholders.

Work has intrinsic value because it seeks common goals through collaboration with other people, contributing to personal development and counteracting selfishness. Illuminated, creative, motivated, responsible employees seek meaningful work, personal development and conformity between the company's ethics and their own. People with hope and faith have a vision of

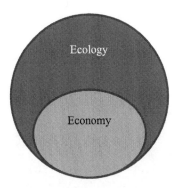

Figure 13.9 Ecology as context

"where they are going, and how they get there, they are willing to face opposition and endure hardship and suffering, to achieve their goals" (Fry 2003, p. 713). Work gives people opportunities to develop and make use of their abilities and skills. Progression from passivity to activity is closely connected to the progression from necessity to freedom. In addition, working together with others helps to develop a feeling of interdependence that reduces selfish tendencies. Sustainability in this perspective is based on freedom, justice and welfare.

People in business may find their inspiration in both Western and Eastern philosophy. Value-based leadership involves dialogue, responsibility and ethical reflection. Dialogue-based cooperation characterizes organizations anchored in value-based leadership. The main challenge of leadership today is bridging the gap between ecosystem reality and ego-system awareness. By releasing policy-makers from learned forms of understanding and established solutions we get access to a virtually unlimited source of creativity. However, if we are to develop the creative potential in the networks of actors we must accept turbulences and complexities.

Creative thinking can be combined with practical experimentation. We must switch our understanding toward wholeness and coherence and away from a focus on atomized parts. Resilience depends on diversity; therefore the local economy must avoid too much specialization and monocultures. Through specialization the whole is lost by focusing on the parts. The goal of economic development is to encourage fair trade through cooperative networking. Business is oriented toward self-organizing local markets in which companies secure their supplies through fair and equal exchange. If we don't give people opportunities to release their personal potential we cannot expect them to perform any better than robots. Instead of using one-dimensional instrumental thinking aimed at increased growth and profits, our energies and efforts are aimed instead toward greater complexity, beauty and harmony. We have, with tragic results, organized our economic thinking around the very bad, old and tired idea that we work for money.

In Utopia VSO the product is defined as a dynamic phenomenon, integrated in societal and ecological networks. Values such as responsibility and fairness cannot be separated from the product. "Being aware of product as process leads to acceptance of the actors co-responsibility for the whole lifecycle of the product they use or produce" (Ims, Jakobsen and Zsolnai 2015, p. 12). Social and the biophysical realities are interconnected and facts about reality are inseparable from values.

Products are not at any stage in the lifecycle harmful to the environment. The precautionary principle is based on the reverse burden of proof. The person performing the action must demonstrate that it has no negative impact on the social or natural environment. Products are not allowed to consume large amounts of energy or raw materials, create a lot of waste, inflict animal disorders or make use of resources that are detrimental to endangered ecosystems, plants or animal species. Products must not be harmful to either humans or animals. Food cannot be healthier than the soil it is grown in, and the most reasonable solution is organic farming that contributes to good biodiversity and good health both for the planet and the humans on it.

Technological changes are based on improved resource efficiency and clean technology. Social changes presuppose more emphasis on public goods, fair distribution of benefits and reduced materialism. Villages are to encourage locally based industries and crafts, take pride in using local products and import only what they could not produce themselves. To do this, the economic system consists of small firms and farms owned by individuals and families with a sense of loyalty to their place and their local social networks. Spirituality in the system is stimulated by a creative network of living economic entities (the web of life) owned by living people who depend on them for their own well-being.

All business is integrated into social and ecological networks. The challenge is to find new forms of interaction that allow solutions within a larger ecological and social context. When contact with the local communities and culture is reduced the temptation to forget anything but profits and growth becomes dominating. Leadership with a spiritual grounding provides the best guarantee for not reducing corporate objectives to increasing profits and efficiency. Spiritual leadership helps to give values a deep inner anchoring which reduces the chances that ethics become an instrument for achieving external goals. Responsibility is connected to accepting that we are co-responsible, co-creators of the development and the economic actors experience one another as interdependent partners.

Reflection

Business practice depends on both the economic system and the image of the economic actor. Let's think of them as methodological collectivism and methodological individualism, respectively. On the one hand, methodological collectivism can be characterized as top-down explanations; lower-level practice is explained by reference to the systems level. On the other hand, methodological individualism can be referred to as bottom-up explanation because higher-level practice is explained from the level below. In my interpretation both bottom-up and top-down explanations are essential. A change in business practice depends on change in worldview, economic system and the image of economic man.

Even if it is possible to make small changes within the current business model, using the market economic tool, far deeper change toward a partnership model is necessary to develop economic practices which stimulate resilience in both nature and society.

Many economic functions in modern society do require larger enterprise units. There are many good examples of how we can meet this need in ways consistent with broad, equitable, stable and locally rooted participation in ownership through cooperative ownership structures.

Box 13.4 Characteristics of partnership approach

- The Gaian world order:
  - fair trade
  - GNH
  - decentralized

- Circular value chains:
  - network of mutual dependence
  - small is beautiful

- Arenas for free exchange of ideas:
  - knowledge
  - information

- Spiritual leadership
- Communicative rationality

IMAGE OF MAN

Introduction

John Stuart Mill defined the economic man in 1836. He was inspired by Adam Smith's economic theories. Economic man is a metaphor, indicating that economic actors are supposed to act as ethical egoists. Rational behavior is explained as an ever-present tendency to give priority to alternatives that maximize one's own self-interest. According to Siebenhüner: "The assumption of a rational, self-interested, and utility-maximizing individual is the model of humans underlying standard economic theory" (Siebenhüner 2000, p. 15). The economic man was a "hypothetical subject, whose narrow and well-defined motives made him a useful abstraction in economic analysis" (Persky 1995, p. 222).

Neo-classical economics has a highly reductionist view of human nature in describing economic man as an isolated being, very similar to the mechanical description of an isolated particle moving in space, always maximizing his own utility function. The individual is separated from other people and people are separated from nature. Our identity and our way of being are largely linked to the experience of the separated self.

Economic man is free to make his own choices and be responsible for taking care of himself. The assumption that the actors are rational provides, according to Kahneman, "the intellectual foundation for the libertarian approach to public policy: do not interfere with the individual's right to choose, unless the choices harm others" (Kahneman 2012, p. 11). According to Thaler and Sunstein, government is allowed to "nudge" (any factor that significantly alters the behavior) people to make decisions that serve their own long-term

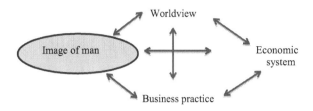

Figure 13.10 Focus on the image of man

interest. This kind of libertarian paternalism is based on the idea that "choice architects can make major improvements to the lives of others by designing user-friendly environments" (Thaler and Sunstein 2008, p. 12).

In contrast to the economic man in mainstream economic theory, ecological economics is based on the assumption of an ecological man who is aware of being integrated in the web of life. Ecological man is described as an integrated, co-responsible person behaving in accordance with fundamental ecological and humanistic values. As noted earlier, the implementation of ecological economics started with a shift from a mechanistic to an organic view of reality. Different institutions are not enough, a different mind-set is required too.

Extended consciousness on the individual level is important, along with a holistic understanding of the social and environmental challenges we face. We must eliminate the idea of separation. There are two different forces which help to create the required shift of direction, external challenges (push factor) and expanding individual consciousness (pull factor). Both factors are present today.

It is often said that most people resist change. In reality they are resistant to change imposed from outside. Success on the systems level depends on success on the individual level. The combination between change and stability is essential to every living society. We have to change our mind-set from fragmentation, competition and humiliation toward a mind-set of integration, cooperation and humility. We must abandon the mechanical ontology of the mainstream economy that presupposes the existence of "discrete, well-defined, rational, self-interested, and autonomous agents" (Storsletten and Jakobsen 2013, p. 365) and introduce the idea of human beings with an ecological mind-set. Life based on purely materialistic values would be deficient. We need a balanced life where material and the spiritual values are combined.

Utopia VSO

If we are to cope with the underlying patterns of the crises, it will be of great importance to change the way we think as economic actors. The transformation of the economic actor, a shift from "economic man" to "ecological man," is at the heart of ecological economics, which sees ecological man as characterized by holistic understanding and social responsibility. Life's goals simply cannot be limited to an endless cycle of production and consumption. Rather, the actor accepts that all forms of life have inherent value. Ethics constitutes the connection between inner and outer reality. Ethics is tied to our ability to develop a notion of the future based on imagination and empathy with all life forms. It is no longer sufficient to choose actions that increase the total utility or benefit for a defined group of people (utilitarianism), or follow ethical principles (duty ethics). It is also essential to develop the moral character of all economic actors (virtue ethics).

With Kierkegaard's three modes of existence in mind, it becomes clear that a move toward the spiritual stage offers an interesting dimension to the image of man embodying a human identity in cooperative partnerships with both culture and nature. This shift in economic practice goes hand in hand with a transition in consciousness, and represents a truly radical shift away from the idea of a rational, self-interested actor toward a human being with holistic concerns embedded in nested networks of social and ecological relations. "The relationship between the human being and nature is described beyond economic self-interest and biological survival" (Ingebrigtsen and Jakobsen 2009, p. 2781).

The economic actor is far from being a one-dimensional consumer. He has become a multifaceted human person socialized in networks of reciprocal social and ecological responsibility. This is what Habermas refers to as the lifeworld, which represents an intuitively pre-understood context for action. The ecological self contradicts the egocentric self, which is self-centered, self-obsessed, attached to hedonistic pleasures and, as a consequence, alienated from itself and from nature and other beings. Through presencing the ecological self makes it possible to break with established patterns of behavior. Presencing is composed of the words "presence" and "sensing" and describes a process leading to an expanded awareness at a deeper level.

To get this change in consciousness going we introduce eco-literacy as a topic in the curriculum in schools from kindergartens to universities. In order to sustain life in nature and develop healthy societies for people with a high quality of life, topics reaching from metaphysical speculation about ontological questions to topics concerning practical behavior are present on all levels of education so that the positive inner nature of a person emerges in a supportive environment. This increase in eco-literacy competence points to better understanding among economic actors of the basic principles of living organisms.

To establish the best atmosphere of purposeful reflection on organic understanding, students are engaged in practical experiences that involve long-term projects in living nature. Slowly but surely the mind-set changes and as a consequence of the process of critical reflection we move from "I" to "We" consciousness. By developing relationships with others and engaging in social networks the individual becomes more responsible. A culture deeply rooted in human relationships makes radical changes in both business practice and in economic systems. A holistic understanding is the aim, an understanding which transforms conflicts of interests into experiences of common interest between the individual, society and nature. Being aware of nature's inherent value makes human beings responsible toward nature.

> At the individual level, flexible framing and the ability to see and consider the complexity of reality reduce the risks of unethical behaviour. Flexible framing is superior to rigid framing, and it makes sense to promote conditions in societies and organizations that foster a climate of tolerance and pluralism instead of fundamentalism and dogmatism.
>
> (Palazzo et al. 2012, p. 335)

It is, furthermore, of great importance to ensure that teachers have the capacity and competence to use different transdisciplinary methods that are particularly appropriate for understanding and experiencing the implications of organic living. As a consequence, reflections on organic worldviews will be introduced in the curriculum at teacher training colleges. Consciousness anchored in eco-literacy is transmitted intuitively from generation to generation. "Memes" is a metaphor often used to describe how cultural information, attitudes, values and behavior patterns are transferred from generation to generation.

In practice ecological man is oriented toward prosperity based on voluntary simplicity. Development of wisdom, empathy and moderation stimulates the elimination of the pathological tendency to extreme individualism, greed and violence and, consequently, individual actions are consistent with the continuation of genuinely human life on Earth. Qualitative individual development is associated with the facilitation of opportunities to develop human potential and to realize and enhance the importance of inherent values in nature and society outside the individual. Personal choice and responsibility, personality growth and positive feelings of self-worth are of great importance, as people with strong intrinsic values are more satisfied and exhibit greater environmental responsibility than people with an exclusive focus on material values. We have a natural tendency toward self-actualization – the realization of our individual potential.

Buddhist concepts such as chanda (wisdom) and tanhã (selfishness) give an illuminating impression of the human condition. As long as tanhã dominates, a pathological situation expressed by physical, developmental, cultural and/or institutional failure will occur. Segregation and separation are the outcomes which affect society internally and the environment externally. It is of great importance to find antidotes to cynicism, frustration and paralysis. In addition to changes at the systems level, the shift in practice depends on extended individual consciousness characterized by a dominance of chanda values.

Even if extended individual consciousness is and will be a complex process, the elimination of the myth of dualism or bifurcation is a massive step forward. Taylor (1991) describes human development as a process in which the individual adapts to a wider horizon of important values and thus

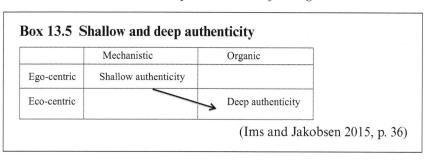

Box 13.5 Shallow and deep authenticity

	Mechanistic	Organic
Ego-centric	Shallow authenticity	
Eco-centric		Deep authenticity

(Ims and Jakobsen 2015, p. 36)

moves beyond the individual self. Authenticity is a relational concept; the individual is strongly embedded in society and nature. Authenticity is cooperation between interrelated, self-realizing subjects. "A deeply authentic person is simultaneously free and committed to society and nature" (Ims and Jakobsen 2011, p. 214). Individual behavior is both multifaceted and context-dependent. Accepting the organic worldview has far-reaching consequences for the interpretation of the individual as a self-realizing person in society.

Deep authenticity depends on "our ability to switch to an organic worldview where the eco-centric self becomes actuality" (Ims and Jakobsen 2015, p. 36). This radical and necessary change in mind-set is visualized in Box 13.5.

Bridging the gap between ego-system reality and ecosystem awareness is the main challenge today. In the land of ecological utopia, well-being is closely connected to moderation in consumption and a life-style based on simplicity and frugality. Well-being is based on moderation in consumption of material goods and increased focus on the development of co-responsibility for all life. Ecological man's life is interconnected in living networks. Creativity is the result of bottom-up initiatives where the potentiality of the social organism is focused. Creativity is always reflexive and is exercised over and with respect to the self. Creativity is both self-creative and co-creative.

Reflection and increased self-understanding are important means to develop the individual's positive freedom. Human beings are by nature interdependent and constitute an organic whole. The I & We paradigm or communitarianism is part of the extended self-consciousness. These initiatives presuppose the establishment of arenas for dialogue and cooperative action. Dialogue is essential for qualitative individual and social development (prosperity). The good life cannot be seen in isolation from the development of the good society. Dependent (linked to external objects), independent (linked to peace of mind) and harmonious happiness cultivate the experience of the relationship between I and We. Access to healthy food and clean water, sustainable nature and strong social and cultural identity contribute to high individual well-being. Prosperity is also dependent on a vigorous nature, stable societies, safe communities, social justice, belonging and many other social and spiritual qualities.

Exploration and study of the inner person, that is, one's interior world, is completely impossible without self-awareness. In the absence of self-awareness and self-confidence, we think and act mechanically, like a programmed computer, and have no freedom to act in accordance with our own ideas and intentions. This needs a radical rethink of the way we see the world by opening up to a new holistic framework for our perceptions. These processes have the potential to reveal solutions to the world's most urgent challenges, helped along as they are by a pure moral awareness and acts of will.

Life's spiritual dimension, and its meaning, help us to understand reality.

> This anchoring requires a pervasive change in the levels of consciousness in which mechanical solutions are understood from an organic perception of reality and not the inverted form in which organic solutions are interpreted in a mechanical perception of reality.
>
> (Storsletten and Jakobsen 2015, p. 348)

Reflection

Authentic ecological consciousness is closely connected to shifts at the metaphysical, systems and practice level. Ecological consciousness is based on the idea that economic actors have an ecological perspective simply by having a sense of being part of the whole of life. Ecological man is rooted in the idea that the superior goal of sustainability and quality of life cannot be reached within abstracted mechanistic or social worldviews. Ecological man is a person who is engaged in a fundamental enquiry into the basic questions such as humanity's relationship to the source and ground of its being. Changes in individual consciousness can on the one hand be explained by referring to changes in worldview, at the systems level and in business practice. On the other hand all change is closely connected to furthering individual development. In other words, as everything is interconnected, the change must start on all levels at the same time. Box 13.6 illustrates the sort of concepts to which the image of man in this understanding is connected.

Box 13.6 Characteristics of ecological man

- Eco-centricity
- Extended self
- Co-responsibility

- Recognize the right of each to meet their needs with due consideration for the needs of others

---

- Cooperation
- Political economic person (PEP)

- Authenticity
- Dignity
- "I & We" mind-set
- moral economic man

---

14 Change

We are living in frightening times. According to Korten, "we see a future in which the evolutionary viability of our species is in doubt. Our most powerful and respected institutions are driving rather than resolving the unfolding crises" (Korten 2015, p. 56). To change course we must rewrite the story of our future and this utopian description must include how we structure our relationship to nature and society – the very essence of ecological economics. We must also take the ecological economic story in front of a far wider audience, make it a focal point of discussion in conversations, in mass media and in academic work.

Schopenhauer said that "poor people's lives are a constant struggle against distress; the kingdom of life is a persistent and desperate battle against boredom." How can we develop a dynamic society where everybody becomes better off? Today the gap between rich and poor is increasing, both globally and nationally. Those wealthy few hold the purse strings and are the ones keeping us from changing the system because they have become dependent on and addicted to the existing system for their own survival.

Change is initiated by a situation made up of anomalies, negative unintended consequences or disturbing factors of any kind between worldview, system, practice and individual. Today we face problems on all levels and it is impossible both to understand and explain the problems and to come up with solutions. Ecological economics must be used as an inspiration not only to develop new solutions to the old questions – we have to ask new questions.

Many contributors to ecological economics refer to a mismatch between our worldview and real-life conditions. If we accept that Gaia is like a living organism and that the economic system, business practice and the image of the economic actor are based on a mechanistic pre-understanding we can only conclude that it is no surprise we have ended up in trouble. If we have mistakenly used a misleading map bearing little or no relation to reality, we have to make our own map.

In Part II of this book we looked at thirty different perspectives, almost all of which point to the necessity of re-establishing economic theory and practice within an organic ontology. Conflict between mechanistic and organic philosophy has a history in European culture going back more than

---

Box 14.1 The connection between the four levels

Metaphysics Organic worldview	Economic system Circulation economics	Business practice Partnership approach	Image of man Ecological man
• organic • holistic • process	• economy as a nested system • bottom-up	• the Gaian world order • fair trade • GNH • decentralized	• eco-centricity • extended self • co-responsible
• integrated • relations • non-linear	• economy as networks • associative economics • communitarian approach	• circular value chains • network of mutual dependence • small is beautiful	• recognize the right of each to meet their needs with due consideration for the needs of others
• diversity • resilience • creativity	• economy as an open system • local self-sufficiency • prosperity	• arenas for free exchange of ideas, knowledge and information	• cooperation • political economic person (PEP)
• self- organizing • becoming • meaning	• economy as cognitive interactions • a sense of ethics	• spiritual leadership • communicative rationality	• authenticity • dignity • "I & We" mind-set • moral economic man

---

2,000 years. What's extraordinary is that the mechanistic paradigm has been almost totally dominant for the last 200 years. In other words, we have been through an experiment where we have practiced economy based upon the idea that nature is just an economic resource base and people's happiness depends on the level of their consumption alone. Today we recognize the negative unintended consequences of atomizing nature and reducing human beings to no more than one-dimensional consumers to the extent that we have, quite simply, lost control.

Part of this extremely problematic situation is how science has developed over the preceding 200 years; knowledge has been divided up into a huge number of specialized scientific research programs and the mismatch between atomized knowledge and holistic reality makes it difficult to secure proper solutions to pressing problems. To come up with realistic solutions, transdiciplinarity is only part of the answer. Ecological economics is a new science based on weak and strong transdiciplinarity and the first step is to create arenas for cross-scientific dialogues and dialogues between science and practice. It is also necessary to include art in the dialogue because it is vital to discover and communicate knowledge and wisdom through art.

Mapping out relationships and studying patterns involves visualizing. That is why, throughout our intellectual history, artists have made their best contributions to science whenever the study of patterns was uppermost. Art can be a powerful tool for teaching organic thinking. Arts enhance that emotional dimension which is increasingly being recognized as an essential component of the learning process. A change is possible because, for the first time in history, it has become obvious that individual self-interest coincides with humanity's long-term collective interests.

There is a growing recognition among policy-makers and private-sector decision-makers that the current model of economic growth is socially, environmentally and economically unsustainable and should be replaced by a new organic economy. Empirical studies indicate that stricter environmental regulations, better business practices and more efficient technologies are needed, but they are not sufficient. To solve our problems (e.g. environmental, poverty, war and financial crisis) we need a far deeper systemic change.

To start the change process we must get a few obstacles out of the way; first, we must raise awareness of the fact that despite everything we *can* do something. Next, we must reduce the distance between our actions and the negative effects they have on environment and society. We must realize that what we are doing now creates consequences for our children. Lastly, and possibly most serious, is the problem that today people perceive the challenges we face as being so overwhelming they lose all energy to do anything and don't even know where to start. Radical engagement is the answer and we should implement change on all levels – metaphysical, systems, practice and individual development – and do so at the same time.

I have argued that change must be implemented on all levels at the same time, ontology must be part of the curriculum at universities and business schools, alternative economic systems must be developed based on ontological preconditions, business practice must find a balance between society and nature and we must get rid, once and for all, of the idea of economic man.

It is time to get started!

Bibliography

Albritton, Robert (2012) A Practical Utopia for the Twenty-First Century, in *Existential Utopia: New Perspectives on Utopian Thought*, Patricia Vieira and Michael Marder (eds.), London, Continuum

Anand, Sudhir and Sen, Amartya (2000) Human Development and Economic Sustainability, *World Development* 28:12, pp. 2029–2049

Anshen, Ruth Nanda (1961) *Alfred North Whitehead: His Reflections on Man and Nature*, New York, Harper & Brothers

Atkins, Peter (2010) *The Laws of Thermodynamics: A Very Short Introduction*, Oxford, Oxford University Press

Balachandran, P. K. (2006) Gandhi Proclaimed Himself a Buddhist, *Hindustan Times*, June 14

Barash, David P. and Webel, Charles P. (2014) *Peace and Conflict Studies*, 3rd ed., London, Sage Publications

Beard, T. Randolf and Lozada, Gabriel A. (1999) *Economics, Entropy and the Environment: The Extraordinary Economics of Nicholas Georgescu-Roegen*, Northampton, MA, Edward Elgar Publishing

Becker, C. (2006) The Human Actor in Ecological Economics: Philosophical Approach and Research Perspectives, *Ecological Economics* 69, pp. 17–23

Berry, T. (2007) Teilhard in the Ecological Age, in *Teilhard in the 21st Century: The Emerging Spirit of Earth*, Arthur Fabel and Donald St. John (eds.), New York, Orbis Books

Blaug, Mark (1978) *Economic Theory in Retrospect*, 3rd ed., London, Cambridge University Press

Boukaert, Luk and Chatterji, Manas (eds.) (2015) *Business, Ethics and Peace*, Bingley, Yorkshire, Emerald

Boulding, Kenneth (1968) *Beyond Economics: Essays on Society, Religion and Ethics*, Ann Arbor, University of Michigan Press

Boulding, Kenneth (1970) *Economics as a Science, Morality, Ecology, Evolution, Sociology, Mathematics*, New York, McGraw-Hill Book Company

Boulding, Kenneth (1981) *Evolutionary Economics*, Thousand Oaks, CA, Sage Publications

Buchholtz, Ann and Carroll, Archie (2009) *Business and Society*, Stamford, CT, South-Western Cengage learning

Capra, Fritjof (1996) *The Web of Life: A New Synthesis of Mind and Matter*, London, HarperCollins

Capra, Fritjof (2007) *The Science of Leonardo*, New York, Anchor Books

Capra, Fritjof and Luisi, Pier Luigi (2014) *A Systems View of Life: A Unifying Vision*, Cambridge, Cambridge University Press

Carroll, A. B. (1987) In Search of the Moral Manager, *Business Horizons*, March–April, pp. 7–15

Carroll, A. B. (1991) The Pyramid of Corporate Social Responsibility: Toward the Moral Management off Organizational Stakeholders, *Business Horizons*, July–August, pp. 39–48

Carroll, A. B. (1998) The Four Faces of Corporate Citizenship, *Business and Society Review* 100:1, pp. 1–7

Chouinard, Yvon, Ellison, Jib and Ridgeway, Rick (2011) The Sustainable Economy, *Harvard Business Review*, October, pp. 52–62

Cobb Jr., John B. (2000) Economic Aspects of Social and Environmental Violence, presented at the Buddhist-Christian Conference in Tacoma, Washington, August 2,000, www.religion-online.org/showarticle.asp?title=1092, accessed December 6, 2016

Costanza, R. (2008) Stewardship for a "Full" World, *Current History*, January, pp. 30–35

Cyert, Richard M. and March James, G. (1963) *A Behavioral Theory of the Firm*, Englewood Cliffs, NJ, Prentice-Hall

Czarniawska, Barbara (2004) *Narratives in Social Science Research*, London, Sage Publications

Daly, Herman (1996) *Beyond Growth: The Economics of a Sustainable Development*, Boston, Beacon Press

Daly, Herman (2007) *Ecological Economics and Sustainable Development: Selected Essays of Herman Daly*, Northampton, MA, Edward Elgar

Daly, Herman and Cobb Jr., John B. (1994) *For the Common Good: Redirecting the Economy toward Community, the Environment, and a Sustainable Future*, 2nd ed., Boston, Beacon Press [first published 1989]

Darwin, Charles (1982) *The Origin of Species*, London, Everyman's Library [first published 1859]

Darwin, Charles (2007) *The Descent of Man*, New York, Penguin Group [first published 1871]

Dasgupta, Ajit K. (1996) *Gandhi's Economic Thought*, London, Routledge Research

Davis, Laurence (2012) History, Politics, and Utopia: Toward a Synthesis of Social Theory and Practice, in *Existential Utopia: New Perspectives on Utopian Thought*, Patricia Vieira and Michael Marder (eds.), London, Continuum

Dawson, J. (2006) *Ecovillages: New Frontiers for Sustainability*, Dartington, Devon, Green Books

Eisendrath, Craig, R. (1999) *The Unifying Moment: The Psychological Philosophy of William James and Alfred North Whitehead*, Cambridge, MA, Harvard University Press

Eisenstein, Charles (2007) *The Ascent of Humanity: Civilization and the Human Sense of the Self*, Berkeley, CA, Evolver Editions

Eisenstein, Charles (2011) *Sacred Economics: Money, Gift, and Society in the Age of Transition*, Berkeley, CA, Evolver Editions

Eisenstein, Charles (2013) *The More Beautiful World Our Hearts Know is Possible*, Berkeley, CA, North Atlantic Books

Elkington, John (1997) *Cannibals with Forks: The Triple Bottom Line of 21st Century Business*, Oxford, Capstone

Elkington, John and Burke, Tom (1987) *The Green Capitalists*, London, Gollancz

Emmet, D. M. (2012) *Whitehead's Philosophy of Organism*, London, Forgotten Books [first published 1932]

Encyclopedia of Philosophy (1967) Paul Edwards, editor-in-chief, vols. 1 and 2, New York, Macmillan Publishing

Etzioni, A. (1988) *The Moral Dimension: Toward A New Economics*, New York, The Free Press

Etzioni, A. (2002) Towards a Socio-Economic Paradigm, *Socio-Economic Review* 1:1, pp. 105–118

Etzioni, A. (2009) A Crisis of Consumerism, in *Aftershocks: Economic Crisis and Institutional Choice*, Anton Hemerijck, Ben Knapen and Ellen van Doorne (eds.), Amsterdam, Amsterdam University Press

European Fair Trade Association (2001), *Fair Trade Yearbook: Challenges of the New Millennium 2001–2003*, available at www.european-fair-trade-association.org/efta/Doc/yb01-en.pdf, accessed December 6, 2016

Fabel, A. and St. John, D. (eds.) (2007) *Teilhard in the 21st Century: The Emerging Spirit of Earth*, New York, Orbis Books

Finlayson, James Gordon (2005) *Habermas: A Very Short Introduction*, Oxford, Oxford University Press

Ford, Lewis, S. (2002) Two Types of Creationist Philosophy: Thomas and Whitehead, *Encounter* 63:4, pp. 385–396

Francis, Pope (2015) *Laudato si': On Care for Our Common Home. Encyclical Letter*, London, Catholic Truth Society

Frank, Robert H. (2011) *The Darwin Economy: Liberty, Competition, and the Common Good*, Princeton, NJ, Princeton University Press

Fry, Louis (2003) Toward a Theory of Spiritual Leadership, *Leadership Quarterly* 14, pp. 265–278

Galtung, Johann (1985) Twenty-Five Years of Peace Research: Ten Challenges and Some Responses, *Journal of Peace Research* 22:2, pp. 141–158

Galtung, Johan (1996) *Peace by Peaceful Means: Peace and Conflict, Development and Civilization*, London, Sage Publications

Galtung, Johan (2012a) *Peace Economics: From a Killing to a Living Economy*, Transcend University Press

Galtung, Johan (2012b) *A Theory of Peace: Building Direct Structural Cultural Peace*, Transcend University Press

Galtung, Johan (2014) *A Theory of Civilization: Overcoming Cultural Violence*, Transcend University Press

Georgescu-Roegen, Nicholas (1971) *The Entropy Law and the Economic Process*, Cambridge, MA, Harvard University Press

Georgescu-Roegen, Nicholas (1975) Energy and Economic Myths, *Southern Economic Journal* 41:3, pp. 347–381

Georgescu-Roegen, Nicholas (1999) *The Entropy Law and the Economic Process*, Lincoln, NE, iUniverse Press

Gerber, Julien-François and Steppacher, Rolf (eds.) (2012) *Towards an Integrated Paradigm in Heterodox Economics*, Basingstoke, Palgrave Macmillan

Giddens, Anthony (1990) *The Consequences of Modernity*, Stanford, CA, Stanford University Press

Goheen, John (1991) Whitehead's Theory of Value, in *The Philosophy of Alfred North Whitehead*, Paul Arthur Schilpp (ed.), Chicago, Open Court

Grewal, Singh (2003) Johan Galtung's Positive and Negative Peace, www.scribd.com/document/122966768/Johan-Galtung-Positive-and-Negative-Peace, accessed December 6, 2016

Griffin, David Ray (1985) Bohm and Whitehead on Wholeness, Freedom, Causality, and Time, *Zygon* 20:2, pp. 165–191

Griffin, David Ray (1991) Steiner's Anthroposophy and Whitehead's Philosophy, *ReVision* 13:4, pp. 1–22

Guruge, Ananda W. P. (2008) *Buddhism, Economics and Science: Further Studies in Socially Engaged Humanistic Buddhism*, Bloomington, IN, AuthorHouse

Harding, Stephan (2009) *Animate Earth: Science, Intuition and Gaia*, Totnes, Devon, Green Books

Harman, Graham (2009) *Prince of Networks: Bruno Latour and Metaphysics*, Melbourne, re.press

Hausman, Daniel M. (2013) Philosophy of Economics, in *Stanford Encyclopedia of Philosophy* (Winter 2013 Edition), Edward N. Zalta (ed.), https://plato.stanford.edu/archives/win2013/entries/economics, accessed December 6, 2016

Higgins, Polly (2010) *Eradicating Ecocide: Exposing the Corporate and Political Practices Destroying the Planet and Proposing the Laws Needed to Eradicate Ecocide*, London, Shepheard-Walwyn Publishers

Higgins, Polly (2012) *Earth is Our Business: Changing the Rules of the Game*, London, Shepheard-Walwyn Publishers

Holbæk-Hanssen, Leif (1973–1976) *Metoder og modelleri markedsføringen Bind 1–3* Oslo, Tanum

Holbæk-Hanssen, Leif (1984) *Et samfunn for menneskelig utvikling*, Oslo, Tanum-Norli

Holbæk-Hanssen, Leif (2009) *Økonomi og samfunn: Når mennesket blir viktigst*, Oslo, Antropos

Hopfenbeck, W. (1992) *The Green Management Revolution: Lessons in Environmental Excellence*, New York, Prentice-Hall

Hopkins, Rob (2009) *The Transition Handbook: From Oil Dependency to Local Resilience*, Foxhole, Devon, Green Books

Hosinski, Thomas E. (1993) *Stubborn Fact and Creative Advance: An Introduction to the Metaphysics of Alfred North Whitehead*, Boston, Rowman & Littlefield

Hughes, Gertrude Reif (1995) Introduction, *in* Rudolf Steiner, *The Philosophy of Freedom: Intuitive Thinking as a Spiritual Path*, Hudson, NY, Anthroposophic Press

Ims, Knut and Jakobsen, Ove (2006) Cooperation and Competition in the Context of Organic and Mechanic Worldviews: A Theoretical and Case Based Discussion, *Journal of Business Ethics*, 66, pp. 19–32

Ims, Knut and Jakobsen, Ove (2010) Cooperation or Competition? A Required Shift in the Metaphysics of Economics, in *The Collaborative Enterprise: Creating Values for a Sustainable World*, Antonio Tencati and Laszlo Zsolnai (eds.), Oxford, Peter Lang

Ims, Knut and Jakobsen, Ove (2011) Deep Authenticity: An Essential Phenomenon in the Web of Life, in *Business Ethics and Corporate Sustainability*, Antonio Tencati and Francesco Perrini (eds.), Northampton, MA, Edward Elgar

Ims, Knut J. and Jakobsen, Ove (2015) Peace in an Organic Worldview, in *Business, Ethics and Peace*, Luk Boukaert and Manas Chatterji (eds.), Bingley, Yorkshire, Emerald

Ims, Knut J., Jakobsen, Ove and Zsolnai, Laszlo (2015) Product as Process: Commodities in Mechanic and Organic Ontology, *Ecological Economics* 110, pp. 11–14

Ingebrigtsen, Stig and Jakobsen, Ove (2006) Economics and Culture, in *Business within Limits: Deep Ecology and Buddhist Economics*, Laszlo Zsolnai and Knut J. Ims (eds.), Oxford, Peter Lang

Ingebrigtsen, Stig and Jakobsen, Ove (2007) *Circulation Economics: Theory and Practice*, Oxford, Peter Lang

Ingebrigtsen, Stig and Jakobsen, Ove (2009) Moral Development of the Economic Actor, *Ecological Economics* 68, pp. 2777–2784

Irvine, A. D. (2003) Alfred North Whitehead, in *Stanford Encyclopedia of Philosophy* (Winter 2015 Edition), Edward N. Zalta (ed.), https://plato.stanford.edu/archives/win2015/entries/whitehead/, accessed December 6, 2016

Jackson, Ross (2000a) *Kali Yuga Odyssey: A Spiritual Journey*, San Francisco, Robert D. Reed Publishers

Jackson, Ross (2000b) *And We ARE Doing It: Building an Ecovillage Future*, San Francisco, Robert D. Reed Publishers

Jackson, Ross (2012) *Occupy World Street: A Road Map for Radical Economic and Political Reform*, Totnes, Devon, Green Books

Jackson, Tim (1996) *Material Concerns: Pollution, Profit and Quality of Life*, London, Routledge

Jackson, Tim (2009) *Prosperity without Growth? The Transition to a Sustainable Economy*, London, Sustainable Development Commission

Jackson, Tim (2011) *Prosperity without Growth: Economics for a Finite Planet*, London, Earthscan

Jakobsen, Ove (2013) Economical, Social and Ecological Challenges Enlightened by Ecological Economics, in *Sustainability Ethics: Ecology, Economy and Ethics, SusCon III*, Sanjoy Mukherjee and Christoph Stückelberger (eds.), Shillong, New Delhi, McGraw-Hill

Johnson, A. H. (1962) *Whitehead's Philosophy of Civilization*, New York, Dover Publications

Jones, W. T. (1970) *A History of Western Philosophy: The Classical Mind*, New York, Harcourt Brace Jovanovich Publishers

Jones, W. T. (1975) *A History of Western Philosophy: The Twentieth Century, Wittgenstein to Sartre*, New York, Harcourt Brace Jovanovich Publishers

Kahneman, Daniel (2012) *Thinking Fast and Slow*, London, Penguin Books

Kellner, Douglas (2012) Ernst Bloch, Utopia and Ideology Critique, in *Existential Utopia: New Perspectives on Utopian Thought*, Patricia Vieira and Michael Marder (eds.), London, Continuum

Kennedy, Margrit (1995) *Interest and Inflation Free Money: Creating an Exchange Medium that Works for Everybody and Protects the Earth*, [n.p.], Seva International

Kennedy, Margrit (2012) *Occupy Money: Creating an Economy Where Everybody Wins*, Gabriola Island, BC, New Society Publishers

Kertman, Cynthia Earl (1974) *Creative Tension: The Life and Thought of Kenneth Boulding*, Ann Arbor, University of Michigan Press

Korten, David C. (2010) *Agenda for a New Economy: From Phantom Wealth to Real Wealth*, San Francisco, Berrett-Koehler Publishers

Korten, David C. (2015) *Change the Story, Change the Future: A Living Economy for a Living Earth*, Oakland, CA, Berrett-Koehler Publishers

Kourdi, Jeremy (2015) *Business Strategy: A Guide to Effective Decision-Making*, 3rd ed., London, Public Affairs

Kuhn, Thomas S. (1962) *The Structure of Scientific Revolutions*, Chicago, University of Chicago Press

Latour, Bruno (2011) Foreword: What is Given in Experience, in Isabelle Stengers, *Thinking with Whitehead*, Cambridge, MA, Harvard University Press

Latour, Bruno (2014) On Some of the Effects of Capitalism, Lecture, Royal Academy, Copenhagen, February 2, 2014

Lee, Chong Soon (2006) *Alfred North Whitehead and Yi Yolgok*, Maryland, MD, University Press of America

Levitas, Ruth (2011) *The Concept of Utopia*, Oxford, Peter Lang

Levitas, Ruth (2012) Secularism and Post-Secularism in Roberto Unger and Ernst Bloch: Toward a Utopian Ontology, in *Existential Utopia: New Perspectives on Utopian Thought*, Patricia Vieira and Michael Marder (eds.), London, Continuum

Levitas, Ruth (2013) *Utopia as Method: The Imaginary Reconstruction of Society*, New York, Palgrave Macmillan

Lietaer, Bernard (2001) *The Future of Money: Creating New Wealth, Work and a Wiser World*, London, Random House

Lietaer, Bernard and Dunne, Jacqui (2013) *Rethinking Money: How New Currencies Turn Scarcity into Prosperity*, San Francisco, Berrett-Koehler Publishers

Lindner, Evelin (2009) *Emotion and Conflict: How Human Rights Can Dignify Emotion and Help Us Wage Good Conflict*, Westport, CT, Greenwood Publishing Group

Lindner, Evelin G. (2011) *A Dignity Economy*, Doerzbach, Germany, Dignity Press

Lovelock, James (1979) *Gaia: A New Look at Life on Earth*, Oxford, Oxford University Press

Lovelock, James (1988) *The Ages of Gaia: A Biography of our Living Earth*, Oxford, Oxford University Press

Lovelock, James (2006) *The Revenge of Gaia*, London, Penguin Books

Lowe, Victor, Hartshorne, Charles and Johnson, A. H. (1950) *Whitehead and the Modern World: Science, Metaphysics and Civilization*, Boston, Beacon Press

McGrath, Alister (2007) *Dawkins' God: Genes, Memes, and the Meaning of Life*, Oxford, Blackwell Publishing

Makower, Joel, Elkington, John and Hailes, Julia (1993) *The Green Consumer*, London, Penguin Books

Mannheim, Karl (1936) *Ideology and Utopia*, New York, Harcourt, Brace and World

Marcuse, Herbert (2002) *One-Dimensional Man*, London, Routledge

Martinez-Allier, Joan (1987) *Ecological Economics: Energy, Environment and Society*, Oxford, Basil Blackwell

Martinez-Alier, Joan and Røpke, Inge (eds.) (2008) *Recent Developments in Ecological Economics*, vol. 1, Northampton, MA, Edward Elgar

Maslow, Abraham (1971) *The Farther Reaches of Human Nature*, New York, Viking Press

Matthews, Layth (2014) *The Four Noble Truths of Wealth: A Buddhist View of Economic Life*, Victoria, BC, Enlightened Economy Books

Max-Neef, Manfred (1981) *From the Outside Looking In: Experiences in Barefoot Economics*, London, Zed Books

Max-Neef, Manfred (2005) Foundation of Transdisciplinarity, *Ecological Economics* 53, pp. 5–16

Max-Neef, Manfred (2010) The World on a Collision Course and the Need for a New Economy, *AMBIO* 39, pp. 200–210

Max-Neef, Manfred (2014) The Good Is the Bad That We Don't Do. Economic Crimes against Humanity: A Proposal, *Ecological Economics* 104, pp. 152–154

Mayumi, Kozo and Gowdy, John M. (eds.) (1999) *Bioeconomics and Sustainability: Essays in Honor of Nicholas Georgescu-Roegen*, Northampton, MA, Edward Elgar

Merton, R. K. (1936) The Unanticipated Consequences of Purposive Social Action, *American Sociological Review*, 1:6, pp. 894–904

Merton, Robert (1948) The Self-Fulfilling Prophecy, *Antioch Review* 8:2, pp. 193–210

Midttun, Atle (ed.) (2013) *CSR and Beyond: A Nordic Perspective*, Oslo, Cappelen Damm Akademisk

Moylan, Tom and Baccolini, Raffaella (eds.) (2011) *Utopia, Method, Vision: The Use Value of Social Dreaming*, Oxford, Peter Lang

Mukherjee, Sanjoy and Stückelberger, Christoph (eds.) (2013) *Sustainability Ethics: Ecology, Economy and Ethics, SusCon III*, Shillong, New Delhi, McGraw-Hill

Northrop, Filmer S. C. (1991) Whitehead's Philosophy of Science, in *The Philosophy of Alfred North Whitehead*, Paul Arthur Schilpp (ed.), Chicago, Open Court

Ormerod, P. (1994) *The Death of Economics*, London, Faber and Faber

Palazzo, G., Krings, F. and Hoffrage, U. (2012) Ethical Blindness, *Journal of Business Ethics* 109, pp. 323–338

Pandey, B. P. (ed.) (1991) *Gandhi and Economic Development*, London, Sangam Books

Parekh, Bhikhu (2001) *Gandhi: A Very Short Introduction*, Oxford, Oxford University Press

Patnaik, S. C. (1991) Gandhian Economic Framework, in *Gandhi and Economic Development*, P. B. Pandey (ed.), London, Sangam Books

Payutto, P. A. (1994) *Buddhist Economics: A Middle Way for the Market Place*, Bangkok, Thailand, Buddhadmamma Foundation

Pearce, J. (2001) *Small is Still Beautiful*, London, HarperCollins

Persky, J. (1995) Retrospectives. The Ethology of Homo Economicus, *Journal of Economic Perspectives* 9:2, pp. 221–231

Popper, Karl (2002) *The Poverty of Historicism*, London, Routledge Classics

Powdyel, Thakur S. (2014) *My Green School: An Outline*, Timphu, Bhutan, Kuensel Corporation

Priddle, John (1994) Marketing Ethics, Macromarketing, and the Managerial Perspective Reconsidered, *Journal of Macromarketing* 14:2, pp. 47–62

Pruzan, Peter (1998) From Control to Values-Based Management and Accountability, *Journal of Business Ethics* 17, pp. 1379–1394

Pruzan, Peter (2011) Spirituality as the Context for Leadership, in *Spirituality and Ethics in Management*, Laszlo Zsolnai (ed.), New York, Springer

Pruzan, Peter and Mikkelsen, Kirsten Pruzan (2007) *Leading with Wisdom: Spiritual - Based Leadership in Business*, Sheffield, Greenleaf Publishing

Ray, Paul H. and Anderson, Sherry Ruth (2000) *The Cultural Creatives: How 50 Million People Are Changing the World*, New York: Harmony Books

Rees, William (2000) Is there Intelligent Life on Earth? Parkland Institute Conference, Edmonton, Alberta, November 18, http://aurora.icaap.org/talks/parklandrees.html, accessed December 6, 2016

Rees, William (2008) Human Nature, Eco-Footprints and Environmental Injustice, *Local Environment* 13:8, pp. 685–701

Restany, Pierre (2011) *The Power of Art. Hundertwasser: The Painter-King with the Five Skins*, Cologne, Midpoint Press

Ricoeur, Paul (1986) *Lectures on Ideology and Utopia*, New York, Colombia University Press

Rose, Philip (2002) *On Whitehead*, Belmont, CA, Wadsworth

Ruggiero, Renato (1966) UNCTAD and WTO: A Common Goal in a Global Economy, press release, October 7, 1966, http://unctad.org/en/pages/PressReleaseArchive.aspx?ReferenceDocId=3607, accessed December 6, 2016

Safranski, Rüdiger (2003) *How Much Globalization Can We Bear?* Cambridge, Polity Press

Samuels, Warren J. (1972) The Scope of Economics Historically Considered, *Land Economics* 48:3, pp. 248–268

Santa-Barbara, J., Dubee, F. and Galtung, J. (2009) *Peace Business: Humans and Nature above Markets and Capital*, Transcend University Press

Sargent, Lyman Tower (2011) Choosing Utopia: Utopianism as an Essential Element in Political Thought and Action, in *Utopia, Method, Vision: The Use Value of Social Dreaming*, Tom Moylan and Raffaella Baccolini (eds.), Oxford, Peter Lang

Scarfe, Adam C. (2002) Whitehead's Doctrine of Objectification and Yogacara Buddhism's Theory of the Three Natures, *Contemporary Buddhism* 3:2, pp. 111–125

Scharmer, C. Otto (2009) *Theory U: Leading from the Future as it Emerges*, San Francisco, Berrett-Koehler Publishers

Scharmer, Otto and Kaufer, Katrin (2013) *Leading from the Emerging Future: From Ego-System to Eco-System Economies*, San Francisco, Berrett-Koehler Publishers

Schilpp, Paul Arthur (ed.) (1991) *The Philosophy of Alfred North Whitehead*, Chicago, Open Court

Schumacher, E. F. (1978) *A Guide for the Perplexed*, London, HarperCollins

Schumacher, E. F. (1993) *Small is Beautiful: A Study of Economics as if People Mattered*, London, Vintage [first published 1973]

Segall, Matthew David (2013) *Physics of the World-Soul: The Relevance of Alfred North Whitehead's Philosophy of Organism to Contemporary Scientific Cosmology*, lulu.com

Sen, Amartya (1987) *On Ethics and Economics*, Oxford, Basil Blackwell

Sen, Amartya (1993) Does Business Ethics Make Economic Sense? *Business Ethics Quarterly* 3:1, pp. 45–54

Sen, Amartya (2004) Why Should We Preserve the Spotted Owl? *London Review of Books* 26:3, February 5, pp. 10–11

Senge, Peter, Scharmer, C. Otto, Jaworski, Joseph and Flowers, Betty Due (2004) *Presence: Human Purpose and the Field of the Future*, New York, Crown Publishing Group

Shaviro, Steven (2014) *The Universe of Things: On Speculative Realism*, London, University of Minnesota Press

Shiva, Vandana (2000) *Water Wars: Privatization, Pollution, and Profit*, Cambridge, MA, South End Press

Shiva, Vandana (2005) *Earth Democracy: Justice, Sustainability, and Peace*, Cambridge, MA, South End Press

Shiva, Vandana (2008) *Soil Not Oil: Environmental Justice in an age of Climate Crisis*, Cambridge, MA, South End Press

Shiva, Vandana (2010) *Staying Alive: Women, Ecology and Development*, Cambridge, MA, South End Press

Siebenhüner, B. (2000) Homo Sustinens: Towards a Conception of Humans for the Science of Sustainability, *Ecological Economics* 32, pp. 15–25

Sivaraska, Sulak (2009) *The Wisdom of Sustainability: Buddhist Economics for the 21st Century*, London, Souvenir Press

Smith, Philip B. and Max-Neef, Manfred (2011) *Economics Unmasked: From Power and Greed to Compassion and the Common Good*, Totnes, Devon, Green Books

Söderbaum, Peter (1993) *Ekologisk ekonomi: Miljö och utveckling I ny belysning*, Lund, Studentlitteratur

Söderbaum, Peter (1999) Values, Ideology and Politics in Ecological Economics, *Ecological Economics* 28, pp. 161–170

Söderbaum, Peter (2000) *Ecological Economics: A Political Economics Approach to Environment and Development*, London, Earthscan

Söderbaum, Peter (2008) *Understanding Sustainability Economics: Towards Pluralism in Economics*, London, Earthscan

Sommer, Mark (1985) *Beyond the Bomb: Living without Nuclear Weapons*, Chestnut Hill, MA, Expro Press

Spash, Clive L. (2012) Towards the Integration of Social, Ecological and Economic Knowledge, in *Towards an Integrated Paradigm in Heterodox Economics*, Julien-François Gerber and Rolf Steppacher (eds.), Basingstoke, Palgrave Macmillan

Spash, Clive L. (2013a) The Ecological Economics of Boulding's Spaceship Earth, SRE-Discussion Paper 2013/02, Institute for the Environment and Regional Development, Vienna University of Economics and Business

Spash, Clive L. (2013b) The Shallow or the Deep Ecological Economics Movement? *Ecological Economics* 93, pp. 351–362

Steeves, James B. (2000) Utopia and Text: Ricoeur's Critique of Ideology, *Symposium* 4:2, pp. 221–235

Steiner, Rudolf (1964) *The Philosophy of Freedom: The Basis for a Modern World Conception*, Forest Row, East Sussex, Rudolf Steiner Press

Steiner, Rudolf (1972) *World Economy*, Forest Row, East Sussex, Rudolf Steiner Press

Steiner, Rudolf (1977) *Towards Social Renewal: Basic Issues of the Social Question*, Forest Row, East Sussex, Rudolf Steiner Press

Steiner, Rudolf (1995) *The Philosophy of Freedom: Intuitive Thinking as a Spiritual Path*, Hudson, NY, Anthroposophic Press

Stengers, Isabelle (2011) *Thinking with Whitehead*, Cambridge, MA, Harvard University Press

Storsletten, Vivi M. L. and Jakobsen, Ove D. (2013) Revolution and Evolution in Economics, Business Management and Leadership Theory, in *CSR and Beyond: A Nordic Perspective*, Atle Midttun (ed.), Oslo, Cappelen Damm Akademisk

Storsletten, Vivi M. L. and Jakobsen, Ove D. (2015) Development of Leadership Theory in the Perspective of Kierkegaard's Philosophy, *Journal of Business Ethics* 128:2, pp. 337–349

Stuckey, P. (2009) Air Money: Or Bringing the Financial Crisis down to Earth, This Lively Earth blog, March 10, 2009, http://thislivelyearth.com/2009/03/10/air-money, accessed December 6, 2016

Tanner, Michael (2000) *Nietzsche: A Very Short Introduction*, Oxford, Oxford University Press

Taylor, Charles (1991) *The Ethics of Authenticity*, Cambridge, MA, Harvard University Press

Tencati, Antonio and Zsolnai, Laszlo (2010) *The Collaborative Enterprise: Creating Values for a Sustainable World*, Oxford, Peter Lang

Thaler, Richard H. and Sunstein, Cass R. (2008) *Nudge: Improving Decisions About Health, Wealth and Happiness*, London, Penguin Books

Torry, Malcom (2013) *Money for Everyone: Why We Need a Citizen's Income*, Bristol, Policy Press

Turner, R. K., Paavola, J., Cooper, P., Farber, S., Jerssamy, V. and Georgiou, S. (2003) Valuing Nature: Lessons Learned and Future Research Directions, *Ecological Economics* 3, pp. 493–510

United Nations Conference on Trade and Development [UNCTAD] (2013) *Wake Up Before It Is Too Late: Make Agriculture Truly Sustainable Now for Food Security in a Changing Climate*, Geneva, UNCTAD

Van Ness, Hendrick C. (1983) *Understanding Thermodynamics*, New York, Dover Publications

Vieira, Patricia and Marder, Michael (eds.) (2012) *Existential Utopia: New Perspectives on Utopian Thought*, New York, Continuum

Wackernagel, Mathis and Rees, William (1996) *Our Ecological Footprint: Reducing Human Impact on Earth*, Gabriola Island, BC, New Society Publishers

Welford, Richard (1995) *Environmental Strategy and Sustainable Development*, London, Routledge

Welford, Richard (2000) *Corporate Environmental Management*, London, Earthscan Publications

Welford, Richard (2007) Examining, Discussing and Suggesting the Possible Contribution and Role of Buddhist Economics for Corporate Social Responsibility, *International Journal of Green Economics*, 1:3–4, pp. 341–350

Welford, Richard and Gouldson, Andrew (1993) *Environmental Management and Business Strategy*, London, Pitman Publishing

Whitehead, Alfred North (1966) *Modes of Thought*, New York, The Free Press [first published 1938]

Whitehead, Alfred North (1967a) *Science and the Modern World*, New York, The Free Press [first published 1925]

Whitehead, Alfred North (1967b) *Adventures of Ideas*, New York, Macmillan [first published 1933]

Whitehead, Alfred North (1977) *Nature and Life*, New York, Greenwood Press [first published 1934]

Whitehead, Alfred North (1985) *Process and Reality*, New York, The Free Press [first published 1929]

Wilkinson, Roy (2001) *Rudolf Steiner: An Introduction to his Spiritual World-View, Anthroposophy*, Forest Row, East Sussex, Temple Lodge Publishing

Wootton, Barbara (1967) *In a World I Never Made*, London, George Allen & Unwin

Zsolnai, Laszlo (2004) The Moral Economic Man, in *Ethics in the Economy: Handbook in Business Ethics*, Laszlo Zsolnai (ed.), Oxford, Peter Lang

Zsolnai, Laszlo (ed.) (2011) *Spirituality and Ethics in Management*, New York, Springer

Zsolnai, Laszlo (ed.) (2013) *Handbook of Business Ethics: Ethics in the New Economy*, Oxford, Peter Lang

Zsolnai, Laszlo (2014) *Beyond Self: Ethical and Social Dimensions of Economics*, Oxford, Peter Lang

Zsolnai, Laszlo and Ims, Knut J. (eds.) (2006) *Business within Limits: Deep Ecology and Buddhist Economics*, Oxford, Peter Lang

Index